COME DOWN, ZACCHAEUS

Adventures in Scripture

Come Down, Zacchaeus

Adventures in Scripture

BY SOLANGE HERTZ

Author of *Women, Words, and Wisdom*

THE NEWMAN PRESS

Westminster, Maryland

1961

Nihil obstat:

EDWARD A. CERNY, S.S., S.T.D.

Censor Librorum

Imprimatur:

FRANCIS P. KEOUGH, D.D.

Archbishop of Baltimore

January 23, 1961

The *nihil obstat* and *imprimatur* are official declarations that a book or pamphlet is free of doctrinal and moral error. No implication is contained therein that those who have granted the *nihil obstat* and *imprimatur* agree with the opinions expressed.

FOR THE ANGELS

ACKNOWLEDGMENTS

THE author and The Newman Press wish to thank the following publishers for their kind permission to reprint quotations from the titles listed below:

B. Herder Book Co., for *The Mysteries of Christianity,* by Matthias J. Scheeben, S.J.

Sands & Co., for *Christ, the Life of the Soul: Spiritual Conferences,* by Dom Columba Marmion, O.S.B.

Burns & Oates, Ltd., for *The Catholic Students' Aids to the Study of the Bible,* by Hugh Pope, O.P., and *Catholicism,* by Henri de Lubac.

Mercier Press, Ltd., for *The Divine Masterpiece,* by Gabriel Roschini.

Sheed & Ward, Inc., for "Demoniacs in the Gospel," by Msgr. F. M. Catherinet, in *Satan,* edited by Père Bruno de Jesus-Marie, O.C.D.; *The Complete Works of St. Teresa,* translated and edited by E. Allison Peers from the critical edition of P. Silverio de Santa Teresa, C.D.; and *The Image of God in Sex,* by Vincent Wilkin, S.J.

Pantheon Books, for *The Christ of Faith: the Christology of the Church,* by Karl Adam.

Bollingen Foundation, for *The Devil's Share,* by Denis de Rougemont.

The Confraternity of Christian Doctrine, for The New Testament and parts of The Old Testament.

The Catholic Record Press, for *Abandonment to Divine Providence,* by Jean Pierre de Caussade, S.J.

TABLE OF CONTENTS

IF YOU INTEND TO READ
THIS BOOK,

IT'S ONLY sporting to tell you nobody asked me to write it. I just went ahead and wrote it anyway without waiting to be asked, because I got so enthusiastic about the Bible I couldn't control myself any longer. Looking back over what I've had the temerity to put on paper, I must also tell you this is anything but a textbook for seminarians, but rather a sort of tabloid for people in the world, like me. As such I present it to the public.

You'll soon see I'm trying to get two points across. The first one is that the Bible must be read "mystically," if it is to be read over and over again as it should be. People who read solely for the literal—or even the moral—meaning of the text will most likely be those who announce, "The Bible? Sure, I've read it!" looking up at it on the shelf as if it were any other book. They see little purpose in constantly trampling the same ground, reading the same old stories, whose gist and moral never change for them. From where they sit, their conclusion is all too correct.

On the other hand, people who read the Bible every day from necessity, to sustain their spiritual life and solve their ever-changing practical problems, and who find in it ever-renewed inspiration and counsel, are most likely those who read it as the saints read it. Using the letter of God's Word as the index of its spirit, they become exuberant explorers in a fascinating land whose charts are allegory and whose land-marks are symbol. These people will never finish reading the Bible because, though they find the terrain literally always the same, they find it spiritually always different; and the horizons widen as they proceed. If this is your method, you need no encouragement from me. God bless you!

The second thing I'm trying to say is that our *Mater et Magistra,* the Catholic Church, like every good mother, doesn't neglect to prepare her children for life by wise sex instruction suited to age and need. We her offspring in a pagan-secular society betray her shamefully when we leave the whole field of sex fair game for the Sigmund Freuds and Grace Metaliouses of this floundering world. We are without excuse, for Scripture as taught to us by our Mother teaches us clearly what sex is, what it's meant to be, and not less important, what it can never be.

Fire must be fought with fire, I'm a-thinking, and not with simpering half-truths mouthed apologetically by Catho-lics so embarrassed by the whole glorious subject they think they're being "modest." If you're one of these, perhaps you had better not read this book, because there's an awful lot about sex in it. I just couldn't help it. There are lots of house-wives in the world, and they all have to come to terms with sex in one way or another. One of them wrote a book called *Peyton Place,* and it shouldn't go unchallenged. It did seem to me another housewife might write a rebuttal. In its oblique small way, this is it.

Because I'm a housewife, my language is simply my own. Some may feel that Scripture should be discussed only in the most formal, elegant phrases at one's disposal. Well, these are just about my most elegant. If I tried to put on airs, people who know me would wonder what came over me. Should my vernacular drive any readers to conclude that I entertain flippant or facetious thoughts concerning God's Word, they misjudge me grossly. If I speak familiarly, it's because I've discovered that God's Word is really and truly *mine,* and *yours,* and everybody's.

That's what this book is about. I submit its every word to the loving infallibility of Mother Church, whose homely daughter I'm honored to be.

I make no personal acknowledgments, because I owe everybody, and if there's anyone to blame, it's me.

At my house,
Feast of St. Jerome, 1961

Behold the days come, saith the Lord, and I will send forth a famine into the land: not a famine of bread, nor a thirst of water, but of hearing the word of the Lord. . . .

AMOS 8:11

COME DOWN, ZACCHAEUS

Adventures in Scripture

IN A WORM'S EYE

Two worms were visiting the Empire State Building. The first worm had prevailed upon his friend to inch his way laboriously to the elevator and ride to the top. After some painful wriggling they got out on a window ledge.

Looking down from the height, the first worm exclaims, "Boy! What a view! Now don't say it wasn't worth the climb. Look at all those little people and things crawling around down there!"

The second worm looks over the edge dubiously and mutters, "If you want to see what's down there, what did you bring me all the way up here for?"

My husband tells me that this is a very old joke: when he first heard it the worms were on the Flatiron Building. It must be older than that. My guess is that the worms were originally on the Tower of Babel. Shortly after that the story must have been translated into all the languages of the earth, because it exemplifies perfectly the only two points of view there ever are on anything: "up there" and "down here."

I repeat this choice chestnut as my opener because this is a book about the Bible, of which I presume to present a worm's eye view. As should be self-evident, this view is the only one proper to "the son of man who is a worm," as Job remarked. We worms can take an elevator to the top of a tower and get a large inclusive view from "up there," or we can stay where we are and look around us for limited but more detailed personal observation.

Both are valid positions. I understand that even in heaven we are to retain them. Theologians call the "up there" view *matutinal:* knowledge of God and creation as a whole. The "down here" aspect is *vesperal,* and deals with particulars. We need apologize for neither. They're ours for eternity. When dealing with interpretations of Scripture, the literal, "down here" view goes under the general heading of "Antiochene School." It is very objective, and leans heavily on grammar and archaeology. The other school, the "Alexandrian," prefers to see everything at once, from "up there." It leans toward the mystics and the operations of one's own soul, making it more subjective. Like man and wife, Antiochenes and Alexandrians need each other desperately precisely because they have their differences.

Our human limitations in this life being what they are, we usually try for the view "up there" first. Take Zacchaeus, for instance. Curious about the Christ, "he was trying to see Jesus, who He was, but could not, on account of the crowd, because he was small of stature." In order to get what he considered a good view of the Lord, he ran on ahead and climbed into a sycamore tree to look down on God and see Him all in one piece as He passed beneath him.

People who begin to read the Bible seriously, really to catch sight of the Christ, often follow Zacchaeus' example. It's the natural thing to do. "On account of the crowd," and knowing ourselves to be short of stature where the things of God are concerned, we run ahead and climb any big sycamores we can find along the way. It's not a bad idea. To get the exhilarating view of Scripture "up there," we have only to read Scripture through the great exegetes who tower above us, the evangelists themselves, for example; they commented on many passages of the Old Testament. Or we can read St. Paul, the fathers of the Church, or simply a good modern commentary—or the mystics.

"Stand in the multitude of ancients that are wise," counsels Ecclesiasticus, "and join thyself from thy heart to their wisdom: that thou mayst hear every discourse of God" (6:35).

Towering above these giants is the Exegete of exegetes, Christ Himself. On the road to Emmaus, "beginning with Moses and all the prophets . . . [he] interpreted to them in all the Scriptures the things referring to himself." Much of His exegesis is recorded for us in the Gospels, wherein He expounded for us numerous passages from Isaias, Deuteronomy, the Psalms and other books. He explained to us the significance of Jonas, of the mysterious cornerstone rejected by the builders, of the smitten shepherd of Zaccharias, and of the voice in the desert—not to mention His own parables.

With these clues to set us on the right track, He continues to expound the Scriptures to us in the Liturgy, through the Holy Spirit. Here, incorporated into our worship of God, we find the high truths of Scripture in their most easily assimilated form: truer, if possible, because applied and distilled. In fact, St. Bernard affirms that the Church "is the Spouse who has wounded His heart, who with the eye of contemplation pierces the abyss of God's hidden designs, and so makes an everlasting dwelling for herself in His heart and for Him in her own."

Echoing St. Augustine, he goes on to say that, *"Whenever,*

therefore, she changes the meaning or the application of a text of Holy Scripture, the words in the accommodated sense possess even greater authority than belongs to them in their primary signification. And perhaps the adapted meaning surpasses the original by as much as the reality excels the image; the light, the shadow; the mistress, the maid-servant."* This makes the Liturgy a giant sycamore indeed, and from up there the Catholic's view will always be un-clouded, for the Holy Spirit Himself guarantees it.

Not that one has to be Catholic, or even Christian or Jewish, to read the Bible. Atheists and agnostics read it, but only as literature, as history, as a quaint primitive social document, or even as semitic propaganda. They admire Job as closet drama, Esther as a good short story, or the Apocalypse as an early experiment in free association; but however unbelievers read it, they must read it "as." Only the believer can just plain read it for what it is—a personal, verbal communication from God to men. And only the Catholic can read it in perfect freedom without fear of missing the point. Like the little boy who proclaimed himself

". . . as brave as brave can be,
When my muvver is wif me!"

the Catholic can run and skip through Scripture under his Mother's watchful eye in perfect security. Nobody can *dare* to read Scripture as a Catholic can, protected by the teaching authority of his Church.

"To you," said Truth made Man, "it is given to know the mystery of the kingdom of God, but to the rest in parables, that 'seeing they may not see, and hearing they may not understand'" (Luke 8:10).

* Third Sermon for Christmas Eve.

The first pope assured Catholics,

> we have the word of prophecy, surer still, to which you do
> well to attend, as to a lamp shining in a dark place, until the
> day dawns and the morning star rises in your hearts. This,
> then, you must understand first of all, that no prophecy of
> Scripture is made by private interpretation. For not by the
> will of man was prophecy brought at any time; but holy
> men of God spoke as they were moved by the Holy Spirit
> (2 Pet. 1:19–21).

How much we absorb of this lofty view, however, depends
to a large extent on how well we see down here. Surveying a
panorama of cars and people from the Empire State Building is after all rather meaningless to anyone not personally
acquainted with cars and people. Who can see forests who
can't see trees? How well can Christ be known from the top
of a sycamore?

So precious did Christ the Exegete deem our humble view
down here that He "emptied Himself, taking the nature of
a slave," even to the point of becoming "a worm and not a
man" to see for Himself what we see and to teach us the
value of the worm's eye view. In fact, when He looks up and
sees a sycamore-climber gazing down at Him from up there,
what does He say?

He says what He said to Zacchaeus, *"Make haste and come
down!"* If we want to see Christ truly, as He is, we must
come down. It's "down here" that, for us, the real exegesis
begins.

Before revealing the meaning of Moses' brazen serpent
to the good Pharisee, Nicodemus, the Lord asks him, "If I
have spoken to you of earthly things and you do not believe,
how will you believe if I speak to you of heavenly things?"
Scripture hangs its messages on personal experiences, as well

as winds, snakes, brass, and all sorts of things found only here below. "Thou art a teacher in Israel and dost not know these things?"

So what we get from St. Bernard or the Liturgy will depend very much on what our view down here happens to be. It will depend upon our humanity, our learning, our joys and sorrows, our experience of life. It will also depend upon how much we have thumbed the Bible for ourselves. For the vesperal look, no elevator, no sycamore, is necessary. It suffices to acknowledge oneself a worm and to take the worm's eye view.

Properly speaking, a worm has no view at all, as any high school biologist can affirm. As a matter of fact, he has no eye. He "sees" by reacting all of a piece to light and dark, and by bumping into what's around him. He does this humbly, because he's a very low form of life. For reading Holy Writ, his is the fundamental disposition required. No one should dare approach the Word of God in any other way. Whether on top of the Empire State Building or down in the traffic, this *is* the worm's eye view. We read Scripture by reading it and read it more by reacting to it and reading it again.

If any soul of good will can't read it profitably, it clearly cannot be God's Word. If it's necessary to pore over commentaries, atlases, ancient history, Hebrew lexicons, and to inspect the diggings at Qumran before tackling the opening lines of Genesis, then God is not the Author of authors, but simply an authors' author, writing for a rarefied public with a special vocabulary. *That,* we know, ain't so!

"For whatever things have been written have been written for our instruction, that through the patience and the conso-

lation afforded by the Scriptures we may have hope!" argues
St. Paul (Rom. 15:4).

Not that the scholarly approach is to be discouraged. Dear
me, no! It's part and parcel of the view down here. Anyone
who aims to dispense with it has no wormly humility at all.
But that doesn't mean we must wait until we are sufficiently
educated to start reading Scripture. That would be like
waiting to be a saint before receiving Holy Communion. It
is the reading of Scripture itself that makes us yearn to be
more educated in order to be able to read it better. It was
only after much reading and meditating on the Old Testament that the Little Flower (hardly a pedant!) longed to
study Hebrew so she could get just that much closer to God's
Word.

Reading Scripture in translation is always just a bit like
going wading with one's socks on. St. Jerome, destined to be
the father of the Vulgate, certainly thought so. He had this
to say about his Hebrew studies: "What a toil it was! How
difficult I found it! How often I was on the point of giving
it up in despair, and yet in my eagerness took it up again!"
And once more he locked horns in mortal combat with those
hydra-headed Hebrew verbs.

"But they that are learned," consoles Daniel, "shall shine
as the brightness of the firmament!" (Dan. 12:3).

Well, I just invested in a Hebrew grammar, so here's
hoping. St. Jerome never got over a holy envy of his friend
St. Paula, whom he pronounced as having "learned it, and
so well she could chant the Psalms in Hebrew, and could
speak it, too, without any trace of a Latin accent!" That's
one accomplishment I can be sure of. If I ever chant Hebrew,
I can guarantee it will be absolutely free of any Latin accent.

But that's just a beginning. St. Jerome also insists, "A man will understand the Bible better if he has seen Judea with his own eyes and discovered its ancient cities and sites either under the old names or newer ones. In company with some learned Hebrews I went through the entire land. . . ." You see what went into the translation of the Vulgate. He was rather short with those who "think that to be without culture and to be holy are the same thing . . . as though they were holy simply because ignorant!"

St. Jerome, pray for us.

The scholarly approach will, unfortunately, not suffice of itself. There is more than scholarship and personal experience to the view down here.

"You search the Scriptures," our Lord tells the Pharisees, who could expound more texts than the devil, "because in them you think that you have life everlasting . . ." but "you have not God's Word abiding in you, since you do not believe in him whom he has sent" (Jn. 5:38-9).

Aha! Didn't our Lord make this clear to Zaccheus too? When He told him to come down from that sycamore, He told him why: "I must stay in thy house today." That's where the real Bible-reading begins, with Christ *in our house.*

Scripture is a vision of God, not a problem in semantics or archaeology. It is a vision accorded to everyone who makes contact with it in faith. As in a true vision, some intermediate species is used by God to establish contact between Himself and the psyche of His creature. In the case of Scripture, the species is simply language, but it is a vision for all that. To borrow Father Tanquerey's definition, visions give us "supernatural perceptions of some object naturally invisible to man." Scholarship can't help us here, except by way of preparation.

Again as in a true vision, contact with Scripture is efficacious. Scripture itself is very clear on this point:

> And as the rain and the snow come down from heaven, and return no more thither, but soak the earth and water it, and make it to spring and give seed to the sower and bread to the eater: So shall my word be, which shall go forth from my mouth. It shall not return to me void, but it shall do whatsoever I please and shall prosper in the things for which I sent it (Isa. 55:10–11).

"For the word of God is living and efficient and keener than any two-edged sword," echoes St. Paul, "and extending even to the division of soul and spirit, of joints also and of marrow, and a discerner of the thoughts and intentions of the heart" (Heb. 4:12), probing deeper than any depth psychology.

"Receive the ingrafted word, which is able to save your souls," advises St. James, for contact with Scripture changes the reader in some mysterious way when he cooperates with its words—the more the cooperation, the greater the acceleration, drawing him closer and closer to the mind of the Author. This sort of change is sanctification. Scripture—the vision of God—makes saints.

Saints are not mass produced. God fashions them individually, lovingly, and with much care. That is why under the broad horizons "up there" will always lie the little fields down here. The Holy Spirit chooses to speak to souls personally, *à même,* as the French say, nakedly. Christ unfolds His greatest exegesis within our own souls, constantly explaining Himself more and more fully. In us, the Word is made Flesh. When disputing with the Pharisees, didn't He ask, "Is it not written in your Law, 'I said, you are gods' . . . to whom the word of God is addressed?"

Speaking of the gift of understanding, through which the Holy Spirit of Christ normally expounds His mysteries in us, Dom Marmion explains:

> Not that this gift diminishes the incomprehensibility of the mysteries or does away with faith; but it goes further into the mystery than the simple acquiescence of faith; it bears upon the appropriateness or the greatness of the mysteries, upon their relations with each other or with our supernatural life. It has also for its object the truths contained in the Sacred Books, and it is this gift which seems to have been granted in a special measure to those in the Church who have shone by the depth of their doctrine, those whom we call "Doctors of the Church"; but every baptised soul possesses within itself this precious gift. You read a text of Holy Scripture; you have read and reread it many times without having been struck by it; but one day, a sudden light flashes, illuminating to its depths, so to speak, the truth set forth in this text; this truth then becomes altogether clear to you and often a principle of supernatural life and action. Is it by your reflexions that you have arrived at this result? No, it is an illumination, an intuition of the Holy Spirit who, by the gift of understanding, makes you penetrate further into the inmost and deep meaning of the revealed truths so that you may hold them the more firmly. (*Christ the Life of the Soul,* Ch. 6.)

No one can read the Bible for anyone else. Because man is existential, in a sense he creates himself progressively, constantly absorbing his particular experience into himself. Like Tennyson's Ulysses, he is always "a part of all that I have met." (Don't you love Tennyson? He has a platitude for every occasion!) A plumber would never read Numbers as an accountant reads it, or a choreographer, or a lawyer. A happy plumber who reads Kipling can't read it the same way as an unhappy plumber who sails a boat on weekends. A man doesn't read it as a woman does. A married man doesn't read it as a priest does. To all these people the Bible has the same great things to say and also different things to say. All are true, universal, and yet special. Obviously, only God could have written such a book! Indeed, "They shall all be taught of God," as Isaias prophesied.

"Do you know how we have to read the holy Scriptures?" asks St. Augustine. "Like someone who reads letters which have come to him from his native land; to see what news we have from Heaven and what they tell us of our fatherland, where we have our parents and brethren and friends and acquaintances, and where we are wishing and longing to go." This is in line with the spiritual adage: When we pray we speak to God; when we read we listen to Him.

How many great saints received their vocations through reading some passage of Scripture which suddenly became luminous and irresistible, and which they felt was directed specifically to them? St. Francis of Assisi, hearing in the Gospel, "Do not keep gold, or silver, or money in your girdles, no wallet for your journey, nor two tunics, nor sandals, nor staff" (Mt. 10:9), took the words to himself. Giving away money and clothes, he settled for one old coat tied around the middle with a length of rope, and became the founder of a multitudinous order of poor men.

Citing St. Anthony of the desert, whose call from God came in the words "Go, sell what thou hast . . . and come, follow me," St. Augustine relates his own similar experience in his *Confessions*. Hearing a little child from a nearby house sing-songing, "*Tolle, lege, tolle, lege*—take up and read," he was moved to look into St. Paul's Epistle lying close at hand. His eyes fell on "Not in rioting and drunkenness, not in chambering and impurities, not in contention and envy, but put ye on the Lord Jesus Christ and make not provision for the flesh and its concupiscences" (Rom. 13:13). "I had no wish to read further and no need," writes the saint. His conversion was immediate and entire, the Word of God having extended well into his joints and marrow.

"*Tolle, lege,* take up and *read!*" he admonishes us in turn, now a doctor of the Church.

We're fools not to.

Speaking of the delights of the contemplative life, the fourteenth-century English mystic Walter Hilton assures us, "It sometimes happens that grace causes a soul to leave vocal prayer and moves it to see God in another way. It sees Him first in the Scriptures, for God, who is Truth, is hidden there under the beauty of the words as under a soft silk."

Then he cautions, "He can only be recognized by the pure of heart, because truth will not reveal itself to those who are hostile, but only to those who love it and seek it with humility." (Believe it or not, the name Zacchaeus means "pure" in Hebrew!)

> For truth and humility are sisters joined by love, and there is no divergence in their counsels. Humility relies on truth and not at all on itself, and truth trusts in humility, and so they agree well together. The soul of one who loves and desires God sees Him in proportion to the degree in which it is made humble by the infusion of grace and the opening of the spiritual eyes, and insofar as it understands that it is nothing of itself but is entirely dependent on the mercy and goodness of God, and that it is upheld only by His favor.

It sees the truth of the Scriptures wonderfully revealed to it in a way that it could not do by study and its own natural intelligence, and this is a kind of experience or perception of God, for God is the source of wisdom, and by imparting a little of His wisdom to a pure soul He can enable it to understand the whole of Scripture. He does not impart this knowledge all at once in a single act of enlightenment, but through His grace the soul receives a new habitual ability to understand the texts which come to its mind.

"This light and clearness in the intelligence is produced by the presence of God," Hilton continues, citing what God's presence did for the disciples going to Emmaus.

In the same way the indwelling of God illumines the intelligence of those who love and ardently desire Him, and brings to their minds by the ministry of angels [Ah!] the words and the texts of Scripture without their searching for them or thinking about them, and it makes their meaning clear however difficult or obscure they may be in themselves. The more difficult they are and the less able to be understood by the ordinary light of reason, the more delightful is their exposition when it comes from God.

The interpretation is literal, moral, mystical, and heavenly, if the matter allows of it. By the literal interpretation, the natural intelligence of man is fortified; by the moral sense of Scripture the soul is instructed about vices and virtues, how to distinguish one from the other. By the mystical sense it is illumined to see the operation of God in the Church, to apply the words of Scripture to Christ our Head, and to the Church, His mystical Body. The fourth, the heavenly sense, is concerned only with the operation of love, and it consists in applying to love all the truth of Scripture. Since that comes nearest to the experience of heaven, I call it heavenly.

Ah, dear reader, why are you reading Hertz when you could be reading Hilton?

Speaking from experience, he says,

> To a pure soul, whose palate is cleansed from the defile-
> ment of sensual love, Holy Scripture is a life-giving and
> refreshing food whose flavor is very agreeable to the mind
> which ruminates it well, because there is hidden in it the
> spirit that informs all the powers of the soul and fills them
> with heavenly and spiritual delight. He has need of good
> teeth who will eat this bread, for lovers of the flesh and
> [formal] heretics cannot reach its inner nature. Their teeth
> are unclean and so they cannot taste it. . . . They can never
> do more than gnaw on the outer bark, and whatever their
> claims, they never taste the inner flavor. They are not humble
> and pure, or friends of God, and therefore He does not reveal
> His secrets to them.
>
> The secret of Scripture is kept sealed with the signet of
> God's finger, which is the Holy Ghost, and so without His
> love and His leave no man may obtain it. . . . And He is
> Himself the key, and He lets in whom He will through the
> inspiration of His grace, and does not break the seal. That is
> what God does to those who love Him. He does not do it to
> all in the same measure. He does it especially for those who
> are inspired to seek truth in the Scriptures and who, *having*
> *applied themselves to serious study, give themselves up to*
> *fervent prayer*. These may find the truth when God is
> pleased to reveal it to them.
>
> See, then, how grace opens the eyes of the spirit and en-
> lightens the intelligence beyond the weakness of corrupt
> nature. Whether the soul reads Scripture, or hears it, or
> reflects on it, it receives, as I said before, a new ability to
> understand it and appreciate its truth. And it gets, too, the
> ability to find a spiritual sense in what is said literally. And
> that is not surprising, for it is the same spirit, namely the
> Holy Ghost, who interprets it for the consolation of a pure
> soul and who originally inspired it.
>
> And through this grace the uneducated can, and in fact, do,
> grasp the substance, the real truth and the spiritual flavor of
> Scripture, as well as the educated. Admittedly they may not
> understand so many details, but that is not necessary. . . .

And only by experience can a soul know what consolation and spiritual joy, what savor and sweetness, these illuminations may bring—interior perceptions, secret knowledge, and sudden touches of the Holy Ghost. And I believe that a man receiving these will not fall into error, if spiritual pride and over-great subtlety of intellect do not cloud his interior senses.

Echoing St. Augustine, he notes,

And indeed the light that grace throws on Holy Scripture and other inspired books is nothing else than a series of delightful letters which pass between God the true lover and the souls which He loves. . . . A very slight taste of this knowledge of Scripture will make a soul that enjoys it set little value on all the seven liberal arts or all worldly knowledge. For the end of this knowledge is the salvation of the soul in everlasting life.*

Peace on earth to men of good teeth! Everyone is invited to savor Scripture. At this banquet God has prepared for us, there is bread for every taste. It is a diet for saints and, please forgive me, also a diet for worms. There is, however, one piece of advice our Lord gives to anybody who accepts dinner invitations.

"When thou art invited," He suggests gently, so as not to hurt our feelings about our ignorance of etiquette, "go, recline at the last place." Come down here, Zacchaeus.

"That when he who invited thee comes in," He continues, "he may say to thee, 'Friend, go up higher!' " I guess that's "up there."

"Then wilt thou be honored in the presence of all who are at table with thee." That means Daniel, St. James, St. Francis, St. Jerome, St. Augustine, St. Paula, Walter Hilton. . . . Think of the conversation, let alone the fare!

* *Scale of Perfection,* Bk. II, Ch. 43.

Dashing for this advantageous last place before somebody beats me to it, I have written a book "down here" about the Bible, brazenly advertising my ignorance and lack of virtue to anyone who flicks these pages. That, I am afraid, is the point of the whole endeavor. I'm not an exegete. I've never been to Judea, nor can I chant Psalms in Hebrew, with or without a Latin accent. This is just my view of Scripture down here at the foot of the sycamore, where I happened to reach the publisher before you did. What was true of Zacchaeus is also true of me. Christ "has gone to be the guest of a *sinner*," as anyone with half an eye can see, now as then.

But of course you know the kind of Man the Christ is.

GOD'S LAUGH

I BELIEVE it was Stephen Leacock who said the first humorist was the savage who first cried "Ha-ha!" as he beat his enemy over the head with a tomahawk. Now Stephen Leacock was a humorist, and he should know, but I make bold to disagree with his theory. That savage could not have been the first humorist. What he is talking about is not humor, but a perversion of humor. Now popularly known as sadism, it often masquerades as humor, but isn't. For something to be perverted, however, it stands to reason there must have been something a whole lot better that went before, and *ersatz* humor is no exception. Where there's counterfeit, as they say, there must be real money somewhere.

Where? Well, even if that savage were not a sadist, he still couldn't have been the first humorist, because Almighty God was. He invented humor. I think everybody recognizes that God's humor is the best there is: our common speech reveals it. When we think anybody really knows what's funny, don't we say he has a simply *divine* sense of humor? God has *the* divine sense of humor, the true coin from which every joke ever told is counterfeited.

Lest we neglect to take His humor into consideration when reading the Bible, the Holy Spirit makes us aware of ts existence at the outset in Chapter Three of Genesis, where there develops before our eyes a comic situation of cosmic proportions, the exemplar of every known burlesque. Like all good comedy, it's rooted in the deepest tragedy of mankind, the Fall of Man. There is, apparently, something terrifyingly fundamental about humor.

"Where are you?" calls the Lord God to Adam in the garden, where our progenitor is hiding among the trees after his sin.

It's a very bad moment, deeply humiliating to Adam, who has only just discovered to his amazement that he is strip, stark naked. Nobody can maintain much dignity when caught in the wrong, and even less when caught without his pants. A few fig-leaves couldn't have helped the situation much.

For a creature made in the image and likeness of God and destined to rule the earth, Adam presents a travesty of deposed kingship. Suddenly, he is every dignitary who ever slipped on a banana peel before the grandstand. He is Canio, Charlie Chaplin, Falstaff and Mr. Macawber all rolled into one. He's the man who buys the Brooklyn Bridge and the gold brick; the sword swallower who chokes to death on a fishbone; the fellow who saws off the limb he is sitting on. He's every deadpan comedian who ever lived, because, of course, Adam isn't laughing.

He can't. There was no laughter in Eden, because who needed it? Everything was pure bliss there, where the Lord God walked in the cool of the day. As Bishop Sheen says, there wasn't even a mother-in-law. Where pain and unhappiness don't exist laughter is superfluous. What would you be laughing at? To exist at all, laughter must stand knee deep in misery, its native soil.

"Where are you?" calls God.

Adam has to show himself. After an unsuccessful attempt to put the whole blame on his wife, poor Adam is sentenced to the natural human condition now prevailing among his descendants. Looking upon him in his nakedness, shorn of all preternatural gifts, cursed and doomed to dust and perspiration, the Lord God can't help feeling sorry for him. Casting His eye on those pitiful fig leaves, He proceeds to clothe Adam and Eve in "garments of skin," to make their shame bearable.

Then, standing back and viewing the lamentable pair, God is represented as quipping sarcastically, "Behold, the man has become one of Us, knowing good and evil!"

And God created Humor. Not levity, mind you, but humor.

The scene is masterly, the work of divinely inspired genius. We can almost see God standing over Adam with His hands on His hips, rocking back on His heels and shaking His head slowly at His foolish creature. Anthropomorphic? I should say so. How else does one write for anthropomorphs? Was there ever a scenarist like the Holy Spirit?

"Behold, the man!"

God invites Adam to take a good look at himself and laugh with Him if he can. Like the skin garments, this proffered laugh is a mitigation of the Fall, an effect of God's inexhaustible mercy. It is medicinal and creative, a healing seed found in the very fruit of pain.

God knew we could probably never find our way back to

Him without laughter. We would die of despair on the road, for "by grief of mind the spirit is cast down," as Proverbs warns. Inability to laugh is very bad for the spiritual life, especially when it is coupled with the mortification and penance God enjoins.

"When you fast," counsels the new Adam, "be not gloomy as the hypocrites."

The Holy Spirit would have us believe that gloom in itself is displeasing to God. It is evident that gladness has a power of impetration second only to humility, for whereas it is true that "the prayer of him that humbleth himself shall pierce the clouds," we are first told that "He that adoreth God with joy shall be accepted, and his prayer shall approach, even *to* the clouds" (Ecclus. 35:21, 20). Though it may not take us through them, joy takes us up to where humility can be effective.

We know Adam accepted God's invitation to laugh, because he has been laughing at himself ever since. It was a gift God gave only to man, because only man needed it, and only man could make use of it. It is necessarily a prerogative of a creature who is adorned with intellect and free will, but who occupies an anomalous position—think, for example, of Aristotle playing hop-scotch, or a king wearing only a few fig leaves.

The philosopher Henri Bergson has something to say along these lines:

> The comic does not exist outside the pale of what is strictly *human*. A landscape may be beautiful, charming and sublime, or insignificant and ugly; it will never be laughable. You may laugh at an animal, but only because you have detected in it some human attitude or expression. You may

laugh at a hat, but what you are making fun of, in this case, is not the piece of straw, but the shape that men have given it—the human caprice whose mold it has assumed. . . .

Laughter has no greater foe than emotion. I do not mean that we could not laugh at a person who inspires us with pity, for instance, or even with affection, but in such a case we must, for the moment, put our affection out of court and impose silence on our pity. In a society composed of pure intelligences there would probably be no more tears, though perhaps there would still be laughter. . . .

The comic will come into being, it appears, whenever a group of men concentrate their attention on one of their number, imposing silence on their emotions and calling into play nothing but their intelligence.

So it would seem that it's the intellectual who laughs best, not the village idiot! Bergson also notes that "The attitudes, gestures and movements of the human body are laughable in exact proportion as that body reminds us of a mere machine"—in other words, in exact proportion as a human being is not what he is. It would appear that the sense of humor is essentially the ability to see incongruity, mentally to place what is alongside of what should be, and then proceed to laugh at the agonizing difference. (Laughter is, I should say, a kind of agony.)

Since the Fall, incongruity *is* the human condition. Because we were made for God, we were fashioned for bliss and were never meant to endure pain. When pain happens to us, we don't know what to do with it. We're not equipped for it. A man in pain, separated from the vision of God, is supremely incongruous. It's understandable that there is no record anywhere in the Gospels of out and out laughter on the part of our Lord. This doesn't mean that His sense of humor wasn't keen, but, given the perfection of the hypostatic union, the psychic release of laughter was simply unnecessary for Him. Surely He often smiled, but for laughter there must be present a certain degree of disintegration. In Him this is unthinkable.

Most of us, at the mercy of what German philosophy calls the *Angst der Kreatur,* would fall apart without rational laughter. As we approach God, we become progressively more serene, more joyous, and we leave giggling and guffaws behind. But never, if we become saints, do we abandon the sense of humor. In fact, isn't deterioration of the sense of humor one of the more reliable signs of insanity? And depravity?

When Adam consented to laugh, something even more marvelous than relief resulted. That cloud-piercer, humility, was born. This was inevitable, for humor and humility are twins, too, and one is never found without the other in this life. To see real humor, one must be humble, for pride never laughs at itself. Pride is capable only of sadism, which is laughing at the other fellow.

Every comedian who ever trod the boards invites us to "behold the man,"—ourselves—and laugh at him. To see what's so funny, we must be able to identify ourselves with him and receive the custard pie, the rubber check, or the perfect squelch as our due. Because all jokes have their roots in the great fiasco in Eden, nothing is ever so funny as humor in dire circumstances—on scaffolds, for example, or in concentration camps. St. Thomas More who fastidiously removed his beard from the executioner's block because, "After all, it is not guilty of treason," gave this line a punch it could have had nowhere else. And St. Lawrence, over the hot coals on his gridiron, asked his tormentors to turn him over "because I think I'm done on this side." This is truly divine humor. Nobody can crack jokes like saints, because they of all people have the strongest sense of the incongruous, knowing better than the rest of us how things *should* be.

They also know how closely the sublime hovers over the ridiculous. Unless handled by experts, tragedies have a way of degenerating spontaneously into comedy, just as comedies can turn into tragedies, so close is pathos to bathos. Let Hamlet trip inadvertently over Yorick's skull, and he's finished as a tragedian. You know what I mean.

Adam's tragedy, the prototype of all, turned into the greatest "comedy" ever put together. This began to happen when God promised He would send Someone to save Adam and Eve.

"He shall crush your head," He told the villain, "and you shall lie in wait for His heel."

A man called Dante wrote about all this, and because he was a great artist, close to truth, he called his work simply "The Comedy." His readers caught on so well to what he was writing about, they renamed it "The Divine Comedy," that being what all real comedy is anyway. Rooted in tragedy, all comedy is characterized by a happy ending, and God's Comedy has a superlatively happy one—God Himself.

God's laugh is like no other. His irony is the woof of redemption. His Bible can be said to be a book written between two "laughs," the first one in Eden, and the last laugh—the apocalyptic one—at the Parousia. In between, the Book is filled with God's "laughter." Doesn't the Psalmist say right out, "He who is throned in heaven *laughs?*" (Ps. 2:4).

And King David:

"The wicked man plots against the just
>and gnashes his teeth at them;
>
>But the Lord laughs at him,
>for he sees that his day is coming" (Ps. 36:12–13).

The ancient prophet Amos calls God,

"He that with a smile bringeth destruction upon
>the strong, and waste upon the mighty" (5:9).

This laughter of God, which can destroy, is therefore not only merciful, it is also just. In it are hidden God's unsearchable judgments.

"I also will laugh in your destruction," says Holy Wisdom, "and will mock when that shall come to you which you feared" (Prov. 1:26).

There is nothing sentimental about this. To be laughed at by God is no trifle. It's Hell. As pure Being, God alone has the right to laugh at His creatures, who can laugh properly only by participation with Him and with one another.

To laugh without God isn't funny: "For as the crackling of thorns burning under a pot, so is the laughter of a fool: now this also is vanity," sighs the forever disillusioned Ecclesiastes (7:7).

But to laugh with God is Heaven:

"When the Lord brought back the captives of Sion
>we were like men dreaming.
>
>Then our mouth was filled with laughter,
>and our tongue with rejoicing!" (Ps. 125:1–2).

Those who sow in tears shall reap rejoicing, because that is exactly what God's humor is like. He sends the big bad rich man to Hell, and Lazarus, whose sores were licked by the dogs, to Heaven. He resists the proud and gives grace to humble nobodies. He takes the stone the builders rejected and makes it the Cornerstone. There is hardly a page of Scripture on which this transcendant "joke" isn't repeated in one form or another.

Ezechiel put it this way: "And all the trees of the country shall know that I the Lord have brought down the high tree and exalted the low tree: and have dried up the green tree and have caused the dry tree to flourish" (17:24).

Our Lord, who withered a green fig tree outside Jerusalem on the eve of His Passion before fructifying the dry wood of His Cross, had already put it this way: "Many who are first now will be last, and many who are last now will be first" (Mk. 10:31).

"Let the brother of lowly condition glory in his high estate, and the rich man in his low condition," quipped St. James, who knew a good "joke" when he heard one. Isn't this transcendentally humorous?

Being a Christian entails catching on to this superlative "humor" and playing along with it. It reduces the trials of this life to little more than so many Perils of Pauline, and what makes these so pleasantly unendurable is our certainty that if we stay on God's side everything will come out right in the end. No matter how close the express train gets to our heroine trussed to the tracks, we know that the villain is licked before the action begins and that the hero will get there in the last reel. We were made for a happy ending, and we crave one with our whole human nature. For us, no story is finished that doesn't have one; and the persevering Christian gets one, no matter what happens.

"Now we know that for those who love God all things work together unto good!" notes that really great humorist, St. Paul (Rom. 8:28).

People who don't believe in God can't see what's funny about a statement like that, and, without God's help, people who do believe in Him can't tell them. There is nothing so frustrating as trying to explain a joke to somebody with no sense of humor. To make matters worse, the Christian missionary finds himself always in the position of having to explain the joke of God's people, which is a family joke. Family jokes are the best kind, but the hardest to get across to outsiders, because, to catch on, prior acquaintance with the whole *esprit de famille* is required.

For instance, at our house we might break into giggles at the phrases "just what I needed," or "dirty filthy thieving paw," or "Daniel J. Boondoggle," but I'm sure you could hardly see why. We have a downstairs closet referred to as Reading Gaol (no, we do *not* incarcerate children in it!). There is also a room called the Dismal, and a part of our lawn designated as Upper Goatland, surely mystifying to anyone not in the know. Just so, without first explaining about Adam and Eve, the devil, and our Lord and Savior Jesus Christ, it is very, very hard for Christians to point out to others the humor hidden in earthquakes, sudden death, infant suffering, or even in bee stings and dented fenders. God's humor makes no sense to them at all.

Yet we are constantly surrounded by it. It envelops us, chides us, instructs us, punishes and encourages us at every moment. If you don't think so, just visit the nearest zoo and look at the giraffes. Giraffe rhymes with laugh, and no wonder. Then look at the monkeys. Whatever other purposes they may serve, certainly monkeys must have been created by God to let us laugh, to let us see what we would be like without spiritual souls.

Then, of course, we can read history books. The rise and fall of dictators is always pretty funny. So is a lot of serious poetry. Or you can pick up the daily paper. I just have, and without even trying, I come upon this caption: "Fabulous Impostor Shot to Death on First Honest Job." The AP release goes on to inform us that this man

> was shot and killed today—apparently dying as the hero he always sought to be in life. Stanley Weyman, 67, who spent half a century posing as everything from a foreign diplomat to the man in charge of Rudolph Valentino's funeral, was slain by robbers while serving as a night motel manager.

A couple of pages away I find this one about a boy angler:

> The biggest fish likely to be caught at the twenty-fifth annual Chesapeake Bay Fishing Fair won't win a prize. It's already been landed—an eighty-five-pound black drum hooked by Joe Cavanaugh, a fourteen-year-old Baltimore boy. The trouble is that Joe didn't even know the fair was in progress. And he caught his whopper while fishing—with perch tackle—from the Emerson Harrison Bridge over the Choptank River. Rules for the contest require that entrants register and do all prize-competition fishing from boats. So far, more than one hundred and fifty fishermen have registered but their best efforts have produced their largest catch eighty-two and one-half pounds lighter than the haul made by young Cavanaugh. The landing of the big black drum, said to be just two pounds under the world record for that species, highlighted the weekend festivities, however. The fish was so big that young Cavanaugh couldn't haul his catch up over the bridge. Instead, he had to trail the fish through the water while he walked along the bridge to shore.

Those who have "toiled the whole night through" and have

caught nothing might do well to become as little children, because I think that's the gist of this story.

I'll never forget one item from South Africa. Some public-spirited fellow, the account read, volunteered to play "casualty" so that a local rescue squad could practice hauling him up and down a cliff to safety on a stretcher. A touch of realism unfortunately marred the proceedings when the rope broke and the unfortunate man plunged to his death, rather more of a casualty than anyone had anticipated. A Christian has to face the fact that God allows this kind of irony every moment. We are all personally familiar with it in one way or another. Unless we have a particularly macabre sense of humor, we don't allow ourselves to roll in the aisles at the fate of the poor South African, but how funny it all becomes if he landed in heaven! If he went to the other place . . . well, that's God's humor. Even we Christians haven't yet been let in on all the family joke.

Until we are, one of the best preparations for the final punch line is certainly Bible reading. It affords us the best possible background for appreciating the family "joke." As we have noted, only believers can simply read the Bible, and we might add that only saints can read it *for laughs*. (If you find this shocking, perhaps you should pray more.) There are plain laughs in the Bible. For instance, in Genesis, the machinations of Jacob and Laban to outsmart each other are impossible to read without at least a smile. In Kings, there is the prophet Elias, whose wit is pretty devastating.

"Let two bullocks be given us," he challenges the priests of Baal, "and cut [one] in pieces and lay it upon wood, but put no fire under: and I will dress the other bullock, and lay it on wood, and put no fire under it. Call ye on the names of your gods, and I will call on the name of my Lord: and the God that shall answer by fire, let him be God!"

The priests leap around their altar, yelling and gashing themselves with knives, but of course nothing happens. Enjoying himself hugely at their expense until noon, "Elias jested at them, saying, 'Cry with a louder voice: for he is a god, and perhaps he is talking, or is in an inn, or on a journey, or perhaps he is asleep, and must be awaked.'"

It doesn't take much imagination to see the great prophet guffawing and slapping his thigh at their desperation. (This was a public contest.) When his turn comes Elias has the satisfaction of bringing down fire from heaven on his offering with the greatest of ease. Being a first class showman, however, he doesn't neglect to douse it with twelve buckets of water first, so as to show off God's power to greater advantage. Don't you think this is humorous? Elias apparently did. And so did the Holy Spirit, who wrote the story and directed Elias in the first place. Not to manage a smile would be hardly polite, and certainly not reverent.

Way before Elias, however, could anything have been more ironic than the beginnings of our redemption? God picked out a childless nomad of ninety-nine called Abraham and promised him: "You shall be the father of a multitude of nations. . . . I will make you exceedingly fruitful; I will make nations of you, and kings shall descend from you." Speaking of Sara his wife, He prophesies, "I will bless her and will also give you a son by her. . . . She shall be the mother of nations!"

Do you remember what Abraham did when he heard this? He laughed. He laughed right smack in the middle of Chapter Seventeen of Genesis, because he knew a good "joke" when he heard one.

"Shall a son be born to one who is a hundred years old? Shall Sara who is ninety bear a child?" Even at this distance we can see his shoulders shaking.

God, who expects humor to be appreciated, replied, "Sara your wife shall bear you a son, and you shall call him Isaac."

Isaac means *laughter*.

When Sara heard about this, she "laughed to herself and said, 'Now that I am grown old and my husband is old, shall I have pleasure?'"

The Lord said to Abraham, "'Why did Sara laugh? Is anything too wonderful for the Lord?' But Sara denied it saying, 'I did not laugh'; for she was afraid. But he said, 'You did laugh.'" Of course she did.

When Isaac was born, "Sara said, 'God has given me cause for laughter, and whoever hears of it will laugh with me.'"

I should think so. I'm with you, Sara! To laugh with Sara is to laugh with the elect the "laugh in the latter day."

Playing the "joke" out further to test Abraham's faith, God soon asked him to sacrifice this only son, upon whom depended the entire posterity Abraham had been promised. Abraham obeyed, for he was the man of faith, worthy to be the father of the blessed.

I wonder, could we prepare the holocaust that he did? Could we sacrifice Laughter?

God, aware of the enormity of such immolation, stayed Abraham's hand at the last minute. He promised him again, "I will indeed bless you, and will surely multiply your descendants as the stars of the heavens, as the sands on the seashore. Your descendants shall possess the gates of their enemies. In your descendants all the nations of the earth shall be blessed, because you have obeyed me."

One of these descendants, sprung from the loins of Laughter, is our Lord Jesus, the Redeemer promised to Adam. The sacrifice of this Son God did not prevent. He was made the butt of jokes, mocked as He hung upon a cross, "laughed to scorn" when He proposed to raise a little girl from the dead, for as Job remarked, "the simplicity of the just man is laughed to scorn."

"I am become a laughing-stock all the day, all scoff at me," foretells Jeremias, not only of the Son of God, but of anyone who follows Him. The Christian has to get used to being laughed at, because he's bound to look ridiculous. This comes of carrying a cross.

Actually, a cross is never carried. Our Lord never commanded us to carry it because that's impossible, and God doesn't command the impossible. If He appears to have said this—as He does sometimes in St. Luke (14:27)—it's because a translator chose to adopt the secondary meaning of βαστάζει, a verb which means primarily "to lift up" or "to raise." Our Lord himself endured the Way of the Cross to prove to us that even He in His human weakness couldn't carry His cross any more than we can ours.

What our Lord told us was, *"Take it up."* Once taken up, a cross is yanked, pulled, kicked, dragged, heaved, pushed or toted uphill. (If you're carrying a cross, put it down. It's not yours; you've picked up somebody else's.) Eventually, like our Lord, you will have to submit to the humiliation of admitting it's too much for you and you'll have to accept help. Even so, you trip over it. You drop it—usually on your own foot—and often fall under it in sight of everybody. At the last, somebody else sets it up for you, nails you to it, and you die on it—slowly—stark naked as Adam. This is living the spiritual life, and the world will always laugh at it. Although transfiguringly beautiful from "up there," down here it's very undignified.

The world's derision of the Christian rose to the surface like putrid foam in Pilate's courtyard. There,

> The soldiers of the procurator took Jesus into the praetorium, and gathered together about him the whole cohort. And they stripped him and put on him a scarlet cloak; and plaiting a crown of thorns, they put it upon his head, and a reed into his right hand; and bending the knee before him they mocked him, saying, "Hail, King of the Jews!" And they spat on him, and took the reed and kept striking him on the head (Mt. 27:27–30).

There he is again, our savage, a whole cohort of him, striking his victim on the head and yelling "Ha-ha!" There is sadism. There is God's gift of laughter turned inside out and become horror. The enormity of its offense here is enough to freeze one's blood. Who will laugh with the savage? Only the damned.

"Upon whom have you jested?" accuses Isaias. "Upon whom have you opened your mouth wide, and put out your tongue? Are you not wicked children, a false seed?" (Isa. 57:4).

Continuing His role in the awful burlesque known as the Passion, Christ, the King of creation, stood before Pilate and the people "wearing the crown of thorns and the purple cloak," emblems of the deposed King Adam.

And, looking upon Him with human pity, Pilate said, *"Behold, the Man!"*

What a stupendous moment! Ignorantly echoing the words first spoken by Almighty God to Adam in Eden, how aptly Pilate might like Him have added, *"He has become like one of us."* Jesus, the descendant of Laughter, had taken on all Adam's guilt and humiliation. Degraded and filthy, He stood in animal skins in his place, as one of us, using for a *crown* the thorns which the earth had brought forth for Adam.

By consenting to become the butt of this farce, He turned humor right side out again and supplied the expected happy ending. Laughter was then turning into joy, for sadism had become its tool. All the merriment of the elect will burst from the pain of the cross!

"Come, beloved of my Father, enter into the joy of your Master!"

"Accipite jucunditatem gloriae vestrae!" shouts the Church on Whit-Tuesday. Receive the joy of your glory! This joy she offers us, this *jucunditas,* has its roots in a *jocus,* as the dictionary reveals. A *jocus,* in Latin or English, is still a "joke." Just as Isaac was a token of Christ, so is laughter a token of joy, a prefiguration of the bliss to come. Useful currency in this life, it can be turned in for real specie in the next.

O felix culpa!

O wondrous condescension of Thy mercy toward us!

That old bad "joke," death, shall be no more, for "Behold, I make all things new," says the Man in Adam's place.

"Have you not read what was spoken to you by God?" He once asked the Sadducees (who didn't seem to have much sense of humor):

"I am the God of Abraham

and the God of Laughter
and the God of Jacob.
He is not the god of the dead, but of the living!"
He who laughs last, laughs best.

ALLELUIA!!!

THE TROUBLE WITH WOMEN

"You have to treat a woman like the devil," remarks my husband. As my brows rise, he adds, "St. Ignatius Loyola said so."

"St. Ignatius could never have said a thing like that," I rejoin—"and still have been canonized!" I try to remain calm.

"He did, though. You can look it up."

You can be sure I do, and I find the passage. It's in the saint's "Rules for the Discernment of Spirits." Here it is:

"The enemy [the devil] conducts himself as a woman." It is only fair, I think, to interject at this point that Iberians have on occasion suggested that the devil *is* a woman—but to continue,

> He is a weakling before a show of strength, and a tyrant if he has his will. It is characteristic of a woman in a quarrel with a man to lose courage and take to flight if the man shows that he is determined and fearless. However, if the man loses courage and begins to flee, the anger, the vindictiveness, and rage of the woman surge up and know no bounds.
>
> In the same way, the enemy becomes weak, loses courage, and turns to flight with his seductions as soon as one leading a spiritual life faces his temptations boldly, and does exactly the opposite of what he suggests. However, if one begins to be afraid and to lose courage in temptations, no wild animal

on earth can be more fierce than the enemy of our human nature. He will carry out his perverse intentions with consummate malice.

"There!" I say. "What he really says is that you have to treat the *devil* like a *woman*. You put the cart a mite before the horse."

"A woman like the devil, or the devil like a woman, what's the difference? The point is, you have to treat them the same. You have to *stand your ground*." My husband doesn't give up easily. "You have to face them boldly," he quotes, doing so.

So goes the battle of the sexes at our house, and a more fascinating game God never invented. Any number can play, anytime, anywhere. It's hilarious, exasperating, educational, and of course, sanctifying. Naturally, the Bible is full of it.

For novices seeking a good grasp of the fundamentals, an excellent starting place is the famous short story in Genesis about Joseph and Phutiphar's wife, which puts before our narrowing eyes a man-woman situation lively enough to elicit first-class interest. The plot is triangular, timeless, and simple. It involves (1) a blameless and handsome hero, (2) a shameless vamp, and (3) her unsuspecting (?) husband. In a frugal twenty verses, the story practically reads itself, so familiar are we with its inevitable course:

As we know, Joseph's brothers sold him to the Ismaelites, and later a high-ranking Egyptian army officer called Phutiphar bought him and took him home with him. Scripture relates,

> The Lord was with Joseph so that he was successful. He lived in the house of his master, the Egyptian. When his master saw that the Lord was with him and prospered all his

undertakings, Joseph found favor with him and became his attendant. He placed him in charge of his household and entrusted all his property to him. From the time he placed him in charge of his household and all his property, the Lord blessed the Egyptian's house on account of Joseph. The Lord's blessing rested on everything that was his, in house and field. He left everything he had in Joseph's charge, and having him, was concerned about nothing except the food he ate (Gen. 39:2–6).

So far so good. Apparently things couldn't have been better. Phutiphar was only too happy to find a steward as competent and honest as Joseph, but the idyllic *ménage à trois* couldn't last long. Scripture sets the action bubbling almost immediately by adding gently, "Now Joseph was well-formed and handsome."

We soon discover that Mrs. Phutiphar is hopelessly taken with him, and what seems to be a happy, placid household is actually seething drama about to boil over. She used every wile to seduce Joseph, only to find him hopelessly virtuous. Being a man, and logical, he took the trouble to explain his reasons for resistance. Not one of them had anything to do with her as a person:

> He refused, saying, "Because of me, my master is not concerned about anything in the house, but has put all he owns in my care. He exercises no greater authority in this house than I, nor has he withheld a single thing from me, except yourself, because you are his wife. How then can I commit this great crime, and sin against God?"

He was facing her boldly. He opposed passion with bare unadorned logic, stating his reasons one, two, three, without any softening appeal to Mrs. Phutiphar's quivering heart. Then, insult of insults, he mentioned her in the same breath with his master's other property—the one item to which Joseph felt he had no right.

The reasons he gave are in themselves excellent and holy. His sense of gratitude, his respect for the married state, and his love of God are indisputable; but women readers sense immediately that he might have softened the blow, perhaps with "I am well aware that you are charming, and I know you must have a pretty dull time of it here," and then have gone on to enlist her sympathy with his own terrible situation, appealing to the mother in her and leading her on from there to respect his ideals. As it is, he sounds a mite priggish, and he succeeded royally in getting her dander up. Joseph was young and inexperienced.

One can, after all, stand one's ground and still be tactful. We know that Joseph's brothers had already found this I-am-better-than-you side of his nature trying beyond endurance and had sold him off. Good people must be especially careful with sinners. When we consider how he flaunted so openly before them his dreams and his coat of many colors, we may wonder whether his sale into slavery wasn't as much a punishment for spiritual pride as a stepping stone to grandeur. Whom God loves, He chastises.

Though we can't deny Joseph's righteousness, it was so righteously righteous! It fell short of that comradely compassion for the difficulties and weaknesses of others which comes with the perfection of holiness. Though quite properly resolved never to temporize with sin, he was still incapable, we suspect, of discerning disfigured goodness in the fallen. Had Mary Magdalene tried to wipe his feet with her hair, would he have kicked her? Well, Joseph lived under the old dispensation. As for Mrs. Phutiphar, she was a scarlet woman, not a bit like his mother Rachel. She was just plain *bad,* and she horrified him.

"Who is weak, and I am not weak?" is a question posed by high sanctity under the new law of love (2 Cor. 11:29).

"Neither will I condemn thee," is the pronouncement of Divinity, whose justice and mercy are one (Jn. 8:11).

Besides, Joseph was a mere man, and a young man at that. Even old men are not noted for their insight into women. Only very spiritual men really understand women, if only because, whether men like it or not, women are "the spiritual sex." Joseph's predicament is actually far from uncommon. Surprisingly enough, it seems to be rather the lot of holy men.

It happened to St. Bernard in his youth, and the great mystical doctor St. John of the Cross was plagued in a similar manner on at least one occasion. In fact, St. John's close companion Fray Juan Evangelista related the following incident in a deposition for the saint's beatification:

> [The saint] was at one time the confessor of some nuns in a certain place and lived in a little house near their convent. A very handsome girl became attached to him, and in order to attain her end, she made use of all possible means [!], none of which was of any avail. She therefore resolved upon a bold attempt against his honor and profession. One night she climbed over the fence into the little courtyard belonging to this house, and thence entered the holy Father's room, where he was alone at supper.
>
> When he saw her, he was astonished, and said that he supposed it to be the devil. [What did we say about Iberians? Devil or woman, what's the difference?] Then with his customary patience, he spoke to her about these things and made

her realize her wickedness; so that she left the room and went back to her house. This witness heard this story from the mouth of the holy Father himself, who was accustomed to speak of it with great frankness. . . .

So we trust he won't mind our mentioning the incident here. Speaking of it elsewhere, Fray Juan says the saint "often told me he had never found himself in a more pressing situation, for she was a girl of good appearance and many good qualities, which made matters worse." And I'll bet she was angry, too.

St. John was a very spiritual man indeed, and understood women so well he had been able to make this one "realize her wickedness." This means he must have been compassionate, but he must have faced her boldly too. Echoing St. Ignatius, St. John is credited with advising confessors that "they should be somewhat stern with (women), for to treat them gently only affected their feelings and they failed to profit thereby."

Anyhow, getting back to the greenhorn Joseph, he continued defending himself against Mrs. Phutiphar as well as inexperience would allow, making it a point never to be caught alone with her. But of course one fine day it happened, and he was doomed. After all, it's almost impossible to face a woman boldly when she is the mistress of the house and you are a slave. Finding him alone and unprotected, she "got physical," as the saying goes.

This is a vulgar expression, and I want to make it plain that it didn't just slip out. I looked for it and used it on purpose. When one wants to get very, very close to truth, to say it as nakedly as possible, it's disconcerting to discover that there is a choice of only two media: a "dead" language which has become stabilized and sacred so that its meanings don't constantly slip out of place—or slang. Anything in between has a habit of falling between the traces.

Because spoken language is a living organism, it grows like all living organisms, from the bottom and inside out, not from the top and outside in—although anything outside may nourish it. As they leave the depths, words lose more and more of their punch until finally they evaporate into bloodless platitudes. To express truth in current coinage, one is constantly chasing words down, not up. When dealing with spiritual topics especially, it's almost impossible not to fall into slang, if not right into the gutter. Doesn't Proverbs tell us "Wisdom uttereth her voice in the streets" (1:20)?

Biblical language, for this reason, is notoriously vulgar in places, though never indecent. So is the language of some of the greatest saints. St. Chrysostom said that the praise of God relieves the heart of man as vomiting relieves an upset stomach. He was very spiritual and obsessed with speaking truly. He could have put it another way, but he wasn't concerned with the genteelness which is only a form of worldliness. Whoever is sick of finicky, pious phrases, turn to the Fathers of the Church, to whom all things are pure!

With their example before me, I now repeat that Mrs. Phutiphar got physical. When a woman gets physical, that means just what the words say: she descends entirely into her instinctual, animal nature. She can be hell on wheels. Ignoring her superior spiritual attributes, she wilfully tries to put herself on a man's level. Unfortunately, she can't. Her emotions are much richer than his, but she isn't equipped with the intellectual ballast which gives his sensual nature balance; therefore she can't "get physical" without falling far beneath him. She disintegrates.

Mrs. Phutiphar did that. Burning with what St. Augustine wasn't too prim to call "the itch of lust," she grabbed poor Joseph. Doing the ignominious best he could under the circumstances, Joseph ran. He wasn't the first man to do this, and certainly not the last. Leaving "his garment in her hand, he fled outdoors."

This was simply too much for the lady, who now became the most formidable opponent a man can have—a woman scorned. In St. Ignatius' words, "if the man loses courage and begins to flee, the anger, the vindictiveness, and rage of the woman surge up and know no bounds." Seething with unrequited affection and smarting from insult,

> she summoned the servants of her house and said to them, "Look! My husband has brought in a Hebrew to insult us. He came in to lie with me but I screamed. When he heard me raise my voice and call out, he left his garment beside me, and fled outdoors."

When Captain Phutiphar returned home, she gave him the same story, which he accepted at face value. With much show of righteous anger, he had Joseph tossed into prison.

Always one to land on his feet, Joseph soon "found favor with the warden," and in no time was running the prison. As he eventually ended up running Egypt for Pharaoh, we begin to guess that being the head of a household can lead to very great things. Joseph was not the only famous executive trained in this lowly manner. His glorious namesake St. Joseph, whom he prefigured, and who is now Householder of the Universal Church, was prepared in the same way for his supernal office.

"A faithful and prudent servant, whom the Lord has set over his household," sings the Church at Matins on his feast. "Amen I say to you, he will set him over all his goods." So we implore you, husbands, take heart. Your struggles with check stubs and windowscreens have mystical significance you don't realize.

We can now dismiss Joseph of Egypt from the triangle. Already well on his way to his high destiny, we know he suffered, learned tact and humility, and forgave everybody. He presents no problem to us.

As for the Phutiphars, well, let's have another look at them. Reading between the lines, the kind of reading women do best, is invaluable here. We note at the outset of this tale that the text runs quite blandly along until we get to the verse about Captain Phutiphar which lets slip the information that he *was concerned about nothing except the food he ate.* Hm-m-m. Moralists, Renaissance painters, Hollywood—in fact, practically everybody—have unanimously agreed that Phutiphar's wife was a shameless hussy, a venomous liar and the obvious villain of the piece.

I'm not so sure. That she is a figure of evil is obvious. I'll grant that. Nor do I want to trample on the beautiful mystical figure Joseph cuts as the faithful steward in the house of a generous God, Mrs. Phutiphar perhaps playing the part of faithless Israel. But Scripture bestows wisdom at every conceivable level. God's Word isn't spoken exclusively to theologians and exegetes; it's spoken to anyone who hears it, even to housewives like me.

Sticking to what I understand about soap opera situations

like this one, I must admit I think the villain is Phutiphar. He's as plain as pudding, as I hope to show in a few masterly strokes of character analysis. Don't try to enlist my sympathy for him. You can tell me he was a pretty good fellow, trusting, goodnatured unless seriously riled, a trifle stupid, no more socially obtuse than most men, hopelessly yoked to a nymphomaniacal shrew and duped by circumstantial evidence—in short, a classical cuckold right out of Molière or Wycherly. I might go along with you but for one thing—that stubborn little phrase: *"was concerned about nothing except the food he ate."*

This reveals him as a man governed entirely by his appetites, sensual or whatever. His god is his belly. Our friends near the roots of vernacular might go so far as to call him a slob. Fastidious or gross, as his case may be, his only purpose in life is self-gratification, and his wife had long ago been tempted to the limit of her meager unenlightened moral strength just living with him. She's a bad girl, no doubt about that, but how did she get that way? Just look at Phutiphar for a minute, ye marriage counselors. *Attendite et videte* where the real blame might lie.

Scripture makes no bones about the fact that Phutiphar eluded every possible responsibility as head of his house. We know, somehow, that he won't end up running Egypt or the Universal Church. Once he found somebody to proxy for him, he placed him without hesitation "in charge of his household and over all his property," including the management of the real estate. He wouldn't even worry about the bills, and certainly he wasn't personally interested in fixing things. Phutiphar didn't face anything, *boldly* or otherwise, if he could possibly get somebody else to do it.

What he did in his spare time, of which he now had plenty, is left to our conjecture. It's possible that he buried himself in his career as captain of Pharaoh's bodyguard, bending his efforts to "getting ahead." I don't think so.

We sophomorons who know a few words of Hebrew can't help noting that in the Hebrew text the word for "captain" is the same as the one used for "warden." Phutiphar and the nameless warden of the prison may have been one and the same man. This makes good sense.* Although Phutiphar imprisoned Joseph and removed him from his household, he had no intention of denying himself the services of anyone so valuable. The sequel would be patently in keeping with the Captain's character. Soon mollified, he put Joseph "in charge of all prisoners: and everything that was done there was done under his management." Characteristically, "The warden did not concern himself with anything in Joseph's charge." As we insist, Phutiphar was congenitally averse to any responsibility he could get out of. Far from being an injured innocent, he was devilishly clever about manipulating circumstances to his own ends.

Aha! Here is corroboration from a most unexpected quarter. My own husband, still facing me boldly, has just handed me a copy of the Koran—into whose pages Joseph and the Phutiphars eventually found their way—and points out the following passage:

> The Egyptian who bought [Joseph] said to his wife: "Use him kindly. He may prove useful to us, or we may adopt him as our son."
> Thus We found a home for Joseph, and taught him to interpret mysteries. Allah has power over all things, though

* Fr. Bruce Vawter espouses this opinion whole-heartedly in *A Path Through Genesis*.

most men may not know it. And when he reached maturity
We bestowed on him wisdom and knowledge. Thus We
reward the righteous.

His master's wife sought to seduce him. She bolted the
doors and said: "Come!"

"Allah forbid!" he replied. "My Lord has treated me with
kindness. Wrongdoers never prosper."

She made for him, and he himself would have yielded to
her had he not been shown a veritable sign by his Lord.
Thus We warded off from him indecency and evil, for he
was one of Our faithful servants.

He raced her to the door, but as she clung to him she tore
his shirt from behind. And at the door they met her husband.

She cried: "Shall not the man who sought to violate your
wife be thrown into prison or sternly punished?"

Joseph said: "It was she who sought to seduce me."

"If his shirt is torn from the front," said one of her people,
"she is speaking the truth and he is lying. If it is torn from
behind, then he is speaking the truth and she is lying."

And when her husband saw Joseph's shirt rent from
behind, he said to her, "This is one of your tricks. Your
cunning is great indeed! Joseph, say no more about this.
Woman, ask pardon for your sin. You have done wrong."

In the city women were saying: "The Prince's wife has
sought to seduce her servant. She has conceived a passion for
him. It is clear that she has gone astray."

The story in the Koran ends with: "Yet though they were
convinced of his innocence, the Egyptians thought it right to
imprison him for a time."

Though necessarily noncanonical, this amusing version
nevertheless gives interesting sidelights which conflict in no
way with Holy Scripture. Joseph's righteous protestation of
innocence rings especially true, considering what we know
about him. As for our friend Phutiphar, he may not have
been as obtuse as he liked to appear where his wife was

concerned. Something of a Pontius Pilate, he simply habitually sidestepped troublesome issues. By publicly accepting his wife's story, he was able to keep up appearances and also to secure Joseph's services in the prison, all the while actually protecting Joseph from Mrs. Phutiphar's vengeance. His reasoning may have been much like Pilate's, who ordered our Lord scourged in a misguided attempt to save him from the wrath of the Jews.

Certainly Mrs. Phutiphar was despised by her husband. Irresponsible and selfish, he couldn't have cared less about her as a person. Maybe in his new-found leisure he took up Egyptian golf, or went on hunting trips with one of those trained Egyptian cats on a leash, which we see pictured on the walls of tombs. Maybe he drank. Whatever he did, we know he didn't spend any time on Mrs. Phutiphar, because the only thing he cared about at home was "the food he ate." She's not only a figure of evil, poor thing. She's a neglected wife.

Captain Phutiphar was a hedonistic worldling, an arch-pagan. His very name means "dedicated to Ra," the false god of the Egyptians. Certainly Mrs. Phutiphar could not have been unaware that he was cowardly, that he was nothing to look up to. She must also have realized that her only share in his life would be catering to his appetites. Deprived of all cherishing, all emotional support or intellectual companionship with her husband, she must have felt her gorge rise as she watched him pleasing his belly day after day like an animal. After Joseph appeared on the scene, maybe he rarely came home at all. Before she was scorned by Joseph, she had first been mortally scorned by her husband. No wonder her rage was so terrible.

Phutiphar may have had other deficiencies. No children are mentioned in his household, and in fact the Koran expressly says Phutiphar thought of adopting Joseph "as our son." This leads us to wonder whether Mrs. Phutiphar, a red-blooded female if ever there was one, may have been denied the normal fulfillment of progeny and all that goes with it. We might also note for what it's worth that the Vulgate calls Phutiphar *eunuchus Pharaonis,* translating a Hebrew word which can mean either eunuch or simply "officer." (This need not surprise us, as officials of oriental courts were often emasculates.) If this is to be taken literally in Phutiphar's case, as the Vulgate may imply, we can see that Mrs. Phutiphar's plight was pitiable indeed. If she was fructified neither spiritually not physically, Joseph's fatal attraction for her is only too understandable. Phutiphar was a husband who took a great deal for granted.

Scripture tells us at the very outset of this domestic tragedy that he did in fact take a great deal for granted where his wife was concerned. It says Joseph "lived in the house of his master," and was given the run of it. This was not common practice, and shows the unusual trust Phutiphar placed in his new slave. It also shows he neglected one of the most important duties of a husband: he provided his wife no protection at all against her womanly weaknesses.

Women are told constantly that rationality is not their strong point, that they are always letting themselves get carried away by their emotions, that they think with their hearts, etc., etc., etc. as if they were in some way to blame for being women. Actually, it is only when a woman is deprived of the loving protection and support of her husband that these wifely characteristics run loose and cause trouble. (We must assume a wife is obedient.) His love is her right, her bulwark.

How well does the Bride of the Canticle know her weaknesses! She begs the bridegroom to bring her more and more fully into his life, saying "Show me, O thou whom my soul loveth, where thou feedest, where thou liest in the midday, *lest I begin to wander after the flocks of thy companions*" (Cant. 1:6). And God Himself, the Husband of Israel, when speaking through Isaias about His chosen vineyard, stresses how first of all He "fenced it in" (Isa. 5:2). When the same God made Flesh repeats this parable of the vineyard, a symbol of the beloved, He marks again how the good householder dutifully "put a hedge about it" after planting it, not leaving it exposed and undefended (Mt. 21:33).

"Where there is no hedge," affirms Ecclesiasticus, "the possession shall be spoiled: and where there is no wife, he mourneth that is in want" (36:27).

Often a husband has only himself to blame.

"I passed by the vineyard of the slothful man," says the Holy Spirit, "and by the vineyard of the foolish man: and behold it was all filled with nettles, and thorns had covered the face thereof, and the stone wall was broken down" (Prov. 24:30–31). This could be a poem about Mrs. Phutiphar.

Like a vineyard, a woman is created to give of herself. She can complete herself only by so doing. She is not the vine-dresser or the fence-builder, and she is harmed psychically, masculinized and degraded, when she is forced to perform these offices for herself. The Bride of the Canticle complains of this too: "They have made me the keeper in the vine-yards," adding sorrowfully, "my vineyard I have not kept" (Cant. 1:5).

A woman loves easily. Her love for man is a love of benevolence, which necessarily includes the gift of self. Man, whose love for woman is a love of concupiscence, must learn this trick of self-giving in the spiritual life. Women do it instinctively.

Women are forever falling in love with their doctors, their bosses, their spiritual directors. Fr. Desurmont, in an authoritative volume on the priestly life, warns priests whose fearsome duty it is to direct women:

> They must not be made even to suspect that one is personally interested in them. Their mentality is so constituted that if they be led to think themselves the object of a particular regard or affection, almost without fail, they descend to a natural plane, be it through vanity or sentimentality.

I think the good Father is trying to say politely that they "get physical." Sentimentality is after all a form of sensuality, and it is always open to "nice" women who are beyond the grosser forms.

There is another reason, too, I think. Women, so easily revolted by carnal men, are by the same token irresistibly attracted to spiritual men, or men they can in any way look up to. That's the way God made women, so there's no reason to be surprised when they act according to their nature. Should there be any doubt in our minds concerning the nature of the Magdalene's first attraction to the Person of our Lord? Never underestimate the power of a man over a woman—especially a good man! Though it pains me to say so, a woman can only be described as a heart forever in search of a head. She yearns for her husband as the heart of the Church yearns for Christ, her Head. These verities can't be sidestepped by irresponsible husbands without dire consequences.

Poor Mrs. Phutiphar was no exception to all this. There is, furthermore, no reason to believe that she wasn't young and beautiful. We may even affirm she was, so unbelievable does she find Joseph's rejection. She was bored. She was utterly denied the stability we have been talking about. She was probably a woman of fire and sensibility, with yearnings for higher things of which her husband refused to take cognizance. Not one to do things by halves, yet frustrated and trammeled, she was burdened with an enormous and undirected power of loving, whose strength can be gauged by the magnitude of the hate it engendered. She was ruthless, of the stuff of saints . . . and devils. Had she been stupid or phlegmatic, her lot might have been bearable, but the forceful way in which she tried to settle Joseph's hash proves otherwise.

When, one fine day, that male paragon walked into the vacuum of her life, we can't wonder at the consequences. Here was everything Mrs. Phutiphar could possibly desire in a man; he took on responsibility, ran things for the benefit of those in his care, and was not concerned only for the food he ate. He was young and handsome, and he was man enough to resist her!

Without minimizing the gravity of Mrs. Phutiphar's offense, we must allow the staggering force of her temptation. Phutiphar was cruel, and much to blame for her sin, as she herself seems to realize sub-liminally when she screams in frustration, "Look! *My husband* has brought in a Hebrew to us." Here the awful thought occurs to us that Phutiphar may actually have put Joseph in his household to keep his unloved wife happy, never dreaming the young man would resist. Phutiphar may have been a real cold-blooded horror. Or then again, maybe he was just plain weak, and, as the Koran suggests, he had really hoped she would look upon Joseph as a son.

Whatever his design, Mrs. Phutiphar wasn't satisfied. She wanted a husband's love, a head for her heart, and suddenly she thought she saw it right there in her own home, where she had had every right to expect it since her wedding day. She set about ensnaring Joseph by the only means she thought men could be ensnared, knowing Phutiphar. That she herself was gross is doubtful. Few women are so by nature, though they can become so by training. Impurity among women is very much a vice of the unloved. Had she been really impure, she would hardly have appreciated Joseph's superlative qualities. She looked up to him, loved him, and the gift of self followed automatically. "Woman is not independent of man" (1 Cor. 11:11), says St. Paul. Man must play God's masculine role toward her by fructifying and protecting her and by providing for her. *That's* the trouble with women!

Poor Mrs. Phutiphar! Only in the cross could she have found the stability she craved in her sad circumstances. As Fray Juan remarked in that other case, "She was a girl of good appearance and many good qualities, which made matters worse." *Corruptio optimi pessima.* Not only that, but Mrs. Phutiphar was a pagan Egyptian. What inkling could she have had of the Christian marvel yet to be revealed, the Wood that sweetens the bitter waters? How could she have known that behind every husband stands Christ, our God made Flesh? How suspect that this Christ is the fructifier of the unloved, the childless and the barren? How could she have guessed that fidelity to her husband in the face of all his terrible shortcomings would have been simply and nakedly what all fidelity is—a fidelity to God the Husband of husbands?

Speaking to the Mrs. Phutiphars through His prophet Osee, God promises:

> I will allure her and will lead her into the wilderness: and I will speak to her heart. And I will give her vinedressers out of the same place, and the valley of Achor ["misery"] for an opening of hope: and she shall sing there according to the days of her youth, and according to the days of her coming up out of the land of Egypt. And it shall be in that day, saith the Lord, *that* she shall call me: MY HUSBAND. . . . And I will sow her unto me in the earth and I will have mercy on her that was without mercy (2:14–16, 23).

That this spiritual consummation, this sublimation of all her natural instincts, might be substituted for the gift of self she yearned to make on a lower level, was a concept utterly beyond our Egyptian wife. A renouncement of natural satisfactions in return for the supernatural favors of a Divine and Tremendous Lover! Incredible! Yet this is LOVE. This is the cross, the opening of hope in the miserable valley of Achor. It is the treasure of the unhappily married Christian wife, to whom God supplies in the order of grace all that may be lacking in the order of nature.

"Give praise, O thou barren, that bearest not: sing forth praise and make a joyful noise, thou that didst not travail with child: for many are the children of the desolate, more than of her that hath a husband, saith the Lord" (Isa. 54:1).

Mrs. Phutiphar had never heard anything like that!

THE TROUBLE WITH MEN

THIS chapter is bound to be shorter than the last one, because I really don't know what is the trouble with men, not being one. I realize that it's all right for a man to be baffled all his life by women without losing his place in society, but a woman is supposed to be able to figure out any given man in five minutes, read his mind, and then tell him how to live. Well, I can't, even with the help of a husband and three sons. I just live among men as best I can.

For a long time I refused to believe that they are as simple as they appear. (Compared to women, they surely seem uncomplicated.) After twenty years or so, wives tend to lose interest in men as a sex and go on about their business, forgetting that their business is men, that woman was created for man, as St. Paul said. That, I tell myself, should be enough to make men very interesting to any woman. Then, too, their very simplicity should be interesting, if only as a reflection of a Divine attribute. God, who is Supreme Simplicity, will fascinate us for eternity. So why not men?

Come to think of it, it's men's simplicity that is the most fascinating thing about them. Generally, with men, you press button "A," and you get reaction "A." Button "B" gets you reaction "B" and so on. This is utterly amazing! With women, you might also get reactions "A" and "B," but then again, it might be "A²" or "B³" or even "AB" or "BA" or on some days "ZXY." If a small boy lies to his mother, she can expect he is probably telling her the exact opposite of the truth or something invented out of whole cloth to suit his purpose. If a girl lies to you, you can be sure it is either just a trifle to the left or right of actuality, and there will be as much truth as possible mixed in. You can also bet you won't find out the real situation until it's too late. Women baffle even women.

Scripture, which is full of information useful to anyone seriously interested in coping with either sex, certainly bears me out. We must remember that Holy Writ not only reveals truth otherwise inaccessible to our intelligence; it also reveals many truths well within the scope of natural reason, but which we may be too stupid or too preoccupied to discover on our own. A married woman who doesn't read the Bible just likes to do things the hard way.

For instance, let's go back to the Phutiphars—but not all the way back to Egypt. Their home can be found in any suburb upper-middle-class enough to breed servant problems, and where the wife, well-dressed, charming, and left to her own devices, is married to a spineless husband "concerned about nothing except the food he eats." Scholars suggest that this phrase is merely Hebrew idiom meaning he didn't care about anything. I'm not educated enough to argue this point, but there is after all no reason why an idiom can't mean occasionally just what it says. If what it says isn't the essential point, how did it get to be an idiom? Nothing grows from the bottom up if not an idiom. In this case, I do believe Scripture means just what the words say, only more so.

Men care about food. They are more sensual than women. To them, physical appetites are very important. When all their other responsibilities fall away in this life, responsibility to their stomachs remains. It's the last to go. Dear me, could any woman resist noticing that even the mortified St. John of the Cross was "at supper" when the young lady importuned him? She couldn't have been much of a Bible reader if she thought she could make any headway with a man by interrupting his dinner. Men must eat. Not only must they eat, but they care about eating.

This is a very simple truth, and therefore a very great one. We have every right to expect to find it in the Bible. I confess this is absolutely all I have ever been able to learn for sure about men, but I suspect that it's the key to everything that can be known about them. It ushers in the whole of theology—creatureliness, redemption and transfiguration. Not being a theologian, however, I shall confine myself as much as possible to the lower periphery of speculation, which lies somewhere in the kitchen.

Men care about food. This truth is one we hear from the cradle up, because the cradle is the first place men let us know they are hungry. Even so it's extraordinary how many wives don't act on it. Like its Author, however, the Bible stoops to our lowliness. Over and over, in the humblest terms, it continues to bombard us with the enormous implications of the obvious, and this truth about men and food is very obvious.

Like many women, Mrs. Phutiphar allowed herself to be repelled by her husband's sensuality, a force whose strength she could never have felt as a man feels it. (Temptations we never have get pretty short shrift!) I suppose that after

Joseph took over, the Captain still turned up for meals, no doubt getting very bad-tempered if dinner was late or not to his liking. This was Mrs. Phutiphar's last chance, but she evidently muffed it. If a pork chop had become the only bond between her and her husband, well, she had had enough: She lost interest in his food, in his sensual life, and Phutiphar lost all interest in her.

This indifference is fatal for a wife, but not just because it's poor psychology on her part. It's a sin of spiritual pride. Because women are the spiritual sex, they fall easily into spiritual sins. They feel superior at the drop of a hat, and especially superior to sensual men. Mrs. Phutiphar, I'm afraid, must have fallen into that.

But all men are not as sensual as the Egyptian Captain. Shouldn't we amend our great truth to read, "Men *of Phutiphar's type* care a lot about food"? No indeedy, not if I read the Bible correctly. Scripture teaches that just men care about their food too. You can't get anywhere with a just man either, unless you feed him.

The first woman to discover this was the first woman. Adam was in full possession of integrated nature, as "just" as just men have hardly been since, yet *he ate* when Eve handed him the forbidden fruit "good for food, pleasing to the eyes, and desirable for the knowledge it would give." Intellectual hunger is hunger too, but I have determined, as I said, to remain on the outer periphery of this subject! I shall content myself with remarking that it was Adam's stomach, real or figurative, that caused us all the trouble we have ever had.

"But Eve ate the fruit first!" I can hear the men say. (I've played Battle of the Sexes a long time.) So she did, but she wasn't the head of the human race and she was deceived by the serpent. "Adam was not deceived," says St. Paul unequivocally. He "ate" in full possession of the facts. Furthermore, Eve's sin, like Mrs. Phutiphar's, was more spiritual than sensual. She ate the fruit, not only because it was "good for food," but because she wanted to be like God, as the serpent had promised her, and she wanted her husband to be like God, too! All Eve's daughters constantly repeat her sin in one form or another. Only one, the Immaculate One, broke the pattern, and when she did, the door of hope in the valley of Achor was opened for all mankind.

Joseph's grandmother Rebecca mastered the truth about men very early too. Planning to trick her husband into giving Esau's blessing to Jacob, the better qualified second twin, so that he might supplant his brother, how did she go about it? Very simply. Scripture says that she instructed Jacob first of all to "go to the flock and bring me two choice kids that I may make of them savory food for your father, such as he likes."

She didn't say, "Bring me that new Chinese cookbook so I can try out on him that chicken, honey and cashew concoction I ran across the other day." She was too smart for that. She planned to make some savory food "such as he likes." That probably means "with potatoes and brown gravy." Ah, the narrow gate is so often missed because it's so plain! Cooking what a man likes can be very dull, but it's also a school for virtue and the exercise of intelligence. It requires mortification of tastes, submission of judgment, obedience, humility, long-suffering, and heaven knows what all. Rebecca proved right there that she deserved to be the ancestress of the elect.

"Then bring it to your father to eat, that he may bless you before he dies," she told Jacob. This gambit proved completely effective. Although his father Isaac was blind and on his deathbed, he was not dead yet, and still cared about the food he ate. Jacob got the blessing.

In fairness to Jacob and Rebecca, who might be censured for these underhand methods, we must recall that Esau had already sold his birthright to his twin some time ago. For guess what? A plate of bread and lentils. The account reads, "Once when Jacob was cooking some food, Esau came in from the field famished. . . . Esau said to Jacob, 'Let me have some of that red food, for I am famished.'

But Jacob replied, 'Sell me first your birthright.'

Esau said, 'I am dying, of what use to me is the birthright?'"

The exchange was made in short order, proving that even men know that men care about food. Being men, however, they don't operate like women: they are inclined to use food not as an inducement, but as a weapon. Men strike *out*, not in.

Hunger is a powerful weapon. Satan used it mercilessly against our Lord when he tempted Him in the desert, and the reprobate Esau will continue to sell his birthright under its threat. What we see today in totalitarian states was predicted by Dostoevski precisely in these terms: "A time is coming when men will say, 'There is no crime, there is no sin, there is no guilt; there is only hunger.' And they will come crying and fawning at our feet, saying, 'Give us bread!'"

Unfortunately for men, bad women seem to master the finer points of this technique faster than good ones. Didn't our Lord note that the children of this world are wiser in these ways than the children of light? An unscrupulous woman using the full power of feminine radar to discover a man's weaknesses can subject him to herself and rule him utterly by a constant, vicious, and determined catering to his appetites. In this systematic debauchery, food "such as he likes" is only the elementary ploy.

The Bible warns men about this, showing them how a bad woman goes about emasculating a husband. It shows them Jezabel, for instance. Compared to her, Mrs. Phutiphar looks like a blushing schoolgirl in pigtails. With Jezabel's help, Achab distinguished himself as one of the worst kings of Israel, yielding to her to the point of sinking his entire nation into idolatry. Scripture says of him, "Now there was not such another as Achab, who was sold to do evil in the sight of the Lord: for his wife Jezabel set him on, and he became abominable. . . ."

The name *Jezabel,* incidentally, probably means "un-husbanded" in Hebrew, and very apt it is. She herself fell prey to Eve's basic temptation—the desire to rule and stand on her own two feet. She is the acme of the disobedient wife, a real man-hater who enslaves men by pleasing them, gradually usurping all their prerogatives. I'll wager Jezabel never wore slacks. That form of appropriation was too crude for her. My guess is that she specialized in ruffles, teetery heels, cream pies, and sympathetic conversation. No man who for one minute gave in to his inclination to shirk responsibility could have withstood her long. Jezabels must be faced boldly at all times, but especially at the dinner table by candlelight. Thoroughly masculinized in their psyches, they use woman's weapons with deadly aim, as men would.

Jezabel's tactics can be inspected at close range in the matter of Naboth's vineyard. Achab, a sensual man like all men, and no doubt encouraged in his sensuality over the years by his wife, coveted this particular vineyard, which happened to be handy to the palace. He wanted to turn it into an herb garden. (That's what it says. Don't tell me Achab didn't like his food just right!) Unfortunately, Naboth refused to sell his patrimony, and King Achab, "angry and fretting," threw a classical childish tantrum. "Casting himself upon his bed, he turned away his face to the wall, and would eat no bread."

He wouldn't *eat!* It doesn't take a Jezabel to realize that this was serious. Achab was really unhappy about that vineyard, and if his wife was to rule him, he must be kept happy at all costs. Do you have among your acquaintances a husband thoroughly dominated by his wife? If you do, you know he never suspects for an instant that he doesn't rule the roost, because he's always kept tame and satisfied, like a gorilla on exhibition. He is never presented with annoying problems, and assumes that he governs the house well because everything is always just as he likes it. So as not to bother him, his wife makes all major decisions, but rarely neglects asking his advice on the color of the new drapes.

In the matter of the vineyard, Jezabel saw immediately an opportunity to make herself indispensable to Achab and to consolidate her command. She told him not to worry about a thing, poor dear, she would handle the whole vexing situation. Achab, for years a shirker who liked to throw his weight around, asked for nothing better. Jezabel told him, "Thou art a great authority indeed, and governest well the kingdom of Israel. Arise, and eat bread (!) and be of good cheer. I will give thee the vineyard of Naboth." You have to assert yourself, Achab, says she, proceeding to do it for him. "So she wrote letters in Achab's name, and sealed them with his ring," says Scripture. She ordered Naboth stoned to death on the testimony of false witnesses and dutifully presented Achab with the confiscated vineyard so he could get on with his desired herb garden.

I guess St. Ignatius wasn't far off. Theologically there's no reason why the devil couldn't be a woman as well as a man. Being pure spirit, the devil is not so much sexless as both masculine and feminine. Come to think of it, Jezabel cuts a fine figure of the female aspect of the devil, the very arch-adversary of the just man destroyed by false witnesses. Deceit, alas, is what women excel in.

In all fairness, it's probable that from the beginning neither Jezabel nor Mrs. Phutiphar had much to work with when it came to husbands. Neither man could have been exactly uplifting company, but that's no excuse for making bad worse. Lots of women have it as bad as they did. Take Abigail, for instance. Married to a bad-tempered miser called Nabal (which means "fool"), she managed to hew to the path of virtue in spite of him.

Her story is in First Samuel. At sheep-shearing time, David and his men begged food of Nabal in the wilderness. Although Nabal's flocks numbered in the thousands and he could well have afforded to be generous, his reply was, "Who is David? . . . Servants are multiplied nowadays who flee from their masters. Shall I then take my bread, and my water, and the flesh of my cattle, which I have killed for my shearers, and give to men whom I know not whence they are?" Nabal, I'm afraid, would have insisted that charity begins, and stays, at home.

David vowed vengeance on this inhospitable man, who

had never been in any way molested by him or his warriors, but he reckoned without Nabal's wife. Described as "a prudent and very comely woman," she brought five donkeyloads of food to the hungry David and his friends while her husband was busy feasting in his house and getting drunk. She made excuses for the latter, and asked that his inquity be laid to her account, "for according to his name he is a fool, and folly is with him," she admitted. (Mrs. Phutiphar, alas, never thought of taking the Captain's sins on herself.)

David, a typical man, was abruptly mollified by the sight of a pretty woman with so much food. He told her, "Blessed be the Lord the God of Israel, who sent thee this day to meet me, and blessed be thy speech: and blessed be thou, who hast kept me today from coming to blood and revenging me with my own hand!" So great is the power of food at the right time and place!

The next morning, when Abigail dutifully told Nabal what she had done to avert disaster, "his heart died within him and he became as a stone." He had been accustomed to high living, and I daresay this may have been a heart attack brought on by overeating and the sudden thought of the "two hundred loaves, two vessels of wine, five sheep ready dressed, five measures of parched corn, a hundred clusters of raisins, and two hundred cakes of dry figs" which his wife had seen fit to squander on a band of desert ruffians while he was too drunk to know what was going on. He died ten days later.

"Thou Fool," says Truth, "this night do they demand thy soul of thee; and the things that thou hast provided, where will they be?"

The minute David heard of the Fool's death, he proposed

to the rich widow. Being a woman who always placed first things first, she accepted. See? You never can tell where feeding a man will lead.

Then, there is Esther. Since she managed to wind up as queen of Persia, we can trust Esther to give us good advice on getting ahead with men. We know that, after becoming queen, she used her feminine charms to save her people from the persecutions of the king's evil counselor Aman, who had been instrumental in promulgating an edict ordering the destruction of the Jews.

Faced with the problem of persuading King Assuerus to revoke the noxious decree, how did she go about it? The same way Eve, Rebecca and Abigail did, of course. She asked him to dinner. This might have seemed unnecessary, for the king was obviously head over heels in love with her, as we can see:

"And the king said to her: What wilt thou, Queen Esther? what is thy request? If thou shouldst even ask one half of the kingdom, it shall be given to thee."

But Esther didn't take any chances. She replied, "If it please the king, I beseech thee to come to me this day, and Aman with thee to the banquet which I have prepared."

> So the king and Aman came to the banquet which the queen had prepared for them. And the king said to her, after he had drunk wine plentifully: What dost thou desire should be given thee? and for what thing askest thou? although thou shouldst ask the half of my kingdom, thou shalt have it.

Esther didn't think the time was ripe, however. She asked him to come again to dinner the next night. Apparently even beloved queens have to be careful.

Being a man, the king accepted again.

> So the king and Aman went in, to drink with the queen.
> And the king said to her again the second day, after he was
> warm with wine: What is thy petition, Esther, that it may
> be granted thee? And what wilt thou have done? Although
> thou ask the half of my kingdom, thou shalt have it.

This time, judging him to be sufficiently softened—putty
in her hands, I'd say—she asked Assuerus to revoke the
decree. As we could easily have predicted, he did so. Aman
got hanged.

Leaving Persia, we can go to Bethlehem and look in on
Ruth the Moabitess. As you will recall, Ruth was a young
widow in search of a husband, who eventually set her sights
on the rich and charitable Booz, her late husband's cousin.
As near next of kin, he could be held responsible for her
under Mosaic law, but Ruth was a foreigner, and maneuver-
ing him into dutifully marrying her required finesse.

Luckily she had the able help of her experienced mother-
in-law Noemi, who wasn't born yesterday. Noemi had had
a husband and sons herself, and she knew men. She told
Ruth how to go about catching Booz, step by step, even
before the thought had occurred to Ruth—let alone poor
Booz—finally making it plain to her daughter-in-law that he
would have to be proposed to.

Now, I am quite certain that this sort of thing happens far
more frequently than we ladies intend to admit. It might
therefore not be amiss to note here a secondary truth about
men to be found in the Bible: they can be rather obtuse upon
occasion. Because they have less intuition than reason, they
must often have situations spelled out to them where people
are concerned. Certainly a clever woman can become adept

at revealing them their own minds, as Ruth did for Booz. Apparently he wanted to marry her all along, but he didn't know it until she told him.

Before this final throw of the dice, however, Noemi told Ruth to put on her best clothes and pretty herself up. Then she added this emphatic warning: "Do not make yourself known to the man before he has finished eating and drinking!" and cautioned her to let him go to sleep.

The docile Ruth did as she was told, and in no time at all Booz was hooked. Already aware that she was a woman of great good sense, he was now confirmed in his opinion. He told her, "May the Lord bless you, my daughter!" and complimented her on not chasing after younger men. (His mature qualities were being appreciated.) In a high good humor, he went the limit, just like King Assuerus: "I will do for you whatever you say; all my townspeople know you for a worthy woman!"

"Ah, who shall find a worthy woman?" we ask with Proverbs. She's priceless!

Booz found her, but only because she found him. "The heart of her husband trusteth in her," who is able to appreciate how simple a man can be. We would know their marriage was serenely happy, even if Scripture didn't tell us so.

"Kissin' don't last; cookin' do!" say the Pennsylvania Dutch.

"Best way to a man's heart is through his stummick," says practically everybody.

If only Mrs. Phutiphar had realized this and had got *really* physical! As long as Phutiphar had a stomach, she still had an entry into his heart, and might have awakened him to a sense of duty. We can't help pondering what heights of spirituality that benighted Egyptian might have reached, had his wife been Ruth, insinuating her noble aspirations into him via that humble organ. A woman who builds her spiritual house on her husband's stomach builds on bedrock.

Mrs. Phutiphar, alas, was too proud. She wouldn't cater to the animal in Phutiphar, and she lost her soul and his too. He was beneath her. Maybe she considered cooking beneath her. Food is so sensual!

And so holy.

"Blessed are you who hunger now," says Christ to Mrs. Phutiphar. "Learn of me, for I am meek and humble of heart."

When He rose from the dead, one of the things He asked His friends was "Have you anything here to eat?" for He was the simplest of men. "And they offered Him a piece of broiled fish and a honeycomb. And when He had eaten in their presence, He took what remained and gave it to them," lest we should think that men and the Son of Man are disembodied spirits who are not concerned about food.

"As long as they care about food, there's hope!" offers Rebecca, speaking from experience.

"The belly will devour all meat," interjects Sirach, that wise old moralist, "yet one is better than another" (Ecclus. 36:20).

"That's what Rebecca means," rejoins Esther the queen. "You have to start somewhere. As long as a man really cares about what goes into him, the rest is up to you. First you give him steak and potatoes, then maybe poetry, then steak and potatoes again, then a dash of dogmatic theology, then . . ."

"Open your mouth wide, and I will fill it," promises the Holy Spirit (Ps. 81:11).

"Oh, come now," sneers Jezabel.

"Show me, O thou whom my soul loveth, where thou feedest," muses the Bride, languishing and gazing off into the distance as usual. "Let my beloved come into his garden and eat the fruit of his apple trees" (Cant. 5:1). The Bride is way "up there." Understanding so much more about men and their food than the rest of us women, she has terrible difficulty putting it into words. Her beloved "feedeth among the lilies."

"Neither is man independent of woman," says St. Paul. Woman plays God's feminine role toward him by cooperating in generating his children, and by *nourishing* him. "For as the woman is from the man, so also is the man through the woman, but all things are from God," both male and female (I Cor. 11:11, 12).

"I don't know about all that," says the ever-practical Ruth, "but when a woman loves a man, she caters to him and feeds him when he's hungry. You might call it a kind of gift of self."

You might. The Man who was God considered food so important that He became Food so as to give Himself.

"For My Flesh is Food indeed, and My Blood is Drink indeed. He who eats My Flesh and drinks my Blood, abides in Me and I in him. . . . He who eats this Bread shall live forever."

"Does this scandalize you?" He asks Mrs. Phutiphar.

"It's a hard saying. Who can listen to it?" replies that lady, whose husband was concerned about nothing except the food he ate.

"I am the Living Bread that has come down from heaven," He tells her again (Jn. 6:51), persistently making His way to men's hearts through their stomachs.

MAN PROPOSES—EVENTUALLY

THE world says it's a man's world, and the world should know. Any woman who thinks it isn't hasn't tried seriously to make her way in it. Even if she takes to cigars and putting lapels on all her suits, she finds that the best cooks are still men. Men get to fly almost all the jets, they can always yell louder than she can at political conventions, and no matter how much she lengthens her stride, men's legs are always longer in proportion to their torsos. It's a man's world because it's a world of sense, and anybody who is bigger, noisier, stronger, thicker-skinned, more logical, and more sensual is bound to come out ahead in it.

As a little girl St. Teresa succumbed to the very common female temptation of trying to do something as a man does it. She ran away from home in Avila to go fight the Moors. A male relative pursued her down the road and brought her back in short order, so she was fortunate in being able to learn her lesson early. She did fight the Moors eventually, very effectively, but only because she learned to fight them as a woman does—spiritually, as a great contemplative. She's still doing it, I'm certain, for we all know "woman's work is never done," here or hereafter. Though it begins here, it continues throughout eternity, for woman's work is simply love. For both Martha and Mary, it's the one thing necessary.

In this life, if it weren't for love, a woman would get trampled by the menfolk at every exit. They have the muscles. It's only when a man tries to be a gentleman that a woman has got him on anything like neutral ground where she stands a fair chance of competing. There is a very good reason for this. When a man tries to be a gentleman, he has taken cognizance of something vast and indefinable that is foreign to his sensual nature. He stands at the threshold of an invisible, interior world, which to his consternation turns out to be a woman's world. In here everything is inside out, and she has all the natural advantages. You can't see this world. It rarely makes the headlines, and without love and intuition you are sure to get lost in it.

A man who faces up to this state of affairs and plows forward is in great danger of becoming a saint, because already a great deal of his pride is gone—at least the kind we call male superiority. Sometimes this takes many years. Abraham was very old and spiritually mature before the Lord could safely counsel him to listen to his wife—a practice Adam had found so disastrous. "Heed all that Sara says to you" (Gen. 21:12), He tells the old man concerning the slave-girl Agar; and Abraham, the man of *great* faith, does as she advises, much against his natural inclinations, but with the happiest results for his descendants.

The best spiritual cooks, a man may discover, are women. Ninety per cent of the great mystics were women. There are three hundred women among three hundred and forty-one known stigmatics, and three times as many women as men enter religious life. *All* housewives are women. We inject these statistics for men readers. Men love statistics. It's characteristic of their world and the way they look at things. Give a boy a bag of marbles; does he start playing? Well, not right away. Nine times out of ten, he'll count them first. (Don't think my knowledge is theoretical.) These particular statistics are just a man's way of saying that a man who wants to come close to God does well to learn how from some woman. He can save a lot of time that way.

Almost any woman will do. He should note that she is smaller, quieter, weaker, and has glass feelings, because she almost always suspects what is really going on in others' minds. She also has short legs, which keep her near the ground, and she is notoriously unreasoning. She spends her life making her way against insuperable odds, attacking Goliath every day with pebbles as a matter of course. She heads for God instinctively if given half a chance, because she can't help looking up to Him as she does to doctors, bosses, spiritual directors or Joseph of Egypt. When God takes an interest in her and gets personal, she's His for life. Oh, I almost forgot to mention: lots of women are pretty, and even if they aren't, they still spend hours on end trying to make themselves so, always finding room for improvement. They will even *suffer* to make themselves beautiful. Men won't. Men are inclined to like themselves as they are, and this is death in woman's world.

Because He is the Supreme Being upon whom all things depend, to God all souls are feminine—even football players'. This is a hard fact for lots of men to swallow and no doubt accounts for so many of them equating "saint" with "sissy." Don't worry, the Tom Sawyers and Huck Finns in every age have been only too quick to recognize spirituality as the natural climate of women and to run headlong in the opposite direction. To an eight-year-old, even cleanliness becomes unmanly, if only because girls tend to this virtue, and mother insists upon it. Yet God likes clean souls, so here again women have a head start.

It's only fair to admit, however, that with all these natural advantages, women have really little excuse for not getting to heaven. I'm afraid that women who don't get there must suffer much deeper hell than lost male souls who went through life lacking such psychological equipment.

"Of everyone to whom much has been given, much will be required," our Lord reminds the ladies (Lk. 12:48).

It's hard for a man to lay aside his muscles and cleave silently to God, but he has to learn. When He wrote the Bible, therefore, God did not neglect to teach us the value of the feminine attitude toward Him. Nothing so reveals His ways with men as what the world calls the "battle of the sexes." As it develops in Scripture, beginning with Adam and Eve and ending with Christ and His Bride the Church at the end of time, the battle of the sexes can be seen to be nothing less than a delicate lesson in prayer. To learn it well, it is necessary only to be thoroughly human, reminding ourselves that grace builds on nature.

Getting down to essentials, just how does a woman go about catching a man—and therefore God? The answer to this one can't be found in encyclopedias. In case you don't know, or haven't had the opportunity to observe a woman in action—or didn't wake up until you were saying, "I do" —the Holy Spirit wrote the Book of Ruth for us. It tells us exactly how a man is caught, and can be referred to at leisure for holy meditation. The Holy Spirit (may He be forever praised) is no prude! Comprising only four chapters, Ruth is a sort of playlet, crackling with dialogue and, I think, meant to be read joyfully in God's presence *con espressione*. God is the only Author I know privileged to create His characters in the flesh before writing about them. This fact alone might suffice to account for the matchless realism of His work, so supremely above anything any hacks down here could produce on their own!

Ruth was careful not to interrupt Booz at mealtime, as we have seen; but this was only a small part of the tactics she used to ensnare him. The talent she possessed in eminent degree, and used to devastating advantage, was the talent for always being Johnny on the spot, all the while showing herself to be just the kind of woman Booz most admired. We girls all have faced the fact that about all you can do to get asked to dance is to look as pretty as possible, preferably wearing something red, and then make yourself unobtrusively available, appearing at the right place at the right time, and letting the man do the talking. This may sound easy, but it's a very great art, as any wallflower knows.

It is the whole art of great mystics, who know how to wait patiently for God to notice them, all the while making themselves as attractive as possible to Him, suffering to be beautiful and adorning themselves with virtues. They obey His Commandments, not because these are anything in themselves, but simply because they know this pleases Him. Favors can't be forced from God any more than they can be forced from a man, but both God and man can be enticed in much the same way! (Shall we say, *want* to be enticed? Let's). A big brawny contemplative monk and a girl looking for a husband have much more in common than might at first appear. Theirs is a science that women know best, however, and any man who hopes to make headway with God would do well to watch closely the women in the Bible.

Concentrating for the moment on the one spiritual writers seem always to characterize as "the gentle Ruth," let's flashback to the beginning of her story:

> Once in the time of the judges there was a famine in the land; so a man from Bethlehem of Juda departed with his wife and two sons to reside on the plateau of Moab. The man was named Elimelech, his wife Noemi, and his sons Mahalon and Chelion; they were Ephrathites from Bethlehem of Juda. Some time after their arrival on the Moabite plateau, Elimelech, the husband of Noemi, died, and she was left with her two sons, who married Moabite women, one named Orpha, the other Ruth. When they had lived there about ten years, both Mahalon and Chelion died also, and the woman was left with neither her two sons nor her husband. She then made ready to go back from the plateau of Moab because word reached her there that the Lord had visited his people and given them food (Ruth 1:1-6).

On the road back Noemi told her daughters-in-law to return to their Moabite kinfolk, as she had nothing to offer them in the way of future homes or husbands. Orpha, an ordinary soul, left. Ruth replied with the beautiful and much-quoted:

> "Do not ask me to abandon or forsake you! for wherever you go I will go, wherever you lodge I will lodge, your people shall be my people, and *your God my God*. Wherever you die I will die, and there be buried. May the Lord do so and so to me, and more besides, if aught but death separates me from you!" (Ruth 1:16-17).

This isn't a simple instance of beautiful filial piety. It's a total conversion. The pagan Ruth, following the plain lead of virtue, accepted the true God. Ruth was ruthless. Already a widow, but now leaving behind her everything she had known heretofore, she showed herself capable of that radical detachment which is the preamble to high sanctity. Orpha couldn't take it; she returned to familiar, carnal surroundings. That's why the story is about Ruth and not about Orpha.

"Every one of you who does not renounce all that he possesses cannot be my disciple!" says Ruth's new God.

Ruth did, and she thereupon entered the mystical life. "Noemi then ceased to urge her [to go back] for she saw she was determined," says Scripture. It is clear that Ruth did not follow Noemi because hers was a dependent personality. Strong-willed as she was, however, she was no Mrs. Phutiphar. She was obedient. Arriving in Bethlehem at the time of the barley harvest, she asked her mother-in-law for permission to "go and glean ears of grain in the field of anyone who will allow me that favor" (Ruth 2:2).

This was no unusual course of action, for Leviticus prescribes, "When you reap the harvest of your land, you shall not be so thorough that you reap the field to the very edge, nor shall you glean the stray ears of grain. . . . These things you shall leave for the poor and the alien. I, the Lord, am your God" (19:9).

Noemi thought Ruth's idea a good one. "Go, my daughter," she said. Then Scripture, in one of those ordinary-seeming little asides, tells us, "The field she entered to glean after the harvesters *happened* to be the section belonging to Booz of the clan of Elimelech." I'm sorry, but I can't help detecting Noemi's "fine Italian hand" here. I firmly believe that she pointed Ruth in that direction, probably saying nothing more suggestive than, "That looks like a pretty good place to start, right over there!" Oh, didn't I say even women can't figure out women until it's too late? Ruth, obedient even to suggestions, sets to, and the action begins.

Not only obedient, faithful, detached, and determined, she now proves herself to be industrious. More important still, she turns out to be poor and humble. Quite content with the leavings of others, she doesn't mind gleaning in any field where the harvesters will allow it, after the custom of the indigent in those days. Booz, coming to inspect the work, soon notices her and asks his overseer who she is. The man informs him, and adds, "Ever since she came this morning she has remained here until now, with scarcely a moment's rest."

Who are Booz' harvesters in the allegory? That's easy, with the New Testament to help us. Doesn't our Lord point out "the fields white for harvest" to the apostolic labors of his disciples? These harvesters can't be other than the hierarchy of His Church. Ruth asked their permission to glean in Booz' field, and they readily granted it. Developing the analogy, we might say here that Ruth represents a good soul who comes humbly to vocal prayer, industriously says her beads, meditates, performs her religious obligations dutifully, laboriously perfects herself in the virtues, gathers the gleanings stalk by stalk into sheaves, and does not expect any special favors for herself.

Then what happens? She catches Booz' eye. In the midst of her wearisome spiritual drudgery, he comes to her and speaks to her personally. This means, if I understand the battle of the sexes aright, that the soul has been granted some direct knowledge of God. This need not surprise us. "Lest you think that you will draw little benefit from perfect vocal prayer," says the experienced St. Teresa, "I assure you that it is quite possible that, if you say the Our Father or some other vocal prayer well, God will raise you to perfect contemplation."

Doesn't God tell us over and over again that He gives His grace to the humble? Isn't this the Divine Sense of Humor at work? And who has more opportunity to practice humility than the weaker sex? Just being content to be a woman in this exterior world, it seems to me, is humility good enough for a start.

Men learn to rely on their own strength in their sense world, and they tend to do likewise in the spiritual one. As long as prayer is still to some degree "active," they are hard to beat. It's only proper that the record for aspirations (some 100,000 per day, I'm afraid!) should be held by a man, the Jesuit World War I Chaplain Father William Doyle. Lots of women couldn't even count that far, let alone *aspire*.

When prayer becomes what the books call "passive," however, women come into their own, because being passive is what they are good at. They learn the hard way not ever to rely on their strength or knowledge, but only on their weaknesses. If she is out to catch a man, a woman soon sees that weight-lifting or analyzing the economic situation in prewar Manchukuo doesn't get her nearly as far as just being herself—weak, loving, and avidly uninformed. In the spiritual life, she soon sees that God is attracted in the same way.

The Abbé Huvelin, director of Charles de Foucauld, used to capsulize the whole of Christianity in a loving humility, and all the saints bear him out. It is a basic attitude of soul which must never be relinquished for an instant. The Little Flower, whose "little way" is nothing else, said our only problem in drawing God's favor was to become little enough:

> To love Jesus, to be His victim of love, the weaker one is, without desires or virtues, the more apt one is for the operations of that consuming and transforming love. The desire to be a victim is enough of itself, but one must consent to stay always poor and without strength, and that is the difficulty, for where are we to find the man truly poor in spirit? He must be sought afar, says the psalmist.

"Have humility and again humility!" cries St. Teresa. "It is by humility that the Lord allows Himself to be conquered so that He will do all that we ask of Him."

In the days of the judges, He allowed Himself to be conquered by Ruth the gleaner. In the New Days, He succumbs again, this time to a gleaner of crumbs. Called a Syro-Phoenician, she is, like Ruth, a foreigner with no influence, but humble and determined. As we know, she doggedly follows our Lord, penetrating even into a house where He "wanted no one to know it," and falls at His feet, importuning Him for the cure of her little girl.

"It is not fair to take the children's bread and to cast it to the dogs," says He to this pagan.

"The dogs under the table get the crumbs!" she retorts valiantly, and God made Man can resist her no longer.

"Because of this answer, go thy way; the devil has gone out of thy daughter" (Mk. 7:26).

As they say in man's world, it's the squeaky wheel that gets the grease.

"I was wondering once," remarked St. Teresa,

why our Lord so dearly loved this virtue of humility; and all of a sudden—without I believe, my having previously thought of it—the following reason came into my mind: that it is because God is Sovereign Truth and to be humble is to walk in truth, for it is absolutely true to say that we have no good thing in ourselves, but only misery and nothingness; and anyone who fails to understand this is walking in falsehood.

Ruth, a poor pagan widow with no standing in the world, is a perfect example of humility. She cuts a pathetic figure, working so hard for so little in the hot sun; and of course, she must have been pretty. The rich Booz couldn't stand that. His protective instincts thoroughly aroused, he tells her, "Listen, my daughter! Do not go to glean in anyone else's field; you are not to leave here." Poor fellow, it's the beginning of the end for him. "Stay here with my women servants," he insists. "Watch to see which field is to be harvested, and follow them; I have commanded the young men to do you no harm. When you are thirsty you may go and drink from the vessels the young men have filled."

Hereby God promises sustenance to the humble soul. He takes a personal interest in her and will protect her against evil. Overcome at this condescension on his part, Ruth "casting herself prostrate upon the ground, . . . says to him, 'Why should I, a foreigner, be favored with your notice?'" As the doctors teach, all genuine mystical graces bring not pride, but more humility with them. Again, I must let St. Teresa explain:

When the Spirit of God is at work, there is no need to go about looking for ways of inducing humility and confusion; for the Lord Himself reveals these to us in a very different manner from any which we can find by means of our puny reflections, which are nothing by comparison with a true humility proceeding from the light given us in this way by the Lord. The bestowal upon us of this knowledge by God so that we may learn that we ourselves have nothing good is a well-known experience, and the greater are the favors we receive from Him, the better we learn it (*The Complete Works of Saint Teresa of Jesus,* Vol. I, *Life,* Ch. XV, translated and edited by E. Allison Peers, Sheed & Ward).

A conversation develops between Ruth and Booz at this point in which it is evident he admires her and wishes her well. She thanks him for his kindness and hints demurely, "Would indeed that I were a servant of yours!"

Humble she is, but clever. This tells him she thinks he's wonderful, without frightening him at all. As we know, men run like deer at the slightest show of aggression on the part of a marriageable female. They are very jealous of their prerogatives as the active sex and will not take any action at all in the face of coercion. Again, men are simple as God is simple, and from them we learn about God's ways with souls.

Like men, God also refuses to be coerced and hides Himself from any creature who becomes aggressive toward Him. "Look that thou have no wonder why I speak thus childishly, and, as it were, foolishly and lacking natural discretion." writes the author of the *Cloud of Unknowing* to an inquirer into the ways of prayer. Speaking of this very thing, he says:

And one reason why I bid thee hide from God the desire of thy heart is this: because I think it would more clearly come to his knowledge, for thy profit and in fulfilling of thy desire, by such a hiding, than it would by any other manner of showing that I trow thou couldst show. And another reason is this: because I would by such a hid showing bring thee out of the boisterousness of bodily feeling into the purity and depth of ghostly feeling; and so furthermore at the last help thee to knit the ghostly knot of burning love betwixt thee and thy God, in ghostly onehead and accordance of will. . . . True it is that all thing is known to God, and nothing may be hid from his knowledge, neither bodily thing nor ghostly. But since he is a spirit, that thing is more plainly known and showed unto him the which is hid in depth of spirit, than is anything that is mingled with any manner of bodilyness. (*Cloud of Unknowing and Other Treatises,* by an English Mystic of the Fourteenth Century, edited by Abbot Justin McCann, O.S.B., Newman).

"Thou shalt not tempt the Lord thy God!" Our Lord quoted Deuteronomy to make this point to Satan, who was desperately trying to make Him force a favor from His Father—in this case, to throw Himself down from the pinnacle of the temple and let the angels catch Him. Our Lord's soul, he knew, was as feminine before its Maker as any other man's. O Wisdom!

But back to our story. Had Ruth actually set her cap for Booz? From what she said, the idea hadn't entered her head, but anybody knows that what a woman says and what she might be thinking are two different things. Obviously, Booz was somewhat like the senior class president taking notice of the freshman girl with the freckles and buck teeth. Then too, this meant that Ruth was looking up to Booz, and as we have seen, when a woman looks up to a man, her heart follows unless she sits on it.

The courtship (is there any doubt that's what it is) accelerates rapidly when Booz asks her to share his dinner with him. Ah! As we have seen, when a girl gets close to a man's food, she's awfully close to his heart. He invites, " 'Come here and have some food; dip your bread in the sauce.' Then, as she sat near the reapers, he handed her some roasted grain and she ate her fill and had some left over." These few words show that on the natural plane Booz is taken with Ruth, and no mistake. Even though he may not be entirely aware of it yet, she must be, or she isn't a woman.

On the supernatural plane, which all this is meant to reveal, several books of mystical theology would be required to explain the situation, so don't expect very much from me. All I know is that when God asks a soul to "dip her bread in the sauce," it must be safe to say she is far advanced in prayer. One misstep and she falls from a great height—as did once an advanced soul invited to share the Last Supper.

"When He had dipped the bread, He gave it to Judas Iscariot . . . and after the morsel, Satan entered into him," relates the beloved apostle.

Again, *corruptio optimi pessima.* So it happens to those who take God's Food lightly. Ruth, a predestined soul, takes care. "She ate her fill and had some left over." There's no spiritual gluttony here. More important still, there's no presumption, for Scripture tells us that when she finished eating, "She rose to glean."

She rose to glean. These simple words exceed my powers of comment. I shall let St. John of the Cross take over. He says,

> . . . There might be raised one question—if progressives (that is, those whom God is beginning to bring into this supernatural knowledge of contemplation whereof we have spoken) must never again, because of this that they are beginning to experience, return to the way of meditation and reasoning and natural forms. To this the answer is that it is not to be understood that such as are beginning to experience

this loving knowledge must, as a general rule, never again try to return to meditation; for, when they are first making progress in proficiency, the habit of contemplation is not yet so perfect that they can give themselves to the act thereof whenever they wish, nor, in the same way, have they reached a point so far beyond meditation that they cannot occasionally meditate and reason in a natural way, as they were wont, using the figures and the steps that they were wont to use, and finding something new in them (*The Complete Works of the Cross,* Vol. I, *Ascent of Mt. Carmel,* Bk. II, Ch. XV, 1, translated and edited by E. Allison Peers, Newman).

Just so Ruth was fed when invited. Otherwise, she gleaned. And see what happens: "Booz instructed his servants to let her glean *among the sheaves themselves* without scolding her, and even to let drop some handfuls and leave them for her to glean without being rebuked." Can anything compare with that sentence? In these homely words God reveals to us the little tricks of a man in love—His own tricks toward a soul He favors.

Most spiritual books make a great deal of the "ordinary or general" help of God in prayer and the one called "extraordinary or particular," categorizing, as humans do, the uncategorizable. In the former, we are told, the soul does most of the work, meditating and multiplying pious acts as best she can on her own, "gleaning." In the latter, the soul becomes more passive, as God gradually does her praying in her. This is fine distinction from a human standpoint, and it looks well in textbooks, labeled 1 and 2, with *a,b,c* subheadings. In practice, it's like trying to distinguish natural from supernatural, or to divorce body from soul. Happy the soul who can kneel to pray and put it all out of her mind!

St. Teresa frequently had occasion to note what God hides

in gleanings. She says this is His usual procedure with souls and tells why:

> Despite their bad disposition and lack of virtues, He gives them favors and consolations, and shows them a tenderness which begins to awake desires in them; He even, very occasionally, lifts them briefly to a state of contemplation. As I said before, He does this to test whether, having enjoyed this sweetness, they will be disposed to seek it often. If they are not, let them be forgiven or rather, do Thou, my God, forgive us, for it is a most grievous thing that Thou shouldst approach a soul in this fashion and that it should thereafter become attached to any earthly thing.
>
> I am convinced, myself, that Our Lord tests many souls in this way and that only a few of them show a disposition to enjoy this favor. When Our Lord gives this grace and we do not hesitate to respond, I feel very sure that He continues to pour forth His favors until He has lifted us to a very high state. But when we fail to give ourselves to His Majesty as wholeheartedly as He gives Himself to us, He yet does a great deal in leaving us to mental prayer and visiting us from time to time, as laborers in His vineyard. But the others are favored children, whom He would have ever near Him, and whom He will not leave, because it is their will not to abandon Him. He makes them sit down at His table and gives them to eat, even taking the food from His own mouth to give to them (St. Theresa of Avila, *The Way of Perfection,* Ch. XVIII, translated by Alice Alexander, Newman).

In Ruth God Himself tells us all this, explaining how Booz "instructed His servants to let her glean among the sheaves . . . and let drop some handfuls." He tells us in these childish terms just how terribly particular his "ordinary" help can be—that high mystical favors can be gleaned by the soul in her humblest vocal prayers without her ever suspecting where they came from, all let drop by His "servants" on purpose.

Mystics have recognized the important part played in human prayer by angels. Like St. Bernard, Walter Hilton ascribed to angels the work of putting ineffable experience into terms intelligible to humans. In the minor work *Qui habitat* he says, "They cleanse the soul from fantasies and vain imaginations, and they form fair likenesses in words and in reasons and temper the light of grace sufferably in feeding thy soul," besides encouraging, scolding and comforting us.

Scripture here and elsewhere upholds this teaching in countless passages. The archangel Raphael, "one of the seven who stand before the Lord," says in so many words to Tobias, "When thou didst pray with tears, . . . I offered thy prayer to the Lord." Both St. Teresa and St. Francis of Assisi were aware of receiving high graces at the hands of seraphim. During Holy Mass, all the faithful say with Mother Church, "Most humbly we implore Thee, Almighty God, bid these offerings to be brought *by the hands of Thy holy angel unto Thy altar above!"*

Ruth, with the help of the angels, gleaned about an epha of barley. This is over a bushel, and, I think, quite a lot for a day's work. When she got home, she gave it to her mother-in-law, along with what she had left over from lunch with Booz. We now know that Ruth is a soul very, very far advanced in prayer. Not only does she get enough to nourish herself, she has more than enough to give to others. Her prayer is not only contemplative, it is apostolic. By playing her passive role perfectly, she has become "more active than all active things." She is now fighting the Moors as St. Teresa fought them.

Noemi, who receives Ruth's overflow, is now completely

unmasked before our eyes. She is Holy Mother the Church, and she has been working quietly behind the scenes the whole time, directing the obedient Ruth's every action. She will now show Ruth how to snare Booz, showing us how the Church brings every pious soul to marriage with God.

She informs Ruth at this juncture that this generous Booz "is a relative of ours, one of our next of kin." This bland remark has explosive force. The phrase she uses is literally in Hebrew, "our redeemer," a label full of meaning for us living under the New Covenant. To Ruth it meant that Booz under Mosaic Law was bound to make provision for her by reclaiming her late husband's land and marrying his widow to raise up male offspring in his name. It now appears the freshman girl has a solid legal hold on the class president —just as, since the Incarnation, the human soul has a valid claim on God!

"He even told me," Ruth confided to Noemi (we can almost feel her breathless excitement), "that I should stay with his servants until they complete his entire harvest!" Of course, foolish girl! Woman's work is never done, as we said. Doesn't the prayer of the blessed continue until the Parousia and beyond? (Was there ever an Author like the Holy Spirit? Why read any other?)

Now see what transpires. At the end of both the barley and the wheat harvests, when the final threshing begins, Noemi judges that it's time for Ruth to lay her cards on the table. This is the time for the chaff to get blown away, the good grain to be stored. We sense expectancy and plenitude. Noemi tells Ruth, "So bathe and anoint yourself; then put on your best attire and go down to the threshing floor," because obviously, this is the way to catch a man—or attract

God. But this is no time for half measures. Noemi tells her further, "When he lies down, take note of the place where he does so. Then go, uncover a place at his feet, and lie down. He will tell you what to do."

"I will do whatever you advise," replies Ruth to Mother Church, and she does so, not even pausing to raise her eyebrows at this extraordinary advice. It's clear that Noemi is no ordinary mother-in-law. Where would Ruth be without her?

"While the king was at his repose, my spikenard sent forth the odor thereof," says the Bride in the Canticle. And suddenly, "in the middle of the night," says Scripture, Booz discovers Ruth near him.

We sense something very mysterious here. There are echoes of the first man who slept "in the beginning," and who wakened to find his wife Eve near him.

"The Lord God cast the man into a deep sleep and, while he slept, took one of his ribs and closed up its place with flesh. And the rib which the Lord God took from the man, he made into a woman, and brought her to him" (Gen. 2:21-22).

Again, we are reminded of another Man, asleep in death on a cross, from whose side was drawn, in blood and water, His wife the Church.

The theme of man and wife, lover and beloved, can be said to underlie the whole of Scripture. De Lubac says,

> From one end of the Bible to the other, there is scarcely a woman of prominence who is not in some way a figure of the Church. . . . It is clear, then, that we have not here just one symbol among many others, characterized merely by the frequency with which it occurs and its preponderant interest. All the others are more or less directly related to it. It is the

central symbol, the guiding spirit, as it were, of the whole interpretation of the Old Testament (Henri de Lubac, *Catholicism*, Burns Oates, pp. 92–94, as quoted by Fr. Wilkin, S.J.).

Like the *"mater et magistra"* she really is, Mother Church doesn't neglect to give adequate sex instruction to her children, explaining its sacredness to them, and not leaving them helpless prey to the false doctors of this world. Male and female He created them, not angels, but mankind. Angels can dispense with the battle of the sexes on physical terms, but creatures wedded to matter can never understand anything about themselves or their relations with God unless they take this fundamental fact about themselves into consideration. It's so obvious that it's easily overlooked, especially by "spiritual" persons who think the first thing that must be laid aside on taking up the spiritual life is precisely *sex*. How foolish.

If they lay aside sex, they may as well lay aside the Bible, because the Bible was written specifically for beings whose sexuality is also mirrored in flesh; it is full of sexual imagery. Whoever neglects this consideration in reading it will never penetrate very far into its mysteries, but will only "gnaw the outer bark" all his life.

According to the Jewish anthropologist Raphael Patai,

> It is an interesting sidelight on the attitude toward sex among the biblical Hebrews that, notwithstanding all the importance attached to this aspect of life, practically no sexual terminology proper is found in the Bible. Reference to sexual activities and sexual organs is always couched in euphemistic terms (Raphael Patai, *Sex and Family in the Bible and the Middle East*, Doubleday).

He notes that words like *flesh, nakedness, thigh,* or *"shames,"* for instance, may often actually refer to the genital organs. Believe it or not, the word *feet* is sometimes so used.

When Isaias, prophesying the Assyrian invasion, says, "In that day the Lord shall shave with a razor . . . the head and the hairs of the feet and the whole head" (Isa. 7:10), he makes more drastic sense than may at first appear. I must ask you to bear this in mind if you intend to read further, for many such allusions can be missed, to the great impairment of meaning of a given passage. Again, for instance, God commanded Isaias, "Take thee a great book, and write in it with a man's pen: Take away the spoils with speed: quickly take the prey."

Isaias was no fool. He understood a sexual metaphor when one came to his mind. He wasn't such a simpleton as to start writing right away. He tells us a couple of verses later:

> *I went to the prophetess, and she conceived, and bore a son.* And the Lord said to me: Call his name, Hasten to take away the spoils: Make haste to take away the prey. For before the child know to call his father and his mother, the strength of Damascus and the spoils of Samaria shall be taken away before the king of the Assyrians (Isa. 8:3–4).

We don't have to point to anything as plain as Canticles or the nuptial Psalm 44 to find a plethora of illustrations of this kind of imagery. Nor do we have to wander down the labyrinthine ways of "archaeological psychoanalysis," which of late have yielded such surprising biblical insights. Following certain rabbinical traditions, proponents of this line of investigation will tell us, for instance, that Noe "lying naked in his tent" is meant to convey that he was engaged in carnal knowledge of his wife—much, I suppose, as God is said to know Israel and dwell in His Tabernacle. Some will go further and aver that the reprobate Ham, who "saw his father's nakedness" was suffering from a terrible Oedipus complex and that he castrated his father at this time, seeking to supersede him. According to this interpretation, it's small wonder that Noe cursed Ham when he "learned what his youngest son had done to him!"

All this is quite outside my limited competence, but even I can catch the overtones in Psalm 23, for example, in which David cries, "Lift up, O gates, your lintels; reach up, you ancient portals, that the king of glory may come in!" This too is sexual metaphor, though highly disguised and spiritual.

This ecstatic psalm is a vision of consummation, of the Lord of hosts, the King of Glory, finally entering holy Sion. Dr. Freud would agree with me very quickly. When he discovered sex to be basic to the life of man, not just physically, but psychologically, he stumbled on Divine Truth without knowing it. Any mystic could have set him straight in five minutes. Dr. Freud, alas, simply didn't go far enough. He was a materialist, and didn't suspect the spirituality of sex. Had he followed the trail he blazed to its logical conclusion, he would have ended at the throne of God. Let's hope he did.

That was where the battle of the sexes led Ruth, as she lay at the feet of Booz, waiting in darkness for him to waken from his "rest." As the prophet Osee said, "I will espouse thee to me in faith." This was her "night," in which she lay silent and hopeful, expecting the best, fearing the worst, her heart probably beating violently. Hers was the spiritual night near the summits of divine contemplation, where the soul is very close to God, but does not see Him. It is a time when all is won or lost, according to those who know.

Did Ruth sleep? How could she? She was hard at work doing what women do best. She was waiting. She was waiting as Penelope waited for Ulysses, as Daisy Mae waited for Li'l Abner, as the Church waits for Christ to return. Like Madame Butterfly waiting patiently for Lt. Pinkerton, hers is the everlasting, *"E aspetto gran tempo, è non mi pesa la lunga attesa!"* Or like the desperate woman in Menotti's opera forever filling out forms, hoping always to see the Consul, she might have said, "My name? Woman. Occupation? Waiting . . . waiting . . . WAITING!" This is the pain of passive love. Patient or desperate, it's awful, and men have little natural aptitude for it.

"We have waited patiently for thee," sings Isaias, a man who learned how to wait, "thy name and thy remembrance are the desire of my soul. My soul hath desired thee in the night, yea, and with my spirit within me in the morning early I will watch to thee."

Commenting on these verses, Walter Hilton says,

> You know well that the night is a space of time between two days. For when one day is ended another does not commence at once, but first there comes the night and separates the days; sometimes it is long and sometimes short, and then there comes another day. The prophet was referring not only to this sort of night; but to a spiritual night. You must know that there are two days or two periods of light; the first is a false light, the second a true one. The false light is the love of this world that a man has because of the corruption of his human nature; the true light is the perfect love of Jesus felt in the soul through grace. . . .
>
> He who loves God dwells in light. The man who perceives that the love of this world is false and does not last, and for

this reason wishes to forsake it and seek the love of God, cannot immediately experience His love, but must stay for a time in the night. For he cannot come suddenly from one light to the other, that is from the love of the world to the perfect love of God. This night consists in nothing else than a withdrawal of the soul from the things of earth by a great desire and longing to love and see and experience Jesus and spiritual things. This is the night; for just as the night is dark and material objects are hidden in it and exterior occupations cannot be carried on, so a man who determines to fix his mind on Jesus and to desire only his love, must give neither his thoughts nor his love to bodily creatures. . . . If he can do this he is in the night, for he is in darkness. . . .

And indeed the darker the night, the nearer is the true day of the love of Jesus. . . . But this night is sometimes distressing, and sometimes easy and comforting. It is distressing at first, when a man is much stained by sin, for grace has not accustomed him to the darkness, and yet he wishes to be in it, and he directs his thoughts and his will to God as far as he is able . . . and because he cannot easily achieve this, he is distressed. . . . What does this darkness consist of then? Truly nothing else than a desire through grace to have the love of Jesus. For its desire and its longing for the love of God, for the vision and the possession of Him, drives out of the heart all worldly interests and all desires of the flesh, and makes the soul recollected and occupied only with how it may come to His love, and so it brings it into this fruitful "nothing." And all is not darkness and nothingness when it is so occupied. For though it is darkness in relation to the false light, it is not all darkness in relation to the true light. For Jesus, who is both love and light, is in this darkness, whether it is distressing or peaceful. He is in the soul making it labor with desire, and long for the light, but He is not yet in it making it rest in love, and He does not yet show His light. . . . It is *waiting* for that blessed love of God which it desires (*Scale of Perfection,* Book II, Ch. 24, Benziger).

"I sleep, and my heart watches," says the Bride of the

Canticle, finding herself in the same dilemma as Ruth, so near and yet so far from the one she loves, thinking of nothing else, and sleep so transparent.

Then, rising suddenly "in the middle of the night," Booz asks Ruth, "Who are you?"

Christ always rises so, as the liturgy for Christmas affirms:

"While all things were in quiet silence, and the night was in the midst of her course, Thy almighty Word, O Lord, leapt down from heaven from Thy royal throne!" (Introit, Sunday within the Octave).

So also did Christ burst from His tomb in the middle of the world's night, and this phenomenon of sudden emergence when things are darkest reverberates through Scripture and every human soul. In the Acts of the Apostles, for instance, we read that in the prison at Philippi,

> at midnight Paul and Silas were praying, singing the praises of God, and the prisoners were listening to them; and suddenly there was such a great earthquake that the foundations of the prison were shaken. And at once all the doors flew open, and everyone's chains were unfastened (Acts 16:25–26).

So shall it be on the Last Day when the foundations of our prison are shaken and the night of this world is finally ended, "And night shall be no more, and they shall have no need of light of lamp, or light of sun, for the Lord God will shed light upon them; and they shall reign forever and ever" (Apoc. 22:5).

"It is true, I come quickly!" says Christ, and "Watch therefore, for you do not know at what hour your Lord is to come. . . . Blessed is that servant whom his master, when he comes, shall find so doing."

"Who are you?" He asks each one of us, as Booz did Ruth. Declare yourself. Who are you?

"I am your servant Ruth," blurts the predestined soul, sealed with the New Name. "Spread the corner of your cloak over me, for you are my next of kin!"

So we see that Ruth ends by popping the question herself, in true female fashion. You can be sure, however, that when a woman goes this far, she is pretty sure of her man—as sure as the baptized soul in grace can be sure of her God.

Booz is captured. He is in love with Ruth and on fire to discharge his obligation as next of kin. He's delighted to discover that it's his simple duty to marry her. His prerogatives are intact, and his male superiority has been effectively appealed to. "May the Lord bless you, my daughter! You have been even more loyal now than before in not going after the young men, whether poor or rich." Who are these young men? I suppose they represent the earthly temptations just mentioned by Walter Hilton.

Booz promises her, "Now though indeed I am closely related to you, you have another relative still closer. Stay as you are for tonight, and tomorrow, if he wishes to claim you, good! Let him do so. But if he does not wish to claim you, as the Lord lives, I will claim you myself. Lie there until morning."

At "morning," which can only be the true light of which Hilton speaks, Booz says to her, "Take off your cloak and hold it out." When she does so, he pours out six measures of barley, and "helped her lift the bundle," before leaving for town. It would seem that God's graces at this stage of the spiritual life require His help to bear, so beyond nature are they. Whatever this barley represents, the dutiful Ruth gives it all to her mother-in-law. Perhaps we can call it "the super-abundant merits of the saints," the treasure we draw on every time we gain an indulgence from Holy Mother the Church.

"He did not wish me to come back to my mother-in-law empty-handed," explains Ruth.

"I am a daughter of the Church!" exclaimed St. Teresa on her deathbed, knowing that God does not grant these favors for ourselves alone.

All that remains now to be done is for Booz to get the mysterious "nearer relative" to relinquish his claim. This fellow, it turns out, means to claim Noemi's land, but when he learns that this would involve marrying Ruth and raising up progeny for her late husband, he refuses. "I cannot exercise my claim lest I depreciate my own estate. Put in a claim yourself in my stead," he tells Booz, "For I cannot exercise my claim."

Who is he, this figure who wants the land but can't supply progeny without detriment to his estate? He is natural man, of course. The fathers draw the analogy finer still by envisaging him as the Old Law, good in itself, but incapable of spiritual generation. Only Booz, "the redeemer," would marry Ruth, figure of predestined Israel. Through levirate marriage, he raised up progeny through her in her husband's name, just as God did for us at the Incarnation, planting immortal seed in Adam's line, to Adam's name. God's marriage with human nature is the exemplar of all levirate marriages in Scripture.

The first child born to Ruth and Booz was Obed. The neighbor women gave him his name, which means "worshipper." Scripture says "Noemi took the child, placed him on her lap, and became his nurse." Uncalled-for interference, you might say. Isn't that just like a mother-in-law! But no. Noemi, we recall, is Mother Church, who nurses all the elect, as does our Lady.

And Scripture adds sweetly that Obed "was the father of Jesse, the father of David." It seems that Ruth is not only a lesson in prayer. As kinfolk are prone to do, we have been delving into the geneaology of our own next of kin, our Lord and Savior Jesus Christ.

"Abraham begot Isaac, . . . Salmon begot Booz of Rahab," reads St. Matthew, "Booz begot Obed of Ruth, Obed begot Jesse, Jesse begot David the King," and on down to "Jesus who is called Christ," just to show what the battle of the sexes can produce.

By the way, did I think to mention what the name Ruth means? I just found out that most scholars believe it to be an old Hebrew contraction for "girl friend"!

E PLURIBUS UNA

THE Bible is in some respects the most shocking book ever written. It easily scandalizes imperfect souls, and horrifies sinners, because of course the more steeped in pride a fellow gets, the more fastidious he becomes. Fastidiousness is the "purity" of the fallen. Atheists find the Bible disgusting in spots and have even used their own disgust to prove no God could have written it.

Though we might expect it to be the other way around, the more innocent and God-fearing a human being is, the harder it is to scandalize him, because scandal is simply a temptation. According to the Catholic Biblical Encyclopedia, the word means literally

> the movable stick or trigger in a trap, that is, any obstacle or snare designed to make another stumble or fall. Thus, Christ is figuratively said to be a rock of scandal, because the Jews who expected a political Messias were scandalized and stumbled at the suffering and crucified Christ, and consequently failed to obtain justification.

"Blessed is he who is not scandalized in me," said this Rock of scandal, well knowing that He is the most shocking fact we can ever meet up with. Whoever can accept Him is blessed indeed, because he is on the way to sanctity. Surprisingly enough, our Lord pronounced these words as a rather

cryptic message to be delivered, not to the Pharisees, but to
the great St. John the Baptist in prison. Apparently even that
spiritual giant was entertaining—well—moments of wonder
at this Man he had publicly called the Lamb of God. As for
the Pharisees, they were hopeless. The Gospels are full of
their skirt-withdrawing and eyebrow-lifting. Truth had
become too indecorous for them.

Because the Bible is Christ, it too may scandalize us, and
I offer this bit of introduction by way of leading up to one
of the most scandalous things in it. I am going to explore
the marvels of polygamy. (If you like, you can skip this
chapter and go on to the next one, but I'm afraid that will
be even more shocking.) You can't sneak around the difficulties in the Bible; you have to hit them head on. I know
that much!

Polygamy is pretty shocking to us modern Pharisees, and
the free and easy way in which the Old Testament seems to
treat it is even more shocking. We have our Lord's word for
it that "it was not so from the beginning," and He quotes
Scripture, saying, "Have you not read the Creator . . . made
them male and female and said, 'For this cause a man shall
leave his father and mother and cleave to his wife, and the
two shall become one flesh'? . . . What therefore God has
joined together, let no man put asunder" (Mt.19:4-6).

He is speaking here specifically of divorce, but divorce and
polygamy are very closely allied; in fact, down here they are
now two aspects of the same thing. In our modern civilized
world, plural marriage is frowned upon as an outmoded
form of morality. It is no longer considered gracious living
to have more than one wife—that is, at one time. Actually
polygamy is still very much with us in its other form—a

number of wives in succession. (I think the current catch-phrase for this sort of thing is "sequential polygamy." I just heard it used on a TV program where five or six celebrities were explaining the state of society to me.) It seems we have simply substituted time for space as our marital dimension and have gotten very righteous about it. Why exactly it should be considered moral for a man to have several wives provided he doesn't live with them all at once has me stumped, given the basic premise. Some materialist will have to take me aside and explain in simple language. In the meantime, I will go on with this chapter.

From the Christian standpoint, divorce necessarily introduces polygamy if the partners remarry, and since the Incarnation, polygamy is necessarily adulterous. A man can have only one living wife in this life, no matter how many others he may live with or promise to be responsible for. From now on, three's a crowd.

I think the most telling analogy of sacramental marriage can be found right where you might expect it—in the very flesh it joins together. To meet the materialists on their own ground—matter—let's pursue the truth beyond the mere bodies of the spouses. Let's track marriage down to sperm and ovum. Truth is true at whatever level we strike it.

Allow me to quote from an elementary biology text. (I'm sure there are many better ones for my purpose but this is the best, because it's the only one I can find on the shelf at the moment.) Here we have the battle of the sexes explained under the heading "A Zygote Is Formed":

> Sperm cells are usually liberated in great numbers in the vicinity of the egg cells. Due to some chemical attraction, the sperm cells swim to the eggs. The first sperm to touch the

plasma membrane of an egg cell enters the egg cell. The tail of this sperm, being no longer of any use, is left outside the egg cell. Immediately after the entrance of the sperm, a *fertilization membrane* quickly forms around the egg cell. This membrane prevents the entrance of another sperm. Then the nucleus of the sperm which entered the egg cell unites with the nucleus of the egg cell, *thereby forming a single nucleus.* The single cell formed by the union of the sperm cell and the egg cell is called the fertilized egg, or zygote (Mark A. Hall, *Reviewing Biology,* p. 212).

What unutterable mystery! If this natural knowledge had been available to St. John of the Cross, what lessons on prayer could he not have drawn from it! Did you mark the tail of the sperm which, no longer of any use after fertilization, just drops off? Doesn't God's grace, useful in this life, give way before the glory of Divine Union?

But I digress. There is so much doctrine in everything! Now, if we accept the materialist's conclusions on marriage, all we have to do to explode this zygote, membrane and all, and make the cells single and free again is to get some Reno judge to say a few words over it and maybe fill out a printed form. They will immediately fly asunder, and they can join up with other cells they feel more compatible with, explaining to their friends that the whole thing was an unfortunate mistake.

Silly? Of course. Any materialist will agree, because under a microscope he can see cells and knows this won't happen. Unfortunately, he has no microscope for spiritual realities, which can't be seen without faith. Because he is a materialist he persists in thinking that anything outside the range of his senses doesn't exist. Only the believer can know that the irreversible union of the sperm and ovum is simply a reflection in matter of a tremendous spiritual fact acted out in flesh. The bond of matrimony excludes all others, as long as the partners are clothed in matter,—*i.e.,* as long as they are on earth. In heaven, as our Lord explained patiently to the Pharisees, things are different. It follows that in normal reproduction, no sperm can unite with two ova.

So in Christian society polygamous unions are similarly outside reality. But the Bible is full of polygamous unions! That, indeed, is true, and shocking. The first inkling we get of this state of affairs is in Genesis, the book of beginnings, in one of those famous first eleven chapters.

Not very long after the Fall, a descendant of Cain the murderer, called Lamech, is mentioned as taking "two wives, the one named Ada, and the other Sella." I think the Holy Spirit hides the clue to this ménage in those names. Ada means "ornament"; that's what a wife is to a man, his "glory," as St. Paul puts it. Sella means "shadow"; as a second wife, she has no real existence. She is the three that makes the crowd. Lamech himself is not presented as a very nice fellow, but he's not meant to be overlooked, for St. Luke saw fit to mention him in his genealogy of our Lord. He is a figure of wrath, saying, "I kill a man for wounding me, a youth for bruising me. If Cain shall be avenged sevenfold, Lamech seventy times sevenfold!" (Gen. 4:23-24). I guess we could expect bigamy here. It was to atone for people like Lamech that our Lord instructed Peter to forgive "seventy times seven," and help him turn sadism inside out.

Scripture subsequently remarks sadly, "The sons of God saw that the daughters of men were fair, and they took wives for themselves, as many as they wished. Then the Lord said, 'My spirit shall not remain in man forever, since he is flesh.' " The Flood wasn't long in coming.

So polygamy had bad beginnings. God frowned on it, we feel, as soon as it made its appearance. But let's not dodge any issues. Even after the Flood, many just men were polygamous. Abraham had two secondary wives. Jacob had Lia and Rachel, plus two lesser ones. Elcana, father of Samuel, had Anna and Phenenna. Then, of course, there was Saul. And David. To cap them all, there was Solomon. Even in Our Lord's time, levirate marriage like Ruth's was still lawful, though monogamy was the rule.

Polygamy, though definitely not willed by God and not looked up to by the Jews as an ideal, was certainly permitted, as was divorce in certain circumstances. Why? As far as I know, there is only one answer to this. Marriage under the Old Dispensation was of the nature of a sacramental, not a Sacrament. Like all the rites of the ancient Covenant, it functioned *ex opere operantis,* according to the faith of the performer looking forward in time to Christ. It was figure, not fact, as a sacrament is.

As we know, a sacrament acts of itself, given no obstacle, *ex opere operato.* Some latitude could be allowed the Jews and mankind in general before the Incarnation, as our Lord put it, "because of the hardness of your hearts," but now no longer. Now marriage represents and draws its life from the union of Christ and His Church, which is a monogamous marriage. Sacramental marriage today must be monogamous to be at all between Christians.

Here is the incomparable Father Matthias Scheeben, who puts it all into correct theological language:

The sense in which marriage is said to be so great a mystery clearly depends on the meaning apprehended in its relationship to Christ and to the Church. This relationship can be understood either as symbolic or as real. According to the first interpretation, the Apostle would depict marriage in its natural character as a symbol of the supernatural union between Christ and the Church; in that case marriage itself would not be mysterious, but would only be a figure, itself empty of content, that would serve to call up before our minds a mystery extrinsic to it, that is, the union of Christ with the Church. Hence matrimony would be the sacrament of a mystery rather than a mystery, and a barren sacrament at that. Such, in fact, is marriage between non-Christians in our day; such was marriage everywhere before Christ, even among the chosen people who still looked upon it as a divine institution, although in this case it could not be regarded as a mere symbol, for it was set up by God as a prophetic type of the union between Christ and the Church, and was therefore brought into closer relationship with this union. Even marriage in Paradise was no more than a perfect type of this mystery, although it possessed a mysterious character; for its mysterious character was not derived from any reference to Christ and His Church, at least not in the same way as Christian marriage.

Christian marriage, on the contrary, has a real, essential, and intrinsic reference to the mystery of Christ's union with His Church. It is rooted in this mystery and is organically connected with it, and so partakes of its nature and mysterious character. Christian marriage is not simply a symbol of this mystery or a type that lies outside it, but an image of it growing out of the union of Christ with the Church, an image based upon this union and pervaded by it. For it not only symbolizes the mystery but really represents it. It represents the mystery because the mystery proves active and operative in it. . . .

How does this take place? The Apostle teaches that baptism makes the Christian husband and wife members in the body of Christ, members of His flesh and bone. They have already been received into the mysterious union of Christ with His Church. As members of the bride of Christ they themselves are wedded to Christ; hence the mystery of the union between Christ and the Church is found in them also. They can rightfully unite with each other in matrimony only for the end which Christ pursues in His union with the Church, that is, the further extension of the mystical body of Christ (*The Mysteries of Christianity,* translated by Cyril Vollert, S.J., B. Herder Book Co.).

Where does polygamy figure in all this? Are primitive peoples who still practice it today hopelessly depraved? Hardly. Outmoded as it is under the New Dispensation, polygamy cannot be dismissed as simply "unnatural," as a sexual perversion. Theologians and Christian jurists are quick to warn us against trying to defend monogamy by any specious appeals to natural law, as if the evils of polygamy were self-evident among all peoples.

God did permit polygamy, but not in the same way He permits sin, for He countenanced it. Why? He certainly never countenaced polyandry. That's hardly fair, you might say, if you are a woman. What's the difference? There's a big difference. In Ruth, we have already detected levirate marriage as a type of the Incarnation. So too *polygamy reflects a truth in the spiritual order;* polyandry does not. The latter is unnatural, a real perversion in itself. Although polygamy among the baptized, clothed in flesh and living in Christian society, has become impossible both sacramentally and practically, the great truth it mirrors is still true. As Father Scheeben says, members of the bride of Christ are themselves wedded to Christ. All of us who are in a state of grace are so many wives in a polygamous union with Almighty God. Because there is only one God, polyandry has been rooted in falseness from the beginning. Polyandry could only reflect a union between a human soul and several gods. These could only be devils.

Individually, we are all brides of Christ. "Blessed is he who is not scandalized in me!" reminds the Lord of this multiple household, who, as Husband of all, is still the Husband of only one—His Holy Church. "With men this is impossible, but with God all things are possible!" So we see that polygamy was, though in a lesser degree than marriage, also a figure of great things to come.

Esther, who captivated King Assuerus and was introduced into his multiple household, can be of great help to us here. In her story, the Holy Spirit presents us with a wealth of fascinating detail about harems, knowing of course that most of us would never get any first-hand experience along these lines. To lay ourselves open to His doctrine, however, we must first rid ourselves of any mental claptrap we may have picked up from grade B movies on the subject of harems. Dim lights, silken veils, hookahs, tambourines, beaded curtains, and stilettos should be quietly returned to the prop rooms where they came from.

King Assuerus' harem was a highly respectable place. Anyone trying to force his way in would have been killed on the spot, no doubt. The word *harem* doesn't mean "Minsky's Pleasure Dome" in Hebrew. It means "consecrated" or "sacred." In the true sense, therefore, convents and monasteries are harems, as is the Church. Its members are wedded to the King and are set apart, provided for and protected by Him from the advances of the world. They must love and obey Him alone, for they have been raised to a high estate in His Kingdom. Like convents, harems were locked and guarded, not to keep the inmates in, but to keep intruders out.

"A certain man," said our Lord, "gave a great supper and he invited many," who scorned the invitation. Eventually he commanded his servants to "go out quickly into the streets and lanes of the city, and bring in here the poor, and the crippled, and the blind, and the lame." Then, "Go out into the highways and hedges, and make them come in, so that my house may be filled. For I tell you that none of those who were invited shall taste of my supper."

King Assuerus, as we have already seen, was also fond of banquets. Now identified as the Persian monarch Xerxes I, he gave one once that lasted seven days, and the guest who refused to come, believe it or not, was the official hostess herself, Queen Vasthi. Her husband ordered her to appear, "with the crown upon her head, to show her beauty to all the people and the princes: for she was exceeding beautiful." (Vasthi, as a matter of fact means "beautiful" in Persian.)

She refused point-blank, declining to be seen by "all the people that were found in Susan, from the greatest to the least." She refused in spite of the fact that the king summoned her specially for his grand finale on the last day of the feast, sending word through "the seven eunuchs that served in his presence" figures, no doubt, of the seven spirits who stand before the throne of God, mentioned by Tobias' angel. Vasthi, I'm afraid, represents Mother Eve, who, though called to be the spiritual mother of mankind as well as its physical ancestress, refused her vocation. Like Vasthi, she was too uppity.

As Eve, the model of all disobedient wives, couldn't be allowed to get away with it without reversing the order of creation, neither could Vasthi. Assuerus agreed with his counselor, who pointed out that

> Queen Vasthi hath not only injured the king, but also all the people and princes that are in the provinces of King Assuerus. For this deed of the queen will go abroad to all women, so that they will despise their husbands, and will say: King Assuerus commanded that queen Vasthi should come in to him, and she would not! (Est. 1:16-17).

This was mutiny. No doubt about it, a queen more obedient—and more democratic—had to be found. Assuerus therefore set about advertising for a more dutiful one:

> And let some persons be sent through all the provinces to look for beautiful maidens and virgins. And let them bring them to the city of Susan, and put them into the house of the women under the hand of Egeus the eunuch, who is the overseer and keeper of the king's women; and let them receive women's ornaments, and other things necessary for their use. And whosoever among them all shall please the king's eyes, let her be queen instead of Vasthi. . . .
>
> And when the king's ordinance was noised abroad, and according to his commandment many beautiful virgins were brought to Susan, and were delievered to Egeus the eunuch; Esther also among the rest of the maidens was delivered to him to be kept in the number of the women. And she pleased him, and found favor in his sight. And he commanded the eunuch to hasten the women's ornaments, and to deliver to her her part, and seven of the most beautiful maidens of the king's house; and to adorn and deck out both her and her waiting maids. . . .
>
> Now when every virgin's turn came to go in to the king, after all had been done for setting them off to advantage, it was the twelfth month. So that for six months they were anointed with oil of myrrh; and for other six months they used certain perfumes and sweet spices. And when they were

going in to the king, whatsoever they asked to adorn themselves they received. And being decked out, as it pleased
them, they passed from the chamber of the women to the
king's chamber. And she that went in at evening, came out
in the morning; and from thence she was conducted to the
second house, that was under the hand of Susagaz the
eunuch, who had the charge over the king's concubines.
Neither could she return any more to the king, unless the
king desired it, and had ordered her by name to come (Est.
2:3, 8–9, 12–14).

Dear me! What does God mean to teach us by inspiring a
Hebrew historian to give us all this intimate information?
If I were a saint and knew "the secrets of the king," I could
explain so many things here! Unfortunately, I'm not, and
can pass along only a few "gleanings." The deep meanings
in Esther will yield themselves only to prayer, and in this
field, every reader travels alone.

Who are the eunuchs Egeus and Susagaz, who supply the
maidens with necessities and proper ornaments? I confess
I'm not sure. Perhaps you can say. The outstanding lesson
that emerges from the verses just quoted, however, is simple
enough: No one comes into the king's chamber without
preparation and suitable attire!

"Friend, how didst thou come in here without a wedding
garment?" asks the king in our Lord's parable to the guest
who arrives at the marriage feast in everyday clothes (Mt.
22:12). This is a terrible breach of spiritual etiquette and
accounts, says our Lord, for so few being chosen out of the
many invited. I find it amusing to note that it's a male guest
who is so remiss. Certainly it would be hard to imagine a
woman who "hadn't a thing to wear" ever going to a big
wedding reception without going shopping first!

We are told that it took a whole year for a concubine to prepare herself in King Assuerus' harem. "For six months they were anointed with oil of myrrh, and for other six months they used certain perfumes and sweet spices." The medicinal and bitter myrrh, figure of suffering and purgation, must necessarily precede the perfumes and spices of what theology calls the "illuminative" and "unitive" stages in the soul's journey to God. Then we note that in answer to their prayer, the maidens are adorned with virtues, the "ornaments" provided by the king through his eunuchs, much as Ruth received the bounty of Booz through his servants and harvesters.

This preparation period St. John of the Cross interprets as

the lofty state of spiritual betrothal of the soul with the Word, wherein the Spouse grants the soul great favours, and visits it most lovingly and frequently, wherein the soul receives great favours and delights. . . . Though it is true that they come to the soul when it is completely purged from all creature affection (for spiritual betrothal, as we say, cannot take place until this happens), nevertheless the soul has need of other and positive preparations on the part of God, of His visits and gifts whereby He purifies the soul ever more completely and beautifies and refines it so that it may be fitly prepared for such high union. In some souls more time is necessary than in others, for God works here according to the state of the soul. This is prefigured in those maidens who were chosen for King Assuerus; although they had been taken from their own countries and from their fathers' houses, yet, before they were sent to the king's bed, they were kept waiting for a year, albeit within the enclosure of the palace. For one half of the year they were prepared with certain ointments of myrrh and other spices, and for the other half of the year with other and choicer ointments, after which they went to the king's bed. . . . Oh, how good a place would this be to warn souls whom God is leading to these delicate anointings to take care what they are doing and into whose hands they commit themselves, lest they go backward! (*The Complete Works of St. John of the Cross, The Living Flame of Love,* Stanza III, 24, 26, translated and edited by E. Allison Peers, Newman).

Their preparation completed, like Ruth, these maidens "went in at evening and came out in the morning" from the king's chamber; for as Walter Hilton explained, our spiritual life on earth is a night of faith. They entered the king's chamber at the close of one day, the "false light" of this world, and emerged after night into the true light of the next day.

"We have three gates to pass through before we enter within, brother," wrote Blessed Alonso de Orozco,

for like Queen Esther, we must proceed in an orderly way if we are to come to contemplate King Assuerus, Jesus Christ our God, seated on the throne of His majesty which is His holy cross. The first gate through which we have to pass to contemplation is holy reading. The second is unceasing meditation. The third is fervent prayer—to which contemplation is closely allied (*The Mount of Contemplation,* Ch. 7).

Then Scripture tells us that once a soul had visited the King, "neither could she return any more to the king, unless the king desired it, and had ordered her by name to come." It would take many theologians to expound this verse to the bottom, for it leads us fully into the mysteries of passive prayer, where God is absolute master of His gifts, where above all "no one can come to me unless the Father draw him." Like Ruth at the feet of the sleeping Booz, here the soul is utterly at the beck and call of God and can do nothing to bring supernatural favors on herself.

Between visits lie the long waitings, the patient desolations and emptinesses of the mystics, until God "orders her by name to come." Being ordered by name is sanctity, the unique perfection of the individual, her "name" having been written by Almighty God on the white pebble, "which no one knows except him who receives it" (Apoc. 2:17). It is a personal apocalypse, for how can we know who we are until we know who God is?

"Then will the kingdom of heaven be like ten virgins who took their lamps and went forth to meet the bridegroom (and the bride)" says the Bridegroom Himself. I confess I feel the words "and the bride" make little sense here, and it's comforting to learn that they are conspicuously absent from the best manuscripts. Apparently some ancient glossator found our Lord's parable too much of a shocker without them and proceeded to slip them in. May God forgive him if he did! "Blessed is he who is not scandalized in me!"

Five of these virgins were wise, says our Lord, and five foolish.

> "But the five foolish, when they took their lamps, took no oil with them, while the wise did take oil in their vessels with the lamps. Then as the bridegroom was long in coming, they all became drowsy and slept. And at midnight a cry arose, 'Behold, the bridegroom is coming, go forth to meet him!'"

Didn't Booz awaken "in the middle of the night" and ask Ruth *her name?* What incomparable craftsmanship! Who can write like the Holy Spirit?

"Then all those virgins arose and trimmed their lamps. And the foolish said to the wise, 'Give us some of your oil, for our lamps are going out.' The wise answered, saying,

'Lest there may not be enough for us and for you, go rather to those who sell it, and buy some for yourselves.' [Or, perhaps ask Egeus or Susagaz!] Now while they were gone to buy it, the bridegroom came; and *those who were ready* went in with him to the marriage feast, and the door was shut. Finally there came also the other virgins, who said, 'Sir, sir, open the door for us!' But he answered and said, 'Amen I say to you, I do not know you.' Watch therefore, for you know neither the day nor the hour" (Mt. 25:1-13). You don't know when the middle of your night is.

Whoever finds this parable "difficult" may not be reading it by the light of Esther's lamp, so delicately do the Old and New Testaments illumine each other's depths. Scripture soon tells us specifically about the wise virgin Esther's own preparation for this Bridegroom:

> And as the time came orderly about, the day was at hand when Esther . . . was to go in to the king. But she sought not women's ornaments, but whatsoever Egeus the eunuch the keeper of the virgins had a mind, he gave her to adorn her. For she was exceeding fair: and her incredible beauty made her appear agreeable and amiable in the eyes of all. So she was brought to the chamber of king Assuerus the tenth month, which is called Tebeth, in the seventh year of his reign. And the king loved her more than all the women. . . . And he set the royal crown on her head and made her queen instead of Vasthi.
>
> And he commanded a magnificent feast to be prepared for all the princes and for his servants, for the marriage and wedding of Esther. And he gave rest to all the provinces, and bestowed gifts according to princely magnificence (Est. 2:15-18).

To understand these verses, it is necessary to turn to the fathers of the Church and many other great exegetes, who recognized Esther as a type of the Blessed Virgin, who replaces the disobedient Vasthi—figure of Eve—as the favorite in God's harem of beatified souls. It is of her the Bridegroom in the Canticle says:

> There are threescore queens, and fourscore concubines, and young maidens without number. One is my dove, my perfect one is but one, she is the only one of her mother, the chosen of her that bore her. The daughters saw her, and declared her most blessed: the queens and concubines, and they praised her (Cant. 6:7–8).

Let him who will, try to tell us the bride of the Canticle wasn't being welcomed into a marvelous harem! Likewise in the person of Esther the Blessed Virgin surpasses all her competitors in heavenly wisdom and beauty. Whereas we are told that the maidens who passed on to the king "decked out as it pleased them," Mary on the other hand "sought not women's ornaments, but whatever Egeus . . . had a mind, he gave to adorn her."

"Be it done to me according to thy word," she said quietly at Nazareth, not seeking anything special for herself beyond God's naked Will. To us she counseled the same behavior at Cana, saying, "Do whatever He tells you." This is spiritual direction of such sublimity, it's no wonder the Liturgy sings of her, "After her shall virgins be brought to the King!" for she can bring us all in her train if we will heed her. Wasn't Esther given "waiting maids?"

"For the King hath greatly desired thy beauty!" adds the Liturgy. Already on seeing her, he had ordered his eunuch to "hasten the women's ornaments and to deliver to her her part," so that she was united to him after only ten months' preparation instead of the usual twelve. Scripture says her nuptials occurred in the month of Tebeth "in the seventh year of the king's reign." This would be the dead of winter, but the fullness of time. God is in love with Mary, and it would seem that for her He might hasten the Parousia as He hastened it once before for her at Cana.

"Hasten the time!" we pray at the Communion of the Mass of Our Lady of the Miraculous Medal, feeling somehow that He will do it.

The Book of Esther is full of the glory of Mary and simply exceeds my poor powers of comment. As we have already touched upon, Esther succeeded in persuading King Assuerus to reverse the wicked Aman's edict of death against her people, just as Mary, the new Eve, succeeded by her *fiat* in rescuing us from Satan's sentence of death. She did this, not for herself, but for us, for as King Assuerus told her, the edict didn't apply to her at all. "Fear not," he said. "Thou shalt not die: for this law is not made for thee, but for all others!"

So did the Holy Spirit tuck away in the depths of the Old Testament the dogmas of Our Blessed Lady's Immaculate Conception and her Assumption. This verse occurs, incidentally, in a chapter of Esther which Jews and Protestants today do not allow in their canons. They hold it "apocryphal." Mary and heresy have never mixed.

> The entire Old Testament, St. Paul affirms, is a figure of the New. . . . Many people and especially Our Lord and His Blessed Mother have been prefigured and symbolized in the Old Testament. We can discover figures and symbols of Mary . . . in numerous persons and things. One thinks, after all, of what one loves; one speaks of what one thinks

when the occasion presents itself. But Mary was the creature most loved by the Holy Spirit. Continually He must have thought of her. No wonder then, if the Divine Spirit, condescending to speak to men, as He has done by the inspired Scriptures, should have spoken and frequently spoken of His beloved spouse. (Gabriel Roschini, *The Divine Masterpiece*, Mercier Press.)

The Holy Spirit vouchsafed Esther's uncle, Mardochai, a dream concerning her great destiny as Mediatrix of Grace. Mardochai saw the people of God crying to Him in distress, whereupon, "As they were crying, a little fountain grew into a very great river, and abounded into many waters. The light and the sun rose up, and the humble were exalted, and they devoured the glorious."

"He has put down the mighty from their thrones and has exalted the lowly," echoes Mary in her Magnificat.

Mardochai himself soon understood that "The little fountain which grew into a river, and was turned into a light, and into the sun, and abounded into many waters, is Esther, whom the king married and made queen."

At Lauds on the Feast of the heavenly Esther's Assumption, the whole Harem sings, "The Virgin Mary has been taken into the heavenly bridal chamber, where the King of kings is sitting on a starry throne!"

In the Book of Esther, at her accession, the King "gave rest to all the provinces," because He is Lord of the Sabbath, and His Peace, through the Blessed Esther, He has given unto us.

Mary, Queen of Heaven, pray for us, intercede for us! "Return, return, O Sulamitess, Woman of Peace: return, return that we may behold thee!"

"Hasten the day, bring on the time!" (Ecclus. 36:10).

___

THE TROUBLE WITH THAMAR

IF GENEALOGY is your hobby, the chances are you're getting along in years. It's also likely that you scan the finer print with a magnifying glass and have considerable free time on your hands, since if you talk about what interests you, you'll have acquired a solid reputation as a bore. Your obituary may read, "Dedicated Genealogist Joins Ancestors," if the editor has the nerve.

This is inevitable, of course, because lots of people, especially younger ones, can't appreciate the finer points of this demanding science. When they read the Bible, they probably just skip the *begats,* and when they don't, they can't keep their eyes open. This is rather sad, but then, young people have never had much sense of humor. They haven't suffered enough. It takes time to see what's funny in genealogies, mostly because it takes time to know people, and that, of course, is what genealogies deal in.

Nowhere can God's laugh be heard more plainly than in St. Matthew's genealogy of our Lord. It rings loud and exuberantly, but if you skip the *begats* you are sure to miss it. St. Matthew compiled with care, and I suspect his tongue may not have been far from his cheek in the process. Though tracing our Lord's descent according to the male line, he apparently still couldn't help mentioning four women.

Ruth, we have seen, was one. The others were Thamar, Rahab and Bethsabee. These all had one characteristic in common: not one of them was quite respectable. According to Hebrew standards, none was quite "in." They were all "out." Ruth was a foreigner; worse still, a Moabitess. Her forebears were traditional enemies of Israel who had caused the Jews endless trouble from their earliest days in Chanaan. According to Mosaic Law Moabites were outcasts of the first water: "No Ammonite or Moabite may ever be admitted into the community of the Lord, nor any descendants of theirs even to the tenth generation. . . . Never promote their peace and prosperity as long as you live!" warns Deuteronomy (23:4, 7). (You see now what a Romeo and Juliet affair was the romance between Ruth and Booz.)

Rahab, also a foreigner, was even worse off. She was a harlot. She kept a public house built into the city wall of Jericho, and she too was a convert. She harbored the two spies sent ahead into Jericho by Josue as he prepared to take the city, saving them from certain capture by letting them down over the wall at dark by a rope through her window. To these two men she had already made her profession of faith:

> . . . The Lord, your God, is God in heaven above and on earth below. Now then, swear to me by the Lord that, since I am showing kindness to you, you in turn will show kindness to my family; and give me an unmistakable token that you are to spare my father and mother, brothers and sisters, and all their kin, and save us from death (Jos. 2:9–13).

The men promised, and told her, "When we come into the land tie this scarlet cord in the window through which you are letting us down; and gather your father and mother, your brothers and all your family into your house. . . . We shall be responsible if anyone in the house with you is harmed."

She tied the scarlet cord in her window, and when Jericho fell and was sacked, the promise was made good. Scripture says, "Because Rahab the harlot had hidden the messengers whom Josue had sent to reconnoiter Jericho, Josue spared her with her family and all her kin, who continue in the midst of Israel to this day" (Jos. 6:25).

I'll say they continue to this day! Harlot or not, Rahab is an ancestress of the Mystical Body! St. Paul, who had once been "in" but chose to side with the "outs," and as a consequence had to be sneaked over a city wall out of a window on the end of a rope himself on one occasion, warmly commends Rahab the harlot for her faith in his Epistle to the Hebrews. St. Matthew's genealogy lets slip the fact that Rahab settled down and married an Israelite named Salmon and became the mother of—guess who? Booz! So we understand how he could afford to be so partial to Ruth, after all.

When it comes to Bethsabee, wife of the Hittite Urias, her story is too well-known to need recapitulation. Apparently one of those women congenitally irresistible to men, she succeeded in attracting Ruth's great-grandson, King David, by the simple expedient of getting him to look at her, ultimately driving him to break five if not all of the Commandments to get her for himself. She was an adulteress. Had her paramour been anyone but the king, she would no doubt have been stoned or burned according to due process of law. She is a mystical figure of gigantic stature, precisely because she is so outrageous and leaps so far beyond our view down here. A female figure who, like Esther, attracts a king as easily as she did bears meditating on, once we penetrate beyond the obvious moral aspects of her story.

Of all four ladies, however, I like Thamar best, because she's the worst. She's so marvelously bad, I can't talk about her right away without warming to my subject a little. Just let me say that if she or the other three just enumerated had called singly or in a body on any Pharisee lady whose reputation was above reproach, the amenities would no doubt have been preserved, but the call, alas, would most likely never have been returned.

St. Matthew's pointed inclusion of their names in the Messias' genealogy was after all something like giving exclusive prominence to the unfortunate Uncle Eb who was hanged, or the "other" grandmother who sought to recoup the family fortunes by spying for the Kaiser at military balls —all the while perversely ignoring the great uncle who got nominated for President or the cousin who held Pasteur's test tube at the historical moment. Had St. Matthew been a Pharisee, he might indeed have included the four ladies for the sake of accuracy, but he would certainly have softened the truth by scattering their names as inconspicuously as possible among others more illustrious by conventional standards. He would no doubt have dwelt instead on the four—and justly so—irreproachables: Sara, Rebecca, Lia, and Rachel. Their virtues were more domestic, more tractable, and well, let's say it—*duller*.

I'm afraid St. Matthew didn't do this because St. Matthew wasn't very respectable himself in the pharisaic sense, and it's obvious he was intent on making a point. He tells us straight out that he was a publican, so we know right away that in pharisaic society he had little social standing. Like Zacchaeus, he was of the breed of tax gatherers who, though not necessarily dishonest, lived by collecting money from their own people for the hated foreign overlords. Farmed out at auction to the highest bidders, the publican's concession was a cutthroat business, lucrative in direct proportion to the degree of extortion, for the publican's fee was simply the difference between the actual levy and the amount gathered.

To Matthew the publican, sitting one day in his tax collector's booth, our Lord said simply, "Follow me." And Matthew, whose equivocal position in society had long ago endowed him with a salutary detachment from what people might think, "arose and followed him" without more ado. Our sins are educational if nothing else, and God draws us to Himself by our vices when He can't draw us by our virtues!

Shortly after his call, Matthew tells us, our Lord came to dinner at his house. Although rich and probably fairly well educated, Matthew didn't move in the very best circles. His world was rather *demi-monde* at best, for

> many publicans and sinners came to the table with Jesus and his disciples. And the Pharisees seeing it, said to his disciples, "Why does your master eat with publicans and sinners?" But Jesus heard it, and said, "It is not the healthy who need a physician, but they who are sick. . . . For I have come to call sinners, not the just" (Mt. 9:10–13).

This dinner must have made a profound impression on the new disciple at the outset, for ever afterward he remains dumbfounded and lost in admiration at the shocking way God loves bad people, for whom the fires of hell are nothing else than "negative transfiguration," the fires of God's unrequited mighty love, eternally seeking His beloved miserable little creature against its miserable little human will. "For I have come to call sinners, not the just," He said, putting respectability in proper perspective. He loves sinners so much, He even permits *sin*.

Teaching "the just" in the Temple one day, He tells them, "Amen I say to you, the publicans and harlots are entering the kingdom of God before you . . ." for "the publicans and the harlots believed . . ." Rahab believed, and Matthew who reports the incident believed. Oh, how he must have loved hearing such remarks! Writing his Gospel, he repeats this message over and over again as simply as possible "in the Hebrew tongue" to any fellow Jews who might be induced to acknowledge themselves sinners and to accept as Messias the One who was the least respectable of them all. This Messias, he keeps insisting, was so disreputable He was crucified by the just as a common criminal; He was descended from people like Ruth, and Bethsabee, and Rahab and Thamar.

This is God's laugh on the Pharisees, and St. Matthew heard it when his Lord said, "Follow me" to a tax collector. He must have heard it even before that when he first heard about Thamar. Anyway, we know she made an impression on him strong enough to get herself included as one of only four women in the Messias' genealogy. She certainly made a strong impression on me, and at the risk of acquiring an unenviable reputation as a writer of religious pornography, I should like to dwell on her for a few pages.

Not daring to improve on her story as related by the Holy Spirit, here it is, from God to us:

Juda took a wife for Her his first-born. . . . Her . . . was wicked in the sight of the Lord, so the Lord killed him. Then Juda said to Onan, "Go to your brother's wife, perform your duty as brother-in-law, and raise up descendants for your brother." Onan knew that the descendants would not be his own, so whenever he had relations with his brother's wife, he wasted his seed on the ground, in order not to raise up descendants for his brother. What he did was evil in the sight of the Lord, and he killed him also.

Then Juda said to his daughter-in-law Thamar, "Remain a widow in your father's house until my son Sela grows up"; for Juda feared that Sela too would die as his brothers had. So she went away and dwelt in her father's house.

After a long time Juda's wife, the daughter of Sue, died. After the time of mourning, Juda went to Thamna with his friend Hiras, the Adullamite, to superintend the shearing of his flock. When Thamar learned her father-in-law was on his way up to Thamna to shear his flock, she put off her widow's garments, put on a veil, wrapped herself up and sat at the gateway of Enaim on the road to Thamna; for she was aware that Sela had grown up, yet she had not been given to him in marriage.

When Juda saw her, he thought she was a harlot; for she had covered her face. He went over to her at the roadside and said, "Come, let me have intercourse with you," not knowing that she was his daughter-in-law.

She asked, "What will you give me to have intercourse with me?"

He answered, "I will send you a kid from the flock."

She responded, "Provided you give a pledge until you send it."

Juda said, "What pledge shall I give you?"

She replied, "Your signet and cord, with the staff that you are carrying."

He gave them to her, and had relations with her, and she conceived by him. Afterward she arose and went away. She took off her veil and put on her widow's garments.

When Juda sent the kid by his friend the Adullamite, to recover the pledge from the woman, he did not find her. So

he asked the men of the place, "Where is the temple-prostitute who was by the roadside at Enaim?" They answered,
"No temple-prostitute has been here."

He returned to Juda, saying, "I did not find her; more-
over the men of the place told me, 'No temple-prostitute has
been here.'"

Juda replied, "Let her keep the things; otherwise we shall
be ridiculed. I sent this kid, but you could not find her."

About three months later Juda was told, "Your daughter-
in-law, Thamar, has played the harlot and is pregnant as a
result."

Juda said, "Bring her out to be burned."

But as she was being brought she sent word to her father-
in-law, "I am with child by the man to whom these things
belong; look whose signet, cord and staff these are."

Juda recognized them and said, "She is more in the right
than I; for I did not give her to my son Sela!" But he had
no further relations with her.

Well! I guess it's stories like this that prompt the admoni-
tion from certain tight-lipped quarters never, *never* to put
the Bible in the hands of children! As a matter of fact, this
particular story is the one Paul Blanshard was once heard to
characterize in a panel discussion as "some nasty little incident in Genesis," upon which the Roman Catholic Church
had the temerity to rest her doctrine on birth control. He
was referring to Onan's sin, of course. I'm sorry about Onan,
but he's not the character who fascinates me, nor, do I think,
who fascinated St. Matthew.

We like Thamar. She is the exact reverse of Onan, for
there is certainly nothing negative about her. A wanton?
Yes, if you mean *wantin'*. Let's not quibble, for both words
come from the same stem and it doesn't take a philologist to
see why. As Rachel did to Jacob, Thamar could easily have

exclaimed (and probably did), "Give me children or I shall die!" And like Jacob, her frustrated and bereaved father-in-law might well have answered, "Can I take the place of God, who has made you barren?"

There is absolutely no one harder to sidetrack than a woman intent on having a family, especially a widow with no illusions. On the natural level, Thamar's story deals with elemental femininity, which is complicated enough in itself. I think G. B. Shaw called it "the life force." He explored its dreadful and irreversible potential in "Man and Superman" so well it would be useless for me to add my two bits here. He came to the conclusion that the ordinary man is necessarily helpless against the power which gripped Thamar. I guess this is true, inasmuch as Scripture says so as forcefully as Mr. Shaw. *Tota mulier in utero!*

Scripture, however, goes much deeper than playwrights. The man-woman situation here triggers off a battle of the sexes which takes on all the aspects of guerilla warfare. Thamar's tactics with Juda must somehow teach a daring method for a soul to reach God that is even surer than Ruth's, quicker than Esther's, and which employs means even more deceitful than Rebecca's or Rachel's. It only remains, with the help of the angels, to figure it out.

I shall tell you what little I suspect, which shouldn't take long, but probably will, because it's so hard to put into words. As St. Bernard remarked,

> I make no doubt that many among you possess in themselves a greater abundance of spiritual refreshment than I can communicate, but the little I have is not lost to me by being shared with you. Nay, rather I shall enjoy whatever the Lord may be pleased to bestow with all the more sweet-

ness and security, when I enjoy it in common with you. This kind of treasure is not lessened by communication; it rather increases according as it is dispensed.

Knowing that many of my readers may find what follows all too obvious, I shall continue nevertheless, in hopes of that blessed increase.

The safest place for me to start is with Thamar, whose human character must be ascertained before proceeding, as it is the key to the whole story. I like to think that hers is a temperament which a spiritual director would recognize immediately as the classical "choleric" or "irascible." Its proper virtues are hope and fortitude; its proper vices pride and anger. Its main object is inevitably the *arduum bonum,* for it thrives on obstacles. For an irascible, nothing he wants is ever too difficult. (Modern psychology would say he had drive.) Just tell him there's some goal that's too high for him, or that he hasn't the guts to reach, and he's after it like a shot. Make the goal too accessible and your irascible will fold up, or, more likely, look for another one.

Suicides and martyrs are easily drawn from these ranks. They are the angry. They feel strongly and deeply about everything, and move rapidly, without hesitation, in any chosen direction. An enlightened choleric who learns humility is capable of the most stringent ascesis, for he is as belligerent against the enemy within as without. He has strong desires; what he wants, he gets. If he gambles, he gambles everything. His temptations are likely to be presumption as regards God, and contempt toward neighbors less strongly motivated than himself. St. Peter, an outstanding example of this, tells our Lord only a few hours before he denies Him, "Even though all shall be scandalized because of thee, *I* will *never* be scandalized!" The irascible often gets the feeling that he is a lion alone among a bunch of rabbits. Only bad health could render him tepid about anything, especially religion. As might be expected, many great saints were irascibles.

Some of these saints are women. St. Teresa was certainly one. Listen to the Thamar in her as she says of mediocre souls stuck in the Third Mansion:

> The penances done by these persons are as carefully ordered as their lives. They have a great desire for penance, so that by means of it they may serve Our Lord—and there is nothing wrong in that—and for this reason they observe great discretion in their penances, lest they should injure their health. You need never fear that they will kill themselves: they are eminently reasonable folk! Their love is not yet ardent enough to overwhelm their reason. How I wish ours would make us dissatisfied with this habit of always serving God at a snail's pace! As long as we do that we shall never get to the end of the road (*Interior Castle,* Ch. II, *Complete Works of St. Teresa,* Vol. II, translated and edited by E. Allison Peers, Sheed & Ward).

One doesn't have to be a sissy to be a woman. Thamar wasn't. She exemplifies a kind of aggression peculiar to women, which must be exerted as women exert it, not as men do. Her wantonness is the elemental craving of the human soul for fruition from its God. It is ruthless and persevering, and risks everything, though heavily disguised and its presence often unsuspected until its object has long been reached. Haven't we already noted that men—and God —are repelled by any show of aggression on the feminine side?

Obviously Thamar is a mystical type of a certain kind of

human prayer. She isn't for everybody, perhaps, but she is the only kind for some people. Our Lord was thinking of them when according to St. Matthew He said, "The Kingdom of Heaven has been suffering violent assault, and the violent have been seizing it by force!" Is there any doubt that St. Matthew himself had the choleric temperament? Precisely remarks of our Lord's like this one seem to stick in his mind.

Here is an open invitation to all Thamars to wrest God's favors from Him, if they can. "I refuse you Sela!" God might just as well have said, knowing full well how to attract souls like hers.

To the rabbits He says, as He did to the rich young man, "If thou wilt enter into life, keep the Commandments." Knowing this is no incentive to the Thamars, He adds, "If thou wilt be perfect, go, sell what thou hast, and give to the poor, and thou shalt have treasure in heaven; and come, follow me." This is St. Matthew's Gospel again, of course. Matthew was a Thamar, and he followed. The rich young man, I guess, was a rabbit, because the Gospel says he "went away sad, for he had great possessions." Let's hope he managed to keep on keeping the Commandments.

Thamar is sound doctrine. Her presumption is holy. We must acknowledge that she is detached, in fact, she is *twice* widowed, which in spiritual language might lead us to believe she is a soul completely purified as to both higher and lower faculties. Both husbands, the story reveals, were sinful and "killed" by the Lord. Her, the first one, means "watchful," whereas Onan means "strong," but both died without issue.

No one had to tell Thamar that the primary end of marriage is generation. The author makes plain that she was in no way motivated by lust or promiscuity. She did not seek progeny outside her husband's tribe for this was forbidden. Deuteronomy states, "When brothers live together and one of them die without a son, the widow of the deceased shall not marry anyone outside the family" (25:5). It's clear that Thamar simply wanted her rights in the only way she saw open to her, driven to desperate measures by circumstances.

For her, generation was the essential end that it is, a human husband being merely the means to it. She didn't see marriage in terms of sentimental consolations or companionship, or old age security or as an aid to a professional career or even as means to a nice middle class home where she could entertain her friends in a becoming hostess gown on weekends—though she would probably not have sneered at these benefits if she could have had them. She would have preferred conventional methods had they been hers to use. We know she waited "a long time" for Sela before doing what she did. This doesn't excuse her, of course. Like Mrs. Phutiphar, she was sinful. Let's not whitewash her, but on the other hand let's not overlook the fact that God uses even human sins and sinners to teach human beings sublime truths.

Let the soul to whom circumstances seem to deny the goods and honors of this world, or even Mass and the Sacraments, or who can find no spiritual director, or who is immersed in suffocating worldliness, ponder Thamar's one-track determination! When God denies good human desires, isn't it likely that He is prodding the soul into some desperate higher action? Thamar can easily be taken as a figure of the soul denied human progeny who by holy audacity wrests progeny from God Himself. Let the childless couple or the unwilling bachelor or spinster take notice here. Is this their call to higher fruition? Then again, perhaps the Holy Spirit teaches us here that God is master of His favors and visits what souls He pleases—even those of falsely consecrated pagans—who turn out to be His daughters-in-law in disguise! There is so much to be found in Thamar's indiscretion!

Thamar's yearning for progeny is the eternal yearning of the contemplative for the "fruits that remain." Again like Rachel, another recognized figure of contemplation, Thamar must be given children or die. She must somehow come to union with God, who alone gives fruition of any kind.

"I am the true vine," says Christ,

> and my father is the vine-dresser. Every branch in me that bears no fruit he will take away; and every branch that bears fruit he will cleanse, that it may bear more fruit. . . . He who abides in me and I in him, he bears much fruit; for without me you can do nothing. . . . In this is my Father glorified, that you may bear very much fruit, and become my disciples.

And He concludes, "You have not chosen me, but I have chosen you, and have appointed you that you should go and bear fruit, and that your fruit should remain."

So the end of the soul's union with God is spiritual generation, as children are the end of any marriage. "By their fruits you shall know them," not by the length of time they spend on their knees, or their ethereal smiles, or the kind of Missal they use, or how many afternoons they devote to the poor, or how well they can tell others how to live. "By their fruits. . . ." Ultimately, these fruits cannot be other than human souls, newly generated by God Himself. Using the words of Zacharias, the Liturgy asks, "What is the good thing of Him, and what is His beautiful thing, but the corn of the elect and the wine springing forth virgins?"

Thamar risked everything for these fruits, gambling on one throw of the dice not only her reputation, but in fact her very life. "He who seeks to save his life shall lose it," warned our Lord. (If Christ really didn't rise from the dead, we're sunk, said St. Paul.) This is a very desperate, awesome game. Russian Roulette is mere Blind Man's Buff by comparison. The penalty for sexual irregularity in Thamar's case was simply death under Jewish law, and Juda did, in fact, order her to be burned! Another woman would have settled for a bitter, childless widowhood, but not our Thamar! Denied Sela, she exacted her rights from the head of the clan.

Small wonder that Thamar doesn't bother to collect that kid Juda promised her from his flock. Does any soul intent on laying claims on God Himself stoop to negligible temporal rewards? If Thamar had claimed that little goat with Juda's pledges, look what would have happened to her! Playing the game she was engaged in, Thamar was hardly interested in fringe benefits. If she was successful in becoming a mother, she was bound to be found out. This means that what she was gambling on was Juda's sense of justice and, above all, his mercy.

That puts her in a class with all great saints, especially, I think, with Thérèse of Lisieux, who was a Thamar if there ever was one, and who kept insisting it was *impossible* to have too much confidence in God's merciful love. For her, the whole spiritual life consisted in constantly throwing herself into God's arms and expecting from Him more than she could ever think of asking. She knew God, and certainly Thamar knew Juda, to risk herself as she did! Let's admit it: Thamar and all the elect are betting on a sure thing.

Juda, in fact, lends himself rather easily as a figure of the generative, merciful God. In the story of Joseph, he is distinguished as the brother who offered himself as surety for the young Benjamin and who before that had spared Joseph's life by persuading the others to sell him into slavery rather than kill him. Nor did he join his brothers Simeon and Levi in the disgraceful revenge against Sichem for their sister Dina's rape. Though he visits a pagan prostitute, he is just within certain primitive lights, for he does so as a widower who has waited out the period of mourning. When he discovers Thamar's identity, "he had no further relations with her." Even his penchant for hobnobbing with Adullamites outside his own tribe argues a certain catholicity not at odds with the divine. He is also a man of his word, as his pledges to Thamar certainly testified. Though he was, like her, sinful, this doesn't prevent the Holy Spirit from using him as a divine "type." He bears, you might say, the same sort of relationship to Almighty God that an alcoholic actor might bear to Abraham Lincoln, whose role he interprets on stage.

This is of course over-simplification, for in his prophecy to his sons, Jacob had singled out Juda for a pre-eminent role in the destiny of Israel. In a passage universally recognized as messianic, he said,

> Juda, your brothers shall praise you; your hand shall be on the neck of your enemies; the sons of your father shall bow down to you.

A lion's whelp is Juda; from the prey you have gone up, my
  son.
He crouches and couches as a lion; as a lioness, and who will
  disturb him?
The sceptre shall not depart from Juda, nor the staff from
  between his feet,
Until he comes to whom it belongs.
To him shall be the obedience of nations.
He tethers his ass to the vine; his ass's colt to the choicest
  vine.
He washes his garment in wine, his robe in the blood of
  grapes.
His eyes are darker than wine,
  his teeth whiter than milk (Gen. 49:8–12).

It is by this man, a clear figure of the Messias, that Thamar
conceives when he visits her, disguised as a pagan temple-
prostitute. Incidentally, the polite name for this profession is
hierodule, and implies immediately that, reprehensible as it
is, it still has a sacred character—as all manifestations of sex
must. Isn't that precisely what makes sexual sins the horror
they are? The pledges she demanded of him—the staff and
signet—were extremely important to a Hebrew patriarch.
They are strong masculine symbols. Women didn't use them.
The shepherd's staff, referred to by Jacob in the prophecy, is
particularly a symbol of power and authority. Bishops use it
as such today. The signet, together with the cord by which it
hung around the owner's neck, was a cylindrical seal which
could be used as a binding and valid signature in any legal
commitment. Had she so desired, Thamar could have played
hob with Juda's charge accounts with this seal in hand. We
have already seen what Jezabel did with Achab's!

These were not mere baubles she had extricated from her
father-in-law, and we may be sure he meant seriously to

reclaim them. With these Thamar had a real hold on Juda, if only because they were heavy proof of involvement. When God gives comparable pledges to a human soul—"signet, cord and staff" may be taken as figures of the Persons of the Blessed Trinity dwelling in the soul by grace—He has pledged her His Word, and we can be sure He means to reclaim them as much as did Juda. Redemption is hers if she produces them intact at the time for her "burning." With these in hand at the august last minute, she is in a position to prove that God has indeed been a party to her "sin," who became sin for us, as St. Paul puts it, though He "knew nothing of sin, so that in Him we might become the justice of God."

Even so, doesn't natural reason alone tell us that the horror of human sin hinges especially on the fact that we can perform no act whatsoever—good or evil—without God's immediate concurrence? Certainly God cannot will evil, but we can, and therefore "when a creature acts with God's concurrence . . . God is responsible for the very fact of the creature's activity, and thus accounts for the very existence of the effect" (Frs. Dulles, Demske, and O'Connell, S.J., *Introductory Metaphysics,* Sheed and Ward, p. 187). In this sense God is made a party to all sins we commit. Viewed in this light, Thamar's story teaches an elementary lesson in Christian metaphysics.

So the Divine Magnanimity, having taken on all our guilt, will say, like Juda, "She is more in the right than I!" having, indeed, entered the brothel to unite Himself to Israel disguised in the veil of a harlot.

There are delicate echoes in the story of Thamar, the girl who was willing to be taken for a harlot and to risk her life in order to give birth to an ancestor of the Messias. We know of another who also "was found to be with Child" in highly equivocal circumstances, and whose betrothed husband Joseph "being a just man, and not wishing to expose her to reproach, was minded to put her away privately." In a quandary of love and justice, he could not bear to deliver her to the fate decreed in Deuteronomy for such cases:

> If . . . evidence of the girl's virginity is not to be found, they shall bring the girl to the entrance of her father's house and there her townsmen shall stone her to death, because she committed a crime against Israel by her unchasteness in her father's house. Thus shall you purge the evil from your midst!

declares the Law of Talion.

Let no one ever belittle the courage of the Thamars in such a community. I only mention the parallel, however, for this exegesis I fear belongs exclusively to the pure in heart who can tread lightly on the heights without falling into chasms on one side or the other. Let him explore this interpretation who has been invited to "go up higher."

Whatever applications might be made of this story, one fact always stands out: Juda took pleasure in Thamar. Under cover of sexual imagery, it seems that God may be at pains to reveal here what He repeats over and over again in Scripture, but which His creatures find almost impossible to believe, namely that they are somehow in a position to provide their Creator happiness. This is fantastic! Yet, Holy Wisdom proclaims that her delight is to be with the children of men, and to prove it, she goes down into the pit with them.

This is mystery of course, for it is of faith that God has no need of us and His happiness in Himself can neither be diminished nor increased. But what does Isaias say precisely of God's chosen?

"Thou shalt be called *My-Pleasure-in-Her,*" he says, because she is "called by a new name, which the mouth of the Lord shall name."

How is this possible? The only explanation theology can offer is the obvious one that we must somehow become a part of God by grace in order to share and reciprocate His happiness. Keeping Thamar in mind, this may be viewed in terms, as it were, of a "holy incest," for as adopted children of God, ours is at least a "legal incest" like Thamar's. At the risk of getting scandalized even further, this thought puts us more in a position to appreciate the artistry of her story. There is certainly no indication that she was a blood relative of Juda's; still, no light view of legal incest was taken by the Jews. Leviticus states, "If a man lies with his daughter-in-law, both of them shall be put to death; since they have committed an abhorrent deed, they have forfeited their lives" (20:12). Well might Juda say, "She is more in the right than I!"

As we read, this incestuous relationship is fruitful. Of the spiritual Thamar Isaias predicts, "Thou shalt no more be called Forsaken, and thy land shall no more be called Desolate . . . because the Lord hath been well pleased with thee: and thy land shall be inhabited." Israel is promised fruition because the Lord takes pleasure in her. Not only that, but, like Thamar who was promised a kid from the flock, Israel is promised recompense for the pleasure she gives God, even temporal recompense.

There is such deep wisdom hidden in the sexual relations of man and woman, that it seems the Holy Spirit in the story of Thamar might have wished deliberately to remove these relations for a moment from the framework of marriage so we can contemplate the sexual act, as it were, on its own merits. So withdrawn, this act can be seen first of all as essentially generative. Secondly, this generation results exclusively from the pleasure taken by the man. The woman's pleasure is incidental.

We have already admitted that Thamar was not motivated by lust, but by desire for progeny. Her desire was to *give pleasure in order to be fecundated*. This is true spiritual self-giving. When God created man and woman He made woman's pleasure in marital relations incidental, revealing thereby a spiritual truth pertaining to the human soul's relations with Himself.

Somehow modern sex books overflow with the word "orgasm." Materialists seem to equate it with the end of marriage, as nearly as I can follow their reasoning. Poor, harried, loving wives are daily made to feel hopelessly inadequate, if not frigid, if they don't experience this sensation every time their husbands do (or don't). In other words, here again women are made to feel guilty because they aren't men. The truth is, however, that a man who insists on such in his wife is really wishing he were married to another man, whose reactions are logical, A to A and B to B, and not the inclusive, diffuse response a real woman is designed to give.

In other words, in his sexual relations, he simply is not playing the role of God towards the human soul. God gives pleasure, but according to the nature of the recipient. Saints, who love God very much, receive His will sometimes pleasurably, sometimes not, given our disordered universe. This was true even of our Lord.

Sometimes in great pain saints give God the pleasure of receiving from Him souls generated in the order of grace; for sometimes women conceive in pain. God does not desire our pain. He is not a sadist. He has ordained, however, that through pain we shall defeat the serpent who authored it. Is it surprising, therefore, that we should find pain so often right where life begins—in the marriage bed?

Sometimes, of course, souls are conceived in great joy, for again, women sometimes so conceive. Didn't Sara laugh and say, "Now that I am grown old . . . shall I have pleasure?" Even though it can be a great help, this pleasure on the woman's part is still incidental. It does not have the inevitable connection with procreation that the man's pleasure does.

Just so, almost everything written by St. John of the Cross on asceticism is reducible to one piece of advice: Do not become attached to consolations if you expect to come to fruitful union with God. The only essential, says he, is to be empty and desire Him, and he called this the way of *nada,* "nothing." It is the woman's way, in woman's world.

Thamar's story doesn't inform us whether or not our heroine experienced an orgasm, because obviously this would interest only sensualists who miss the point anyway. We do know, however, that Juda did, for Thamar conceived. To put it bluntly, as Scripture would, no woman bears in whom no pleasure has been taken.

"She shall be called *My-Pleasure-in-Her,*" reminds Isaias.

There is something else we can be sure of, too. Though she may have conceived pleasurably, Thamar's delivery was painful. Ever since Eden, women do not *bear* pleasurably. As the Lord foretold to Eve,

> I will make great your distress in childbearing;
>   in pain shall you bring forth children;
> For your husband shall be your longing,
>   though he have dominion over you (Gen. 3:16).

We have seen how Thamar longed for a husband! What is true carnally, however, is always more true spiritually. Not only does the soul by its nature long for God as a woman yearns for her husband, but like a married woman, the fecund soul espoused to God must suffer as a consequence. Like a married woman, her generative pain is nothing else than an effect of her Husband's love for her. So the soul's birth pangs—her own or for another; purgation here or hereafter—are simply the inevitable pain resulting from loving contact between an all-holy God and His sinful creature—the "harlot" He visits.

"As a woman with child, when she draweth near the time of her delivery, is in pain, and crieth out in her pangs: so are we become in thy presence, O Lord. We have conceived, and been as it were in labor. . . ." groans Isaias.

"A woman about to give birth has sorrow," corroborates the Prophet of prophets, Himself soon to redeem mankind by Church from the agony of the cross. He warns His disciples it will be so with them in their battle for the souls of men.

St. Paul found it out for himself. "My dear children," he addressed the Galatians, "with whom I am in labor again, until Christ be formed in you!" Souls are always born from someone's pain.

DOUBLE TROUBLE

AFTER all this preamble, it's only natural down here to be a mite curious about Thamar's progeny! Offspring conceived at such peril might be expected from natural causes alone to have two heads, or worse. Happily, this was not the case, but our curiosity is not disappointed, because Thamar did have twins. There must have been something unusual about them, for their birth is carefully recorded:

> During the delivery one put out a hand. The midwife took a scarlet thread, tied it on his hand and said, "This one is born first." But as he drew back his hand, his brother was born. Then the woman said, "How have you made your way forth?" For this reason he was called Phares. Afterward his brother with the scarlet thread on his hand was born, and he was named Zara.

A curious little anecdote. We wonder that Scripture should bother with it. What can it mean? I don't know what you get from these details, but I can tell you very quickly what I get: the battle of the sexes doesn't end with Thamar and Juda. It continues in their children and in every creature composed of body and spirit. Figuratively speaking, Thamar's child would have to be twins, just to be human.

Now, when we hear of anything that comes double or by twos in Scripture, we know we are likely to be dealing with the long-standing inseparables which are nevertheless always at odds, action and contemplation. Such are the "double garments" with which the Valiant Woman in Proverbs clothes her household. Such are Lia and Rachel, Elcana's wives Phennena and Anna, Rebecca's twin sons Esau and Jacob, and also Martha and Mary, to mention only the best known ones, all mirroring the active and passive forces in human nature, the very stuff of the battle of the sexes.

The prophet Eliseus, about to receive the mantle of the heavenbound Elias, begs him before he leaves, "I beseech thee that in me may be thy double spirit." Elias replies that he has asked a hard thing, as indeed he has, for this "double spirit," according to Carmelite interpretation at least, is the mixed life, the perfect blend of action and contemplation. natural and supernatural. It can be lived in its full perfection only by the Christ, in Himself or in us. In Him alone is this marriage fully consummated, who sent His disciples out "two by two" like animals from the Ark.

During the courtship there goes on between the two within every human being a ceaseless struggle which began when Adam and Eve forfeited their integration by sin. Ever since, one or the other, action or contemplation, the interior or the exterior force, predominates. They can be reconciled perfectly only in the upper reaches of the Seventh Mansion, or in heaven. Until then, it's double trouble all the way. Like the gingham dog and the calico cat, they can finally settle their differences only by eating each other up.

This is a basic truth at the foundation of all asceticism worthy of the name, and known to serious people from earliest times. Pagan antiquity, though unacquainted with Thamar's twins, had its own twosome called Castor and

Pollux, the *dioscuri,* or "sons of God." Castor was mortal, Pollux immortal. After Castor's death they could be reunited only by a precarious *modus vivendi* whereby Zeus decreed that they live in the upper and lower worlds on alternate days. The Holy Spirit takes cognizance of Castor and Pollux and reveals His secret handiwork in the natural wisdom of mythology, for in the Acts of the Apostles He sends His apostle to the Gentiles to Rome for martyrdom "in an Alexandrian ship with the Twins on the figurehead." Such is the delicacy of detail with which divine Wisdom ordered the journey of one who labored pre-eminently in Elias' "double spirit," and was taken to the third heaven and back again to preaching and tent-making.

Both Hebrews and Greeks were people fundamentally concerned with truth, though they went after it differently. The logical Greeks have always been recognized as a "masculine" civilization which exalted intellect; the intuitive Hebrews, as more "feminine," a people of heart. The languages of both, however, reveal their secure grasp on the basic duality which runs all through creation. For instance, both Hebrew and Greek have not only singular and plural word forms, but duals. They understood that something that comes double is intrinsically different from something that comes singly or severally.

A pair is not the same thing as two. One and one make two. A pair makes three. A pair is creative, because it reflects the life and activity of the Blessed Trinity, which all creation must reflect, however imperfectly, in order to exist at all. The Father, and the Son generated by the Father, together produce the Holy Spirit. Of course no respectable theologian would call what I am talking about the battle of the sexes, or even action and contemplation. Once we leave animal life and mankind and ascend upwards through angelic creation, the battle of the sexes is called "act and potency," but that doesn't change the principle.

Because God is one, act and potency are never separate in Him.

> There is thus no distinction of sex in God, but that which sex differentiates—the function of generation—exists in God undifferentiated, eternal, perfect, infinite. "Genitori, Genitoque laus et jubilatio!" sings the Church while the incense of her praise ascends. And Christ Himself leads the hymn of praise: "When you pray, say 'Our Father who art in heaven, hallowed be thy name,'"—the name of Father, of Generator. Now it is from this perfect generation, this single and infinite point of being, this divine mystery at the heart of all causation, that sex divides and derives (Vincent Wilkin, S.J. *The Image of God in Sex,* Sheed & Ward).

Seeing Thamar's twins by this light, we are in a position to derive an important spiritual lesson from them. Notice that Zara, or contemplation, appeared first. Wishing to establish the right of the firstborn beyond question, the midwife tied a scarlet thread around his wrist. (Would it be introducing an unbecoming note of levity to dub this midwife a spiritual director?) This scarlet thread is no unimportant detail, if we call to mind how Rahab's salvation depended on a similar scarlet cord. The Holy Spirit, I think, excels in these little touches just to delight His readers. I wonder, do you suppose the cord on Juda's signet might have been red? I'll bet it was.

These red cords, probably figures of a later figure of Baptism—the blood on the doorposts in Egypt—are marks of predestination and redemption through the Blood of the

Lamb. Zara, apparently, is elect. His name means "Dawn-
ing." He is a promise. I think he must play the role of the
immortal Pollux who had "the better part." Surprisingly
enough, however, he is not the firstborn. Contrary to the
midwife's expectation, his brother Phares, or natural action,
is born first, being, I suppose, more aggressive by nature. His
name means "Break through." Though caught sight of first,
Zara recedes and is born last.

From what Scripture has already taught us of the interior
vs. the exterior life, this is bound to be so. Jacob had to marry
the weakeyed but prolific Lia before he could have his beloved and long childless Rachel—who was the first to catch
his eye. Phenenna tormented Anna many years before Anna
became the mother of the prophet Samuel. The bustling
Martha upbraided the apparently idle Mary. The Synagogue
precedes the Church, and so on. Even our friend Zacchaeus
had to "come down" from his high sycamore so that Christ
might enter his house.

The same analogy is played out in the account of those
other biblical twins Esau and Jacob. After their mother
Rebecca conceived them, Scripture tells us, "the children
jostled each other within her." She asked God the same question many of us ask who witness the struggle of natural and
supernatural within ourselves, and indeed, within the
Church: "If this be so, why am I pregnant?"

And the Lord answered her: "Two nations are in your
womb; two peoples shall stem from your body. One people
shall be stronger than the other, and the elder shall serve
the younger."

Though properly applied to the struggle between the
predestined and the reprobate, the story illustrates equally

well the relationship of action to contemplation. "When the time of her delivery came," continues the sacred text, "there were indeed twins in her womb. The first to come forth was red. His whole body was like a hairy garment, so they named him Esau. Afterward his brother came forth, with his hand gripping Esau's heel; so he was called Jacob." We know Jacob is the figure of the elect, like Zara being born last.

Let's not, however, fall into mechanical thinking here. Call it Esau or Phares or whatever, let's not identify the active principle with evil, just because Esau also happens to be a figure of the reprobate! We are dealing, after all, with very flexible imagery designed to convey many shades of supernatural meaning, and anyhow, St. Matthew's genealogy will bring us up short, for it is clearly Phares, not Zara, who is mentioned there as the ancestor of our Lord. Phares is active, and is the firstborn, as is our Lord, whom St. Paul calls, "the image of the invisible God, the firstborn of every creature." And God Himself is Pure Act.

The witnesses at the betrothal of Booz and Ruth wished the newlyweds, "May the Lord make this wife come into your house like Rachel and Lia, who between them built up the house of Israel. . . . With the offspring the Lord will give you from this girl, may your house become like the house of Phares, whom Thamar bore to Juda!"

What a deal of wisdom in this happy toast to marital happiness. Booz (a figure of Christ) needs a wife (figure of the Church) who is both Lia and Rachel rolled into one, if she is to present him with suitable offspring. Action and contemplation need each other badly "who between them build up the house of Israel."

Having poor eyesight into supernatural things, Lia may contemn Rachel as Martha did Mary, but Mary and Rachel see too clearly ever to contemn Lia and Martha. Martha, whose vision is limited, always *thinks* she understands Mary, and this is one of Mary's worst tortures, because Martha can be awfully bossy. Mary eventually learns to clutch her "one thing necessary" to her bosom, smile sweetly, avoid polemic, and do her part silently, giving in now and then. (Martha can be pretty loud at dialogue Mass on occasion.) But never mind. As St. Paul says, the spiritual man is a good judge of everything. Mary understands Martha's problems, although Martha doesn't understand hers, and she is so grateful to Martha for doing all those noisy, necessary chores!

To Eliseus' request for the double spirit, Elias said simply, before disappearing heavenward in the fiery chariot, "If thou see me when I am taken from thee, thou shalt have what thou hast asked: but if thou see me not, thou shalt not have it." The test of whether or not one has the spirit of contemplation is therefore equally simple—either one sees supernatural things or one doesn't.

After Eliseus witnessed Elias' departure, his fellow prophets not gifted with his spirit were determined to send fifty men to scour the surrounding terrain, sure that Elias must have been dropped out somewhere. Eliseus knew better, but he had to give in to them. When they returned and reported that Elias really was nowhere to be found, Eliseus replied in effect wearily, "Didn't I tell you so?" Because Phares and Martha don't see, they rarely listen. They have to do everything the hard way, by their own efforts. That's their nature.

A contemplative can no more explain his prayer life to a

thoroughgoing activist than a believer can "explain" the faith to one who doesn't have it. Trying to breeds only frustration. Like Eliseus, the contemplative can only hope that the activist will learn for himself. The same dilemma is reflected on a larger scale between nations. East is East and West is West, and never the twain shall meet, runs the old truism; and the trouble with truisms is that they are true. The phallic, aggressive West can no more comprehend the uterine, encompassing East than a man can understand a woman, though they may manage to get on very well together and between them build up the house of Israel. Of action and contemplation we can only say, like the French, *Vive la différence!*

Little need be said in defense of action. It is well able to take care of itself in man's world, where it is king. It is the contemplative life that must be protected and nurtured, and which our Lord himself felt bound to defend. In practice, there is no such thing as an active soul or a passive soul. There are merely souls in whom one or the other force may be strongly dominant. In most souls the two are forever "jostling each other" unto sanctification. As the biblical imagery suggests, the competition between them is closely allied to the battle between good and evil. "For I am delighted with the law of God according to the inner man," said St. Paul, "but I see another law in my members."

Zara, the timid inner man, always makes his tentative appearance first. "Down here" he is crowded out by the aggressive Phares, but he must see the light eventually, for Zara is contemplation, the prayer of the blessed begun on earth. He is immortal Pollux and "up there." When given a choice of the twins, we have to choose him, for the Lord promised "the elder shall serve the younger." This is doctrine.

Now, like other people, saints have their *bêtes-noirs*. Our Lord was goaded to fury at the sight of money-changers carrying on their niggardly business in sacred precincts, and St. John of the Cross was exasperated by another aspect of the very same thing. He couldn't stand seeing Phares directing Zara's interior life. His hackles rose at the sight of pedestrian spiritual directors who sought to impose the money-changer's spirituality on souls whom God is Himself leading into the Holy of Holies. He wrote many scorching pages on this subject, of which the following is a fair sample. To an advanced soul in whom Phares has long ago been born and in whom Zara is already laboring, he says,

> . . . there will come some director who has no knowledge save of hammering and pounding like a blacksmith, and because his only teaching is of that kind, he will say, "Come now, leave all this, for you are only wasting time and living in idleness. Get to work, meditate and make interior acts, for it is right that you should do these things for yourself and be diligent about them, for these other things are the practices of Illuminists and fools!"

And again,

> Such persons have no knowledge of what spirituality is, and they offer a great insult and great irreverence to God, by laying their coarse hands where God is working. For it has cost Him dearly to bring these souls to this place and He greatly esteems having brought them to this solitude and emptiness of their faculties and operations, that He may speak to their heart, which is what He ever desires. He has Himself taken them by the hand, and He Himself reigns in

their souls in abundant peace and quietness, causing the natural acts of their faculties to fail wherewith they toiled all night and wrought nothing. And He has brought peace to their spirits without the operation of sense, for neither sense nor any act thereof is capable of receiving spirit. . . . And thus one who rashly errs, being under an obligation to give reliable advice—as is every man, whatever his office—shall not go unpunished, by reason of the harm that he has done. For the business of God has to be undertaken with great circumspection, and with eyes wide open, most of all in matters so delicate and sublime as the conduct of these souls, where a man may bring them almost infinite gain if the advice that he gives be good and almost infinite loss if it be mistaken (*The Complete Works of St. John of the Cross, The Living Flame of Love,* Stanza III, *passim,* translated and edited by E. Allison Peers, Newman).

The saint's indignation is unfeigned. It's enough to make any spiritual director tremble in his cassock. Unfortunately, it is directed to a wider public than might be at first supposed, for lots of people are spiritual directors without realizing it, "as is every man, whatever his office." Whether they like it or not, mothers of small children are spiritual directors, and they above all others are in a position to place "coarse hands where God is working." True, they are not dealing with souls such as St. John describes, who are preparing for Zara's final emergence at spiritual marriage, but they are dealing with Zara nevertheless, and what's more, they are dealing with him at the very foundations of the whole spiritual edifice. They are confronted with his first timid appearance, before the reasonable Phares has emerged, and they can do incalculable harm to God's work before it gets off the ground.

Given this difference in degree, the mother stands in the

same relation to the young pre-school child that the spiritual director stands with respect to a soul he is leading to Union. Both can make the same disastrous mistakes—that will not go unpunished, says St. John. Both can pound and hammer like blacksmiths at the unfortunates in their care.

"Say fifteen rosaries every day and meditate for forty-five minutes on the Pharisee and the Publican on Tuesdays and Thursdays. On Mondays and Wednesdays . . ." says the pedestrian director to the soul who can't recite two lines of the *Pater* without being lost in holy wonderment at the goodness of God.

"Now you say after me, 'Angel of God, my guardian dear. . . .' *Will* you stop fidgeting! God *hates* fidgeters! Now, 'Angel *of* God,' not "Angel God." . . . And keep your eyes closed," says dear ole Mom to a four-year-old who thinks God is wonderful and who told Mom only this morning that God is "even in the sugar bowl."

I'll have to hold on to myself here. Not being nearly so mortified as St. John of the Cross, I can get pretty riled at this sort of thing. Just let me state clearly before I go further that I don't know how to direct pre-school children. For this luminous piece of knowledge, I humbly thank God. This means I probably won't do anything right, but on the other hand, maybe I won't do anything too wrong, either. When Zara is in the ascendant, it's plain that God is at work, for Scripture and a Doctor of Mystical Theology say so. This means that in the beginning and in the later stages of the spiritual life, what I don't do is much more important than what I do.

With a clear conscience I can forgo constructing a hand-made Annunciation scene out of a cardboard box with a cardboard angel popping in and out saying, "Hail Mary!" in order to teach devotion to the Blessed Mother, as a pamphlet I once read advised me to do. Instead, I can get to the ironing and iron in the presence of God, with the four-year-old underfoot. Maybe I can be so negligent as just to let the little codger pick up the Hail Mary from us older ones at family prayers in the evening, sort of the way he picks up the commercials word for word on television . . . because he wants to. I'll explain it when opportunity offers. He can fidget, too. (God probably *loves* fidgeters.)

And then I don't have to tell him that praying to God is like talking to somebody you can't see on the telephone, as someone else advised me to do. This might work for Phares, but it will never do for Zara. I ask you, what little child taught to live in the presence of God would pick up a phone to talk to Someone who is everywhere, "even in the sugar bowl?" Adults for whom God may be very far away, but who know God's number and can dial it, might find this concept helpful to their prayer life. If so, they are at liberty to use it, their Zara and his scarlet thread having disappeared for the nonce. Few small children around here can dial, thank God!

One of those souls St. John was talking about could easily have directed his director, and by the same token, almost any unspoiled child is the spiritual master of a benighted mother whose Zara remains sadly unborn. Our Lord was explicit on this point. I didn't make it up, because the people who have taught me most about God have been small children. He didn't take an apostle, place him in a ring of small children, and say, "Now, children, see if you can be like him." He took a little child, says Scripture (for all we know there was a scarlet thread on his wrist), and set him in the *apostles'* midst, to settle an argument about who was the greatest.

In earlier times, monastic communities accepted children into their ranks, the Rule of St. Benedict making special mention of the manner in which they should be treated. The practice was eventually discontinued for sound reasons both historical and moral, but somehow I can't help feeling that this was not without serious spiritual loss—to the monks more than to the children. With a few small children around, many a monastery could dispense with a healthy portion of well-thumbed manuals and get their information live and firsthand. I once presumed to say this to an Abbot. He agreed with me by putting me nicely in my place. "Monks are children," he smiled.

Still, when it comes to the spiritual life, children are the housewife's trumps. No religious gets the instruction she gets! If given half a chance, little children live in God's presence easily, in fact so easily, the observer must be pretty spiritual himself to detect this phenomenon when it presents itself. How often, we wonder, does a child "remain in Jerusalem," when, like Mary and Joseph, "his parents did not know it"? Even more than women, little children have naturally the basic dispositions of great contemplatives.

"Amen, I say unto you, whoever does not accept the kingdom of God as a little child will not enter it!"

The child trusts absolutely. He is poor, having nothing of his own beyond what is given to him. This means he is happily innocent of prejudice or subterfuge. His power of loving far outstrips his intellect, and for him most things are still in primordial unity. A very little knowledge satisfies him, and he believes anyone he loves. He is quite "abandoned" in the spiritual sense.

As the Phares in him develops, however, his intellect grows and reaches out to diversity. He begins to reason. Information becomes vital. (Any mother can check me here.) Gradually he discovers the exterior world, and about school age *formal* Christian education with appeals to intellect begins—in very small doses at first, please! Imagination is still very active. Leading through Bible stories, catechism, perhaps some formal meditation, eventually through theology and more advanced exegesis, always with the life-giving help of prayer and the sacraments, Phares is fully born.

At the same time, however, Zara should be slowly making his way forward, gradually assimilating the adult powers into the spiritual childhood which is full sanctity. When Zara is born, we have a saint in our midst. It should happen all the time, and the tragedy, as Léon Bloy said, is that it doesn't. What is contemplation, after all, but a rediscovery of Zara, who made a first partial appearance "in the beginning"?

I think the Zara-Phares-Zara cycle occurs in yet another way in the spiritual life properly so-called. Many mystical doctors have commented, for instance, on how God sometimes grants very high favors to beginners, favors akin to those they are destined to experience again only in mature perfection. This is taught in Ruth's story, and St. Teresa put the idea in these words:

> Now it quite often happens that the Lord moves a very imperfect soul—though not, however, in my opinion, a soul in mortal sin— permitting it, despite its imperfections, to

have a very lofty vision in order to turn it to Himself. . . .
There are souls which God knows He can draw to Himself
by this means; even though they have lost all touch with
Him, His Majesty will not leave them to the devil. Despite
their bad disposition and lack of virtues, He gives them
favors and consolations, and shows them a tenderness which
begins to awake desires in them; He even, very occasionally,
lifts them briefly to a state of contemplation. As I said before,
He does this to test whether, having enjoyed this sweetness,
they will be disposed to seek it often. . . . I am convinced,
myself, that Our Lord tests many souls in this way and that
only a few of them show a disposition to enjoy this favor
(St. Theresa of Avila, *The Way of Perfection,* Ch. XVIII,
translated by Alice Alexander, Newman).

As a monk friend of ours once said, "The test of a contemplative vocation comes when God takes the lollipop
away." One of my housewife friends who prays puts it this
way: "When you start out God takes you up in a plane to
the top of the mountain so you can see the gorgeous view
from there. Just when you're beginning to enjoy it, He takes
you back to the bottom and says in effect, Now get out and
walk to the top yourself if you want to see that view again!"
That's what happened to three apostles at the Transfiguration. As Scripture seems to indicate, you might think Zara
will be born first, just because he shows his hand, but we have
to wait for Phares before we get Zara for good. Our Lord
bowed to the same spiritual law. Revealing His wisdom and
grace briefly in the Temple at twelve years of age, He "went
down with [His parents] and came to Nazareth, and was
subject to them," disappearing for some eighteen years before
the final emergence in His public ministry. Wasn't this true
also in the history of mankind? Didn't God walk in the
garden familiarly with Adam "in the beginning"? And

hasn't he promised to return some day for good after many long centuries of trial?

A parent who spoils Zara for a small child in his tenderest years leaves him so little to hark back to—or rather, forward to—in later life! He deprives him of what Pope Pius XI pled for in his Encyclical on Christian Marriage, namely that "the home, though it suffer the want and hardship of this valley of tears, may become for the children in its own way a foretaste of that paradise of delight in which the Creator placed the first men of the human race."

Unfortunately, it's not only worldly parents who err in this respect, but also parents who consider themselves spiritual and educated Christians who are offenders. Thinking they know something, they are especially prone to apply to their helpless offspring forms of spirituality meant only for adults *in via,* laying coarse hands on God's work like pounding blacksmiths.

So much of the harm adults do is not direct, but by implication. A little girl I knew was missing a long time one afternoon. Eventually, she was found before the Blessed Sacrament "just sitting with God." She was quite justly given Hail Columbia for needlessly worrying her family, who were too distraught to draw any edifying parallels to the Fifth Joyous Mystery, nor were they aware of any. Unfortunately the child came to the conclusion as a result of the hullaballoo that God punishes little girls who sit in His churches just "doing nothing." (Pious children are unfortunately the very ones who identify God most with the home authority.)

As she couldn't pray vocally and think about God at the same time, she stopped thinking about God so as to get her prayers letter-perfect, the way she thought God liked them. The sequel is obvious. Lacking the sustenance of true prayer, she fell away. It took her twenty-four years to find her way back home before the Blessed Sacrament and "do nothing" again, "that He might speak to her heart, which is what He ever desires." May God have mercy on us all! "The business of God has to be undertaken with great circumspection, and with eyes wide open!"

To understand the prayer of young children, it might be well to study the mystics and read what theologians have to say about the state known as "transforming union." Though children only rarely reach such sanctity, the state of childhood contains the perfection of Zara in embryo, and whereas the child himself can tell his parents nothing of his prayer life, sometimes the books can.

The mother superior of a contemplative secular institute once lent me a thick volume on the mystical life. When I returned it, she asked me pointedly whether I had read it all. Well, not quite all, I admitted. The last chapters dealing with the soul's deportment in the higher brackets of holiness had little practical application in my case and I thought could be safely skipped. I said so.

"Read them!" she replied. "Don't you know light from above illumines everything below it?"

Well, I didn't know, but I do now. This, I think, is the spirit in which all such books should be read, somewhat as we might study the topography of a country we aim to visit, and this is particularly true when dealing with small children, who are displaced natives of the place. Who knows? St. Teresa's *Interior Castle* might make a very practical adjunct to Dr. Gesell's works. If mother takes her spiritual duty seriously, it seems to me a first-grader should set out from the home cloister so firmly established in the one thing necessary that he will always have a yen for Zara. No number of pounding blacksmiths tampering with him in the world of Phares should ever be able to drive him away permanently.

How do we accomplish this? I don't know. Only God can help us. All He said to us directors of small children was what He says in fact to all directors: "Let the little children come unto me and do not hinder them."

DO NOT HINDER THEM.

Apparently, that's all there is to it. But how do we hinder them? Alas, I guess every parent has his own special ways of hindering, of "teaching as doctrine the precepts of men," to the helpless in our care. Each must examine his own conscience, and that courageously.

Do I lose my temper or refuse to answer questions about God because I'm tired, or busy, or haven't bothered to find out for myself?

Do I leave the children home every time I visit the Blessed Sacrament because they're a bouncy nuisance and I can't pray?

Do I impose on their simplicity?

Do I tell them God hates them when they are bad?

Do I ever tell them God said things He never said because I jolly well think He should have?

Do I force them to learn letter perfect some sentimental prayer that rhymes and whose syntax escapes even adults, as if it were of obligation?

Do I teach the Sign of the Cross as if it were a lesson in calisthenics?

Do I obscure their view of God by any false images or my own sinful little peculiarities?

In fact, do I set up *any* obstacles to His grace?

Do I pound and hammer like a blacksmith in their poor little interiors?

Do I deny them solitude?

Do I forget to become like the little children I presume to direct?

Do I neglect to pray without ceasing so that in my company they can breathe in God freely? (Like fish in water, said the Cure d'Ars.)

Do I teach them to say prayers, but not to pray?

Do I asphyxiate them spiritually by my worldliness?

And, of course, do I give bad example? (That scandalizes little children, God told us, and He'll take us in hand for that, but good!)

Do I . . . well, hang it all, do I HINDER?

If not, I can depend on God to do the rest.

What He did for the little children in Judea He will certainly do for all little unhindered children.

"He will put His arms about them, and laying His hands upon them, He will begin to bless them."

Squeeze in if you can.

THE WIDOW'S "MIGHT"

JUDITH is found only in Catholic Old Testaments. If you come across her elsewhere, you will probably find her carefully labeled "Apocryphal," in much the same way that certain medicines carry the warning, "Caution: For External Use Only!" Only Catholics dare take Judith "internally." Along with *Tobias, Wisdom, Ecclesiasticus, Baruch, Macchabees* and parts of *Esther* and *Daniel,* she is firmly barred from other canons.

There are reasons for this. Scholars will give you this one:

> The reason for this divergence lies in the fact that the Protestant Bible only contains those books which are to be found in the Hebrew Bible, whereas the Catholic Bible is based, not on the Hebrew or Jewish tradition, but on the Greek Jewish Bible used by our Lord and His Apostles. After the destruction of Jerusalem in 586 (588) B.C. the Jews were scattered; many of them found their way to Egypt, and there, in course of time, a translation of the Bible into Greek was formed. It seems certain that the list of books considered authoritative in Palestine differed from that accepted in Egypt; hence it is customary to speak of the Hebrew and Greek canons respectively, or of the "first" and the "second" canons. Books found in the Hebrew Bibles as well as in the Greek are called "proto-canonical," as belonging to the "first" canon; while those found only in the Greek Bibles are called "Deutero-canonical," as belonging to the "second" canon. It is these latter books which the Protestant Bibles call "Apocry-

phal," whereas Catholics confine that term to books which are to be rejected as not being inspired, for example, the *Assumption of Moses,* the *Gospel of Peter,* etc.

It has been urged at times that, after all, the Jews were the best judges as to the contents of the Bible. But the Jews of Palestine were not more Jews than those of Alexandria; it remains to be proved, too, that the former did not receive the same books as those of Alexandria. The chief thing to be remembered, however, is that the Church has never tied herself down to the authority of the Jews on this or any other point of doctrine; she depends solely upon Apostolic tradition (Hugh Pope, O.P. *The Catholic Student's Aids to the Study of the Bible,* Burns, Oates and Washbourne, Ltd., p. 133).

This is all a matter of record. From my vantage-point, however, at the housewife's never-failing spring—the kitchen sink—another reason for Judith's absence leaps to mind, and it is supplied by the lady herself: Judith is simply too hot to handle. Only the Church which knows itself infallible and which delights in consistently poising the Truth on the horns of dilemma would dare tangle with Judith. Written in the latter days when the Old Testament was accelerating rapidly toward the fullness of revelation about to burst in the New, Judith presents problems that heresy—which must be superficial—could hardly resolve.

At first reading, Judith appears simple enough. A sort of semitic Joan of Arc, she saved besieged Israel singlehanded by penetrating into the enemy camp and neatly beheading the general. It's a rollicking tale, full of dramatic little scenes, which makes excellent reading even on the purely natural level. One can only wonder that Hollywood hasn't discovered it. To accomplish her feat, however, Judith proves herself a first-rate vamp and an accomplished liar. More delicate consciences wouldn't hesitate to call her a cold-blooded murderess. If ever a book seemed to teach that the end justified the means, that book is Judith. That is where the difficulty begins.

Not that this is the first time the Bible reveals the deception of which good women are capable. Rebecca went in for some pretty fancy trickery in that matter of the birthright; Rachel we know stole from her father and then covered up the theft with what may have been a big whopper; Thamar pulled a very fast one indeed; and Jahel, an early type of Judith in the days of the Judges, didn't mind driving a tent-peg through the head of a Chanaanite general, after enticing him to rest a while in her tent. There is really no end to female deceit in Scripture. These women, however, are never held up to us as paragons of virtue. They are simply figures of wonders to come.

Judith is different. She's in a class with the holy angel Raphael in Tobias (to be sure also considered apocryphal by non-Catholics!), who apparently tells outright lies. Trickier than all the other women put together, she is nevertheless presented to us as a holy woman very close to God; a saint. Apparently she was a consecrated and cloistered widow in the full religious sense. We are told

> she made herself a private chamber in the upper part of her house, in which she abode shut up with her maids. And she wore haircloth upon her loins, and fasted all the days of her life, except the sabbaths, and the new moons, and the feasts of the house of Israel. And she was exceedingly beautiful: and her husband left her great riches. . . . And she was greatly renowned among all, because she feared the Lord very much, neither was there anyone that spoke an ill word of her (Jud. 8:5-8).

When the story opens, a king called Nabuchodonosor is cutting a very wide swath through the ancient world. He had just overcome the Mede king, and is preparing to swallow the rest of the nations. Appointing his general Holofernes to implement the project, he easily subdues most of Palestine—with the lone exception of stubborn little Israel, which prepares to resist.

Whether or not this is actual history and Judith a genuine historical person has long been debated. That an event of this kind must have taken place is most likely, but facts and names have probably been juggled or fictionalized. Judith is therefore best approached as an historical novelette wherein considerable liberties may have been taken to serve the author's real purpose. As elsewhere in the Bible, this purpose is didactic, as we soon discover.

The action perhaps took place during the Persian domination, in the third century B.C. Holofernes and his officer Vagao are known from extra-biblical sources to have been actual members of the court of the Persian King Artaxerxes III, and this Holofernes undertook campaigns in Palestine and Syria. Nabuchodonosor, however, described as "king of the Assyrians who reigned in Nineveh," must have been a fictitious name, probably symbolic. Actually king of Babylon, he is used as a figure of evil, and in this guise he springs the plot. Through his puppet Holofernes, he lays siege to the (perhaps) fictitious Bethulia ("God's House"), which is Judith's home town. Good and evil lock in the customary mortal combat, and the story really gets under way.

The implications in Judith for our day are so striking it would be easy to relate the tale entirely to modern events. Nabuchodonosor, or Satan, supplies his general with all the materiel of this world. Call Holofernes Anti-Christ, Hitler, atheistic Communism or what you will, here he is:

> And he made all his warlike preparations to go before with a multitude of innumerable camels, with all provisions sufficient for the armies in abundance, and herds of oxen, and flocks of sheep, without number. He appointed corn to be prepared out of all Syria in his passage. But gold and silver he took out of the king's house in great abundance. And he went forth he and all the army, with the chariots, and horsemen, and archers, who covered the face of the earth, like locusts (Jud. 2:8–11).

What a picture!

Most of the nations he encounters give in without a fight. Their ambassadors couch cowardliness in the usual terms: "It is better for us to live and serve Nabuchodonosor the great king, and be subject to thee, than to die and to perish, or suffer the miseries of slavery!" (Jud. 3:2). In terror of Holofernes the populations "received him with garlands, and lights, and dances, and timbrels, and flutes" (Jud. 3:10). Unfortunately their collaboration got them no more then than it does now, for

> though they did these things, they could not for all that mitigate the fierceness of his heart: For he both destroyed their cities, and cut down their groves. For Nabuchodonosor the king commanded him to destroy all the gods of the earth, that he only might be called God by those nations which could be brought under him . . . (Jud. 3:11–13).

We could almost be reading this from the evening paper, so familiar is it to all of us.

Only the people of God dared resist this juggernaut. Though as terrified as the others, they did what they could.

Using natural means, "they sent into all Samaria round about, as far as Jericho, and seized upon all the tops of the mountains: And they compassed their towns with walls, and gathered together corn for provision for war" (Jud. 4:3–4). Then taking up supernatural weapons, "all the people cried to the Lord with great earnestness: and they humbled their souls in fastings, and prayers, both they and their wives. . . . And they cried to the Lord the God of Israel" (Jud. 4:7–9).

Balked of his prey, Holofernes "was transported with exceeding great fury and indignation, and he called all the princes of Moab and the leaders of Ammon" to explain these impudent Jews. The author puts into the mouth of Achior, the Ammonite captain, a long speech recapitulating the glorious Israelite past, dwelling on God's special care of His chosen. Achior assures Holofernes that no one ever "triumphed over this people, but when they departed from the worship of the Lord their God." He counsels Holofernes to inquire carefully into their present spiritual state, because "if there be no offence of this people in the sight of their God, we cannot resist them . . . and we shall be a reproach to the whole earth" (Jud. 5:25). We know already that the book of Judith will have a moral, if nothing else.

Achior's suggestion of possible defeat throws Holofernes and his officers into a rage. They want to kill him on the spot, but Holofernes' cruelty is more refined. "To show thee that there is no God, but Nabuchodonosor," Holofernes

> commanded his servants to take Achior, and to lead him to Bethulia, and to deliver him into the hands of the children of Israel, . . . that when he should overcome the children

of Israel, then he might command Achior also himself to be put to death by diverse torments, for having said: The God of heaven is their defender (6:7, 13).

Speaking the truth in Satan's camp always leads to trouble —and a reward. Because Truth said, "Everyone who is of the truth hears my voice" (Jn. 18:37), this Achior, a good pagan like Ruth, bears close watching. According to the Law, Ammonites were in the same class as Moabites— absolutely beyond the pale—so he is sure to prove interesting. Executing their chief's orders, the Assyrians go as far as the Bethulian mountainside, where "they tied Achior to a tree hand and foot, and so left him bound with ropes." Already he bears unwittingly a strong resemblance to crucified Truth, "tied to a tree."

Soon found by the Bethulians, he acquaints them with the latest state of affairs. All return to their prayers and weep with renewed vigor, but assure Achior, "The God of our fathers, whose power thou hast set forth, will make this return to thee, that thou rather shalt see their destruction," also they extend to him a share in their life: "Let God be with thee also in the midst of us!" In our day, this sort of thing is called "the propagation of the Faith." Sealing the promise, King Ozias invites Achior home with him. He "made him a great supper." Supping with the people of God is proper to anyone crucified for Truth, and Achior the Gentile accepted the invitation. He continues to develop through the story like an embryo in the womb of God's providence, though as yet unaware of his destiny.

Meanwhile, Holofernes lost no time in laying siege to Bethulia. No novice in logistics, he "found that the fountain which supplied them with water, ran through an aqueduct without the city on the south side: and he commanded their aqueduct to be cut off." Up to this point, we might have looked upon the book of Judith as nothing more than a good story teaching confidence in God in the face of evil. From now on, however, the depths in Judith yawn openly before us, and a marvelous spiritual allegory, deploying on several levels, begins to emerge. Only the eyes of faith can see through what follows.

Water has just been prominently mentioned. Whenever this happens in Scripture, we can suspect that the Divine Author is about to teach us something concerning grace or sacramental life. He has already used for this purpose the Rivers of Paradise, the Red Sea, the Flood, the Jordan, and the water Moses struck from the rock. We have every reason to believe the Bethulians' aqueduct will be no exception.

When Holofernes, the Anti-Christ, cuts off the water supply, he strikes at the source of sacramental life of God's people, just as he did in Eden. Always his first move, this tactic of his remains the same today. He imprisons bishops and cardinals on false charges. He forbids religious instruction in the schools. He closes churches and pronounces religion "the opiate of the people."

Faced with this situation, the ancient Bethulians did just what Bethulians always do in like circumstances. They ran to the hidden springs: "Nevertheless there were springs not far from the walls, out of which they were seen secretly to draw water, to refresh themselves a little rather than to drink their fill." In many parts of the world today they attend an occasional clandestine Mass, make a hurried confession to a priest disguised perhaps as a peddler. They sneak under cover of darkness to have their children baptized. They meet in basements to pray, always running the risk of arousing Holofernes.

The outcome of this unequal battle is inevitable: Holofernes

> placed all round about a hundred men at every spring. And when they had kept this watch for full twenty days, the cisterns, and the reserve of waters failed among all the inhabitants of Bethulia, so that there was not within the city enough to satisfy them, no, not for one day, for water was daily given out to the people by measure.

The Israelites have come to the end of their resources. They are religious souls of solid piety, and in this harsh emergency, they have done all that souls of ordinary prayer can do. They have used all natural means possible, arming themselves and fortifying their positions. Not neglecting supernatural means, they have fasted, done penance, wept, watched and prayed. They have confessed their sins before God, but He has sent no help, and now they have reached their limit of endurance. They murmur against Ozias their king, whom they now blame for not having bowed to Holofernes.

Even the king has little hope left. "Rising up all in tears," he says, "Be of good courage, my brethren, and let us wait these five days for mercy from the Lord. For perhaps He will put a stop to his indignation, and will give glory to his own name" (Jud. 7:23–24). If God doesn't act in five days, Ozias promises, Bethulia will surrender to the enemy.

In this atmosphere of thirsty despair, halfway through the story, Judith makes her entrance at last. It's a very quiet entrance, characteristic of a powerful contemplative soul with no need of dramatic effects. Never leaving her house

(Ah, the trademark of the soul of prayer!), she calls to her Ozias and the ancients Chabri and Charmi. With some indignation, she asks them, "What is this word, by which Ozias hath consented to give up the city to the Assyrians, if within five days there come no aid to us? And who are you that tempt the Lord?" (Jud. 8:10-11).

In the face of their silence, she delivers them a gentle lecture. It's a masterpiece of spiritual direction, whose main points are uncompromising conformity to God's Will and patience in suffering. It applies to any soul anywhere, in any circumstances this side of Heaven. She says in effect what all mystics preach, that God is God, and He should be allowed to act.

"But esteeming these very punishments to be less than our sins deserve," she adds, "let us believe that these scourges of the Lord, with which like servants we are chastised, have happened for our amendment, and not for our destruction" (Jud. 8:27).

Bowing to her incontestable judgment, the elders ask her intercession. "Now therefore pray for us, for thou art a holy woman, and one fearing God."

She answers, "As you know that what I have been able to say is of God: So that which I intend to do, prove ye if it be of God, and pray that God may strengthen my design" (Jud. 8:29-31).

She intends to save the people of God by a daring plan already formulated, and which she means to carry out immediately. For the prayerful, there is no time but the present. Before we follow Judith into action, however, and before all the aforementioned difficulties in her regard arise, it's essential to ascertain who Judith really is. What is she? A female Samson? The "strong woman"? Her name means simply "the Jewess,"—a rather vague title which could apply to any Israelite woman—and there, I believe, is a clue. Judith, like Mary, is something all-encompassing.

It's already clear from the story that here is no soul of ordinary prayer. Unlike the run-of-the-mill Bethulians, her sackcloth and ashes aren't reserved for national emergencies. Her fasts are year-round and her prayer unceasing. She herself is the answer to the multiplied prayers of the Bethulians, who have been driven to beg God for help. She is the help He has sent, although they don't know it yet, and she rises from their very midst, where she had lain hidden all the time. Judith comes forward when common means can go no further.

I think it's safe to say that Judith is no gleaner. She is contemplation, the prayer of the perfect. She is the prayer toward which all the elect must eventually come, for it is the prayer of the beatified begun on earth. Far from being a "strong woman," Judith is on the contrary the weak woman unarmed destined to destroy Anti-Christ, "the strong man armed," much as Esther destroyed the conniving Aman.

"Who is she that cometh forth as the morning rising," asks Canticles, "fair as the moon, bright as the sun, terrible as an army set in array? . . . What shalt thou see in the Sulamitess but the companies of camps?" (Cant. 6:9, 7:1).

So Judith is also a type of the Blessed Virgin, the Queen of Contemplation, as the fathers of the Church were again quick to tell us. Can't we say truly that to ignore the Scriptures is also to ignore Mary? Who else but she has destroyed

Holofernes for us by her perfect prayer and a simple *Fiat?*
In the Marian Age which is upon us, what treasures must lie
still undiscovered in the Books of Esther and Judith!

St. John of the Cross wrote his comments on Canticles
while kneeling. One can hardly do less for Judith. Reading
through these verses, one is often painfully aware of gross
intrusion on the ineffable. Judith, like Esther and Canticles,
can hardly be read at all outside prayer. When I called her
too hot to handle, I meant just that. She burns with the fire
our Lord came to cast on the earth and resists "handling."
Only to the Canon of the true Church could God possibly
have entrusted her.

Judith's luminous identity as contemplation breaks
through the surface of the text in many places, but I am able
to indicate only a few. For instance, she is designated "a
widow" at the outset. This makes her a figure of detachment, of one removed from the world.

In a letter of direction to an earthly widow, Francisco
Ortiz once wrote,

> Your first and greatest spouse is Jesus Christ, Son of the
> living God, everlasting King of ages, to whom our souls
> promise perpetual fidelity in holy baptism. These espousals
> are so real . . . and so all-embracing that to illustrate the
> sacrament of matrimony St. Paul makes the comparison of
> the above-mentioned espousals between Christ and His
> Church. . . . As it is certain that this heavenly Spouse lives
> and reigns glorious forever, yet is absent in His bodily
> presence, so the souls who have contracted espousals with
> Him, so long as they live in this exile, are called widows
> (*Epistolas Familiares*).

"I am no widow!" says the whore Babylon in the Apocalypse. "I shall not see mourning." I reckon not, for they that mourn are *blessed*.

Scripture is careful to insert some apparently superfluous details about Judith's late husband which are suspiciously un-germane to the plot, and they prove interesting. "Her husband was Manasses, who died in the time of the barley harvest,"—of sunstroke, says the Sacred Text, for "the heat came upon his head." Odd.

Few scriptural names, if any, are meaningless, and it happens that *Manasses* means "he who causes to forget." Coincidence? Well, hardly. All mystics stress this characteristic of forgetfulness in the prayer of contemplation, the abstraction from all creatures, caused by the dark and indistinct knowledge of God flooding the intellect, which drives out all else. *Vacate et videte quoniam Ego sum Deus!*

As for the barley harvest, we have heard a great deal about that already. It was the earliest harvest, taking place in April, and we recall that that other widow, Ruth, first met Booz then. This barley harvest must represent the first fruits of contemplative prayer, which had for "three years and six months" spelled widowhood for Judith, as it does detachment for any soul entering the mystical life.

St. John of the Cross might well have been speaking of Judith when he wrote in the Ascent of Mt. Carmel:

> Hence it comes to pass that the operations of the soul in union are of the Divine Spirit and are Divine. And hence it comes that the actions of such souls are only those that are seemly and reasonable, and not those that are ill-beseeming. For the Spirit of God teaches them that which they ought to know, and causes them to be ignorant of that which it behoves them not to know, and to remember that which they

have to remember, with or without forms, and to forget that which they should forget; and it makes them love that which they have to love, and not to love that which is not in God. And thus, all the first motions of the faculties of such souls are Divine and it is not to be wondered at that the motions and operations of these faculties should be Divine, since they are transformed in the Divine Being (*The Complete Works of St. John of the Cross,* Vol. I, *The Ascent of Mt. Carmel,* Ch. 2, 9, translated and edited by E. Allison Peers, Newman).

This is a description of perfection, of a soul who has reached the summits of transforming union. Her husband long ago has died of sunstroke, and, like Judith, she has "made herself a private chamber in the upper part of her house, in which she abode shut up with her maids." Let him who reads understand.

Judith reveals her perfections more and more fully as the story progresses, and we are privileged to watch her deal with the archfoe Holofernes. This is a lesson in how contemplation battles evil, interiorly and exteriorly, dispatching enemies both domestic and foreign. We might almost say that Judith and Esther should be read together, for they deal with two aspects of the same thing and complement each other's doctrine most marvelously. Esther gives us a positive picture. She tells us how the soul acquires the virtues that lead her to God. Judith gives us the negative. She tells us how to avoid and destroy everything that is contrary to God.

Judith told Ozias, Chabri and Charmi,

> You shall stand at the gate this night; and I will go out with my maidservant. And pray ye, that, as you have said, in five days the Lord may look down upon his people Israel. But I desire that you *search not into what I am doing:* and till I

bring you word let nothing else be done but to pray for me to the Lord our God.

Contemplation works in secret and alone, like Thamar. She takes no one into her confidence. The populace, who can be said to represent the lower powers of the soul, imagination or emotions, are told nothing of Judith's plan. There is, after all, nothing they can do to help. Feeling and images perform no essential function in this perfect prayer. Even the higher powers of the soul, as represented by Chabri and Charmi, are made "to stand at the gate *this night.*" Ah, here is our blessed night again, in which such marvels happen!

When the elders leave, Judith prays for strength. "Bring to pass, O Lord, that his pride may be cut off with his own sword. Let him be caught in the net of his own eyes in my regard, and do thou strike him by the graces of the words of my lips." Judith doesn't need St. John of the Cross to tell her that it is God who must operate through her faculties! "Give me constancy in my mind, that I may despise him," she continues, being a woman whose strength lies in the knowledge of her own weakness and the power of evil to attract. (My, we're a long, long way from Mrs. Phutiphar now!)

"For this will be a glorious monument for thy name, when he shall fall by the hand of a woman," she says.

"I will put enmity between you and the woman, between your seed and her seed," Almighty God had long ago told Holofernes the serpent, so we can't say he wasn't warned. Judith, like all contemplatives, heads straight for her main objective. She will battle Holofernes essentially and utterly. The Bethulians, or souls of common prayer, we have already seen are occupied with fortifying single positions, preparing to fight Holofernes piecemeal, engaging his soldiery one by one in hand-to-hand combat, even though the odds are obviously overwhelming. Just so souls of ordinary prayer battle vices one by one, slowly building up opposing virtues, fortifying single positions. This is the way men fight, and that's why contemplative prayer isn't learned from watching the male sex in the exterior "man's world."

Judith fights as a woman fights. Watch her methods. She doesn't worry with the soldiery, which outnumber, outreach and outweigh her anyway. She heads for the general (here we can call him self-love), knowing that when he falls, his whole army falls with him.

Now, the following should be read every hour on the hour by anyone who has ever accused a contemplative of being an escape artist. See what Judith does next:

> And she called her maid: and going down into her house she took off her haircloth, and put away the garments of her widowhood. And she washed her body, and anointed herself with the best ointment, and plaited the hair of her head, and put a bonnet upon her head, and clothed herself with the garments of her gladness, and put sandals on her feet, and took her bracelets, and lilies, and earlets, and rings, and adorned herself with all her ornaments (Jud. 10:2–3).

Here she is, ready for battle, clad in merits and virtues. The same finery which Esther used to make herself attractive to the King Judith will use to deceive and destroy the Adversary. This can also be said to be Catholic Action in action, making full use of talents natural and supernatural, creatures and opportunities, to implement a purpose whose roots lie in prayer. God seconds this action fully:

"And the Lord also gave her more beauty: because all this dressing up did not proceed from sensuality, but from virtue. And therefore the Lord increased this her beauty, so that she appeared to all men's eyes incomparably lovely" (Jud. 10:4).

"Thou art all fair, O my love, and there is not a spot in thee," Judith Immaculate!

"And she gave to her maid a bottle of wine to carry," continues the text, "and a vessel of oil, and parched corn, and dry figs, and bread and cheese, and went out," because the soul of prayer is careful to carry her own special provisions when she means to tangle with the world and leave her house. Bread, wine, oil—specifically the matter of sacraments, are certainly not put into the maid's basket by accident.

Thus prepared, Judith and her servant pass unhindered through the gates of the city, past Ozias and the ancients, who ask no questions. St. John of the Cross might well have had this very scene in mind when he wrote the beautiful poem, "En Una Noche Obscura":

> On a dark night,
> Kindled in love with yearnings—oh, happy chance!
> I went forth without being observed,
> My house being now at rest.
>
> In darkness and secure,
> By the secret ladder, disguised—oh, happy chance!
> In darkness and in concealment,
> My house being now at rest.
>
> In the happy night,
> In secret, when none saw me,

Nor I beheld aught,
Without light or guide, save that which burned
   in my heart.

St. John explains his meaning, and his words could almost be laid alongside the verses in Judith, so similar is the imagery:

> It is needful for the enamoured soul, in order to attain to its desired end, to do likewise, going forth at night, when all the domestics in its house are sleeping and at rest—that is, when the low operations, passions and desires of the soul (who are the people of the household) are, because it is night, sleeping and at rest. When these are awake, they invariably hinder the soul from seeking its good, since they are opposed to its going forth in freedom. These are they of whom Our Saviour speaks in the Gospel, saying that they are the enemies of man (Mt. 10:36). And thus it would be meet that their operations and motions should be put to sleep in this night, to the end that they may not hinder the soul from attaining the supernatural blessings of the union of love of God, . . . inasmuch as all natural ability is impotent with respect to the supernatural blessings that God, by means of His own infusion, bestows upon the soul passively, secretly and in silence. And thus it is needful that all the faculties should receive this infusion, and that, in order to receive it, they should remain passive, and not interpose their own base acts and vile inclinations (*The Complete Works of St. John of the Cross,* Vol. I, *Dark Night of the Soul,* Bk. II, Ch. 14, 1, translated and edited by E. Allison Peers, Newman).

Judith easily gets by the Assyrian watchmen. "They beheld her face, and their eyes were amazed, for they wondered exceedingly at her beauty." She tells them,

> I am a daughter of the Hebrews, and I am fled from them, because I knew they would be made a prey to you, because

they despised you, and would not of their own accord yield themselves, that they might find mercy in your sight. For this reason I thought with myself, saying: I will go to the presence of the prince Holofernes, that I may tell him their secrets, and shew him by what way he may take them, without the loss of one man of his army (Jud. 10:12–13).

You see what a wonderful liar Judith is, how she lies as a woman lies, consummately mixing fact and fiction. She might shock some people, but I feel certain she never shocked St. John of the Cross or any other mystic, all of whom recognize this marvelous deceitful quality of contemplation when it encounters evil. In his "Spiritual Canticle," St. John has a line which reads, "I will pass by the mighty and cross the frontiers," speaking of contemplation's power to get by evil spirits, represented as Assyrian watchmen in Judith.

These are easily taken in by Judith, who has put off her sackcloth and is disguised in glittering finery calculated to cause only admiration. St. John says about this sort of thing,

> The soul . . . goes forth here disguised with that disguise which most vividly represents the affections of its spirit and which will protect it most securely on its journey from its adversaries and enemies, which are the devil, the world and the flesh. Thus the livery which it wears is of three chief colors—white, green and purple—denoting the three theological virtues, faith, hope and charity. By these the soul will not only gain the grace and goodwill of its Beloved, but it will travel in security and complete protection from its three enemies (*op. cit.* Bk. II, Ch. 21, 3).

St. Paul put it this way:

> Put on the armor of God, that you may be able to stand

against the wiles of the devil. For our wrestling is not against flesh and blood, but against the Principalities and the Powers, against the world-rulers of this darkness, against the spiritual forces of wickedness on high. Therefore take up the armor of God, that you may be able to resist in the evil day, and stand in all things perfect . . . having girded your loins with truth, and having put on the breastplate of justice, and having your feet shod with the readiness of the Gospel of peace, in all things taking up the shield of faith, with which you may be able to quench all the fiery darts of the most wicked one. And take unto you the helmet of salvation and the sword of the spirit, that is, the word of God! (Eph. 6:10–17).

Being a lovely lady, Judith "put a bonnet upon her head, and clothed herself with the garments of her gladness, and put sandals on her feet," these being the way her author chose to represent her theological virtues. Contemplation easily hoodwinks evil because she is so simple, so beautiful, so weak-looking and so inoffensive. She has no visible "works" with which to alarm her enemies. She carries no artillery, and she is quite alone. She deceives in the same way that our Lord's parables deceive, "that seeing they may not see and hearing they may not hear." She travels at night, straight to her target, encountering no opposition, because who would oppose her? "A net is spread in vain before the eyes of them that have wings" (Prov. 1:17). How can the world tempt one who has given up the values of the world? Hers is the prayer of the simple, of the Blessed Virgin, who deceived Satan utterly by her simplicity. Never did he suspect she was the Mother of God until it was too late.

Judith easily reaches Holofernes. In fact the watchmen themselves take her to his tent, where "forthwith Holofernes was caught by his eyes." His goose is cooked. He tells her, "Be of good comfort, and fear not in thy heart: for I have never hurt a man that was willing to serve Nabuchodonosor the king. And if thy people had not despised me, I would not have lifted up my spear against them." Oh, doesn't this line sound familiar!

Judith plies Holofernes with compliments, telling him everything he wants to hear. Doesn't the Holy Spirit tell us that "with the crafty he deals craftily" (Ps. 18:26)? She informs the general that Israel is bound to succumb to him, because in their desperation the Jews have desecrated their holy things, "which God forbade them to touch, in corn, wine, and oil, these have they purposed to make use of, and they design to consume the things which they ought not to touch with their hands." She tells him they have even drunk the blood of their cattle, a serious transgression under Mosaic Law, which regarded blood as a life principle sacred to God.

Of course Judith is lying. Isn't that the point of the whole story, that perfect prayer deceives evil?

Playing further upon Holofernes' superstition, Judith adds demurely, "And I thy handmaid knowing this, am fled from them, and the Lord has sent me to tell thee these very things. For I thy handmaid worship God even now that I am with thee, and thy handmaid will go out, and I will pray to God." There is no prevarication here. Judith, we may be sure, was sent by God, and her prayer is "unceasing."

She then baits the trap, saying, "And he will tell me when he will repay them for their sins, and I will come and tell thee, so that I may bring thee through the midst of Jerusalem, and thou shalt have all the people of Israel, as sheep that have no shepherd."

Holofernes is pleased. He assures her that if this comes to pass, "if thy God shall do this for me, he shall also be my God." It has always been Lucifer's dream to draw Almighty

God into his service. "Bow down and worship me!" he suggested to the Second Person become Flesh. His pride is monstrous.

Holofernes houses Judith "where his treasures were laid up," but always she is careful to eat only the kosher food brought with her. Her request "to go out at night and before day to prayer," is easily granted, for Holofernes is of course persuaded that she is praying for his success. Contemplation often gives the appearance of giving in to evil, because she gives the appearance of doing nothing. Nothing in her exterior conduct can excite its suspicions. Any opposition a contemplative draws is more likely to be from her own lower nature or from good people, who, like Martha, wish she would help with the housework.

Scripture says of Judith, "She went out in the nights into the valley of Bethulia and washed herself in a fountain of water." Confronted by such a verse as this, what can we say? The picture it gives, of Judith slipping out at night to "the valley of Bethulia" to wash in a fountain of water is one of those brushes with the incommunicable.

"As I see it, to be plunged in humility is to be plunged in God," said Sister Elizabeth of the Trinity in her Souvenirs. Her sister in religion, the Little Flower, often pitied the souls who keep looking for God on the heights, when it is in "the valley of humility" that Jesus waits for us. So the valley of Bethulia represents the nothingness and humility from which springs the prayer of a soul united to God. Its washing in a *fountain* of water within the very camp of the enemy, while its co-citizens of ordinary prayer thirst for a few drops in their own city, gives an accurate picture of the contemplative still *in via*, the higher powers of whose soul

are watered and refreshed, while the lower—senses and imagination—are parched. This is also a most truthful account
of the Blessed Virgin's life on earth, full of grace, lived
among compatriots who thirsted in a besieged city. These
things, however, I clearly cannot comment on. Please hold
me excused.

I can comment, however, on what the Bethulians would
have said if they could have seen Judith at this prayer in the
valley. "Traitoress!" "Escape artist!" I can hear. "There you
are praying up a storm and having it easy while we suffer
and die back here in Bethulia where life is *real!*"

Only God can defend Mary against Martha, and in the
Book of Judith He does so. Clearly, she is the only one of
the Bethulians locked in a hand to hand struggle with bare
reality, at grips with the essential. Her danger is far more
terrible than mere thirst or starvation. Her danger is that
of being deflowered by evil. Souls who rise to such heights
are not bothered by *little* skirmishes with the Prince of this
world. They stand to win or lose all. One misstep on Judith's
part now, and she's done for:

> And it came to pass on the fourth day, that Holofernes
> made a supper for his servants, and said to Vagao his eunuch:
> Go, and persuade that Hebrew woman, to consent of her
> own accord to dwell with me. For it is looked upon as
> shameful among the Assyrians, if a woman mock a man,
> by doing so as to pass free from him (Jud. 12:10–11).

How many other Bethulians could have met this situation
with Judith's equanimity and confidence in God? She
answers coolly, "Who am I, that I should gainsay my lord?
All that shall be good and best before his eyes, I will do.
And whatsoever shall please him, that shall be best to me all

the days of my life." Oh dear, if the Bethulians could have heard that! Only the reader is allowed to suspect who her "lord" really is—Almighty God.

Then, "she arose and dressed herself out with her garments," her disguise being all important at this point, "and going in, she stood before his face." The scene which follows is incomparable "theater."

> And the heart of Holofernes was smitten, for he was burning with the desire of her. And Holofernes said to her. Drink now, and sit down and be merry; for thou hast found favour before me. And Judith said: I will drink my lord, because my life is magnified this day above all my days. And she took and ate and drank before him *what her maid had prepared for her.* And Holofernes was made merry on her occasion, and drank exceeding much wine, so much as he had never drunk in his life.

The servants retire, and Judith is left alone to gaze on the unconscious Holofernes, "on his bed, fast asleep, being exceeding drunk." Praying to the Lord, she concludes with, "Strengthen me, O Lord God, at this hour." Then, taking Holofernes' sword from where it hangs at the head of his bed, "she took him by the hair of his head. . . . And she struck twice upon his neck, and cut off his head, and took off his canopy from the pillars, and rolled away his headless body." Whack . . . WHACK!

The deed is done. Holofernes has been destroyed as only Contemplation could have done it. He was the victim of a kind of spiritual judo known to souls of very simple prayer, who innocently trick evil into using its own strength against itself, much in the same way Tweety-Pie always innocently outmaneuvers the bad ole Putty-Tat. This is a high wisdom mastered by the pure in heart, who have given themselves to God completely and have learned to wait on Him, not running around like headless chickens in the meantime. It is the wisdom of Mary, who above all knew how to wait.

Describing the marvels of this supernatural prudence, the spiritual master Father de Caussade says this:

> I fear more my own action and that of my friends than that of my enemies. There is no prudence so great as that which offers no resistance to enemies, and which opposes to them only a simple abandonment. This is to run before the wind, and as there is nothing else to be done, to keep quiet and peaceful. There is nothing that is more entirely opposed to worldly prudence than simplicity; it turns aside all schemes without comprehending them, without so much as a thought about them. The divine action makes the soul take such just measures as to surprise those who want to take it by surprise themselves.
>
> It profits by all their efforts, and is raised by the very things that are done to lower it. They are the galley slaves who bring the ship into port with hard rowing. All obstacles turn to the good of this soul, and by allowing its enemies a free hand, it obtains a continual service, so sufficing that all it has to fear is lest it should itself take part in a work of which God would be the principal, and His enemies the agents, and in which it has nothing to do but peacefully to observe the work of God, and to follow with simplicity the attractions He gives it. The supernatural prudence of the Divine Spirit, the principal of these attractions, infallibly attains its end; and the precise circumstances of each event are so applied to the soul, without its perception, that everything opposed to them cannot fail to be destroyed (*Abandonment to Divine Providence,* Bk. II, Ch. 4, Sec. 6, B. Herder Book Co.).

With sublime poverty of action, Judith allowed Holofernes, really, to destroy himself, to "fall into the pit which he had made." Moved by the Holy Spirit, she trapped him in his own cupidity, his own superstition, pride and lust. She told him only what he wanted to hear. As Judith herself remarked later,

> Judith the daughter of Merari weakened him with the beauty of her face. For she put off her the garments of widowhood, and put on her the garments of joy, to give joy to the children of Israel. She anointed her face with ointment, and bound up her locks with a crown, she took a new robe to deceive him (Jud. 16:8–10).

She waited for him to set the stage. He invited her to dinner; he drank himself insensible; his servants retired on his orders, leaving him at Judith's mercy. Then, and only then, did she strike. Even so, she cut off his head *with his own sword*. (Oh, isn't God's humor at work here!) Scripture says she used two strokes. One began the operation, the second finished it clean.

Doctors of mystical theology have names for these two strokes, and we might apply them here. They are the well-known two purgations of the mystical life which are called "the night of sense" and "the night of the spirit" by St. John of the Cross. Walter Hilton preferred to call them "reform in faith" and "reform in feeling." Whatever called, they are dealt with at length in all spiritual literature treating of the mystical life.

Remembering, however, that Judith also represents the Blessed Virgin, there is a higher interpretation of these strokes. Looking on her Infant at the Presentation in the Temple, the holy Simeon had promised Mary, "Behold, this child is destined . . . for a sign that shall be contradicted.

And thy own soul a sword shall pierce, that the thoughts of many hearts may be revealed."

By consenting to this sword of suffering at the Presentation, Mary turned it against its evil author and delivered the first blow to the pride of Holofernes. She delivered the second and final blow at the foot of the cross when she consented to the Crucifixion in "the hour of the power of darkness." The sword of Holofernes is the Holy Cross, the instrument of Satan's malice which has become the means of redemption for all mankind. Oh, but can't we *really* hear God's Laugh here!

For centuries people good and bad have speculated on the nature of Adam and Eve's first sin. Being all tainted with it, after all, it seems hardly fair that we should not know what it was that is now represented under the symbolism of eating forbidden fruit from a tree. We know it was disobedience, of course, but beyond that, nothing is certain as to details.

Whatever it was, viewing it from our stand down here, the only clues we can pick up must lie with Mary, who, as the new Eve, made restitution for the crime. If we read Scripture aright her temptation at the foot of the Cross must have been something horrible—a close contact with evil as dangerous as was Eve's, as revolting as was Judith's. The enemy must have been allowed very close access to Mary, as close certainly as was Esther's brush with the evil Aman.

Returning to the Book of Esther for a moment, we read that Aman at the last was found "fallen upon the bed on which Esther lay," entreating her for his life. "He will force the Queen also in my presence, in my own house!" cries the king, outraged at seeing this. Immediately he orders Aman hanged, we gather even more for this presumptuous offense than for his promulgation of the wicked edict against Israel.

All this is mystery, but we do know that at the foot of the Cross Mary, like Eve, also stood near a Tree on which hung a most desirable Fruit; but unlike Eve, she didn't appropriate it to her own use. In the face of the most excruciating suffering, she let It hang in obedience to God's will, although she was well aware—certainly since Cana—how great was her power over this Man, greater even than had been Eve's power over Adam. It would have been so easy for her, like the Jews, to wheedle, "Come down from the Cross!" For her, would He have come down? What abysses open before us here.

The serpent, call him Holofernes or Aman or Satan or what you will, must have had his hour with Mary's immaculate soul then, "fallen upon the bed on which Esther lay" and entreating "that Hebrew woman to consent of her own accord to dwell with me." What horror. This seduction is the exemplar of all seduction, for as the devil apes God in every way, wishing to be God, so he too makes love to souls, hoping to possess them as God possesses them.

A love affair with the devil! *That* was the original sin, and so the rabbis and the Church Fathers, who recognized this first "triangle," and who persistently envisaged the first sin as a sexual sin, may not have been wrong after all. Doesn't Scripture in fact call any sin "fornication?" Sexual sin is a deviation in the real meaning of sex, which we now know is something much bigger than the meager physiological play of mere animals. Eve was faithless in her marriage to Adam, but mostly, faithless to God, with whom her soul was at all times united. Is it therefore surprising that this catastrophe should bring in its wake a sense of sexual shame and nakedness in all her descendants? Our sexual powers were seriously disrupted at their highest level by Eve. A new Eve, pure and selfless, was perfectly faithful to her marriage vows in the face of the same kind of temptation.

Mary, we thank thee!

But this is not the end of Judith's story, or the Blessed Virgin's, either. Returning stealthily to Bethulia with her maid, Scripture tells us Judith

> brought forth the head of Holofernes out of the wallet, and shewed it them, saying: Behold the head of Holofernes the general of the army of the Assyrians; and behold his canopy, wherein he lay in his drunkenness, where the Lord our God slew him by the hand of a woman! (Jud. 13:19).

The Bethulians

> all adored the Lord, and said to her: The Lord hath blessed thee by his power, because by thee he hath brought our enemies to nought. And Ozias, the prince of the people of Israel, said to her: Blessed art thou, O daughter, by the Lord the most high God, above all women upon the earth. Blessed be the Lord who made heaven and earth, who hath directed thee to the cutting off the head of the prince of our enemies. Because he hath so magnified thy name this day, that thy praise shall not depart out of the mouth of men who shall be mindful of the power of the Lord, for ever: for that thou hast not spared thy life, by reason of the distress and tribulation of thy people; but hast prevented our ruin in the presence of our God (Jud. 13:22–25).

The Liturgy places some of these verses in Our Lady's Masses, as also the praise of the high priest Joachim, who comes from Jerusalem to tell Judith, "Thou art the glory of

Jerusalem, thou art the joy of Israel, thou art the honor of our people!"

Blessed art thou among women! Hail, Mary, full of grace!

In the midst of Bethulia's rejoicing, our old friend Achior is called for, and upon seeing the head of Holofernes, "his soul swooned away." As Achior is hardly the fainting type, we may suspect that something fundamental, something spiritual, has happened to him, and so it has. "Seeing the power that the God of Israel had wrought, leaving the religion of the Gentiles, he believed God, and circumcised the flesh of his foreskin, and was joined to the people of Israel, with all the succession of his kindred until this present day."

Achior is therefore a convert. In his conversion are hidden the mystery of the apostolate of the contemplative and the spiritual motherhood of Mary. The contemplative penetrates the souls of all men to the degree that she penetrates into God, who is present in all His works. In Him she too is present in the deepest center of all His creatures, and her prayer, as it were, takes place in them. Given no obstacle, grace makes its entry.

Judith was barely aware of Achior's existence. She had given him, I am sure, no pamphlets on apologetics entitled "Is There Salvation Outside the Church?" yet she would have been the first to admit God's pursuit of Achior through her agency. As she herself had remarked, "For all Thy ways are prepared, and in Thy providence Thou hast placed Thy judgments."

Now we see that God deliberately sought the soul of Achior, who is a figure of the Gentiles and whose name, incidentally, means "brother of light." It would be truthful to say He allowed Nabuchodonosor's evil designs to flourish for a time for the express purpose of bringing Achior within range of the grace of Judith and Bethulia—without detriment, of course, to the other unsearchable purposes of Divine Providence. Anyone who has been converted late in life, or who has been privileged to witness another's conversion at close range, will understand how meticulously God chases down His elect. As Francis Thompson put it, how "those strong Feet . . . followed, followed after.

> But with unhurrying chase,
> And unperturbed pace,
> Deliberate speed, majestic instancy,
> They beat. . . ."

Evil always sweats in unknowing service to God. Where would Achior be if Holofernes hadn't thrown him out of his camp? Or if Judith hadn't allowed herself to be drawn into the conflict? Or if the Bethulians hadn't resisted? God seems to lay open here for our inspection the bare bones of His Providence, explaining for us the inexplicable. Nabuchodonosor could hardly have been persuaded that he deployed his military might simply to save Achior's soul, any more than Caesar Augustus could have believed he ordered his census just to ensure that Christ would be born in the city of David, but this is so, and the eyes of faith can see it. On a grand scale, this is the same kind of spiritual judo He teaches His Judiths.

Contemplation doesn't just bring about conversions. She sets in motion entire populations. Hear her:

> Hang ye up this head upon our walls. And as soon as the sun shall rise, let every man take his arms, and rush ye out, not as going down beneath, but as making an assault. Then

the watchmen [Ah, the watchmen again!] must needs run to awake their prince for the battle. And when the captains of them shall run to the tent of Holofernes, and shall find him without his head, wallowing in his blood, fear shall come upon them. And when you shall know that they are fleeing, go after them securely, for the Lord will destroy them under your feet! (Jud. 14:1–5).

The Bethulians respond, and the enemy is alarmed. Their officers run to waken Holofernes, whom they assume to be still asleep with Judith. "For the mice, coming out of their holes," they marvel, "have presumed to challenge us to fight!" (St. Thérèse called these mice her "legion of little souls." They are invincible when thoroughly roused.)

Vagao, dashing into Holofernes' tent, comes out crying, "One Hebrew woman hath made confusion in the house of Nabuchodonosor: for behold Holofernes lieth upon the ground, and his head is not upon him!" A masterly understatement in a crisis, I'd say.

Just as Judith had foreseen, Holofernes' army falls apart. "Then the camp of the Assyrians howled," she recapitulates later, "when my lowly ones appeared, parched with thirst." Routed and despoiled, the Assyrians were totally defeated because they "were not united together, they went without order in their flight; but the children of Israel pursuing in one body, defeated all that they could find."

Novum, again, *in vetere latet.* This one Body, we now know in these latter days, is Mystical. "My perfect one is but one," says the Bridegroom, her Head, who also was "parched with thirst." Being one, this Body acts as one. Our Mother the Blessed Virgin brought it forth once in flesh, and she continues to bring it forth in spirit. Like Judith, she urges it into battle. "See," she tells us mice at Lourdes, at Fatima, at

La Salette, "I have cut off the head of Holofernes, 'now rush ye out, not as going down beneath, but as making an assault!' "

The people give Judith all the spoils of Holofernes, even his arms and emerald canopy. She in turn offers these to God as "an anathema of oblivion," making holy even the goods of evil by a mysterious transmutation known to all souls of prayer. "And the people were joyful in the sight of the sanctuary, and for three months the joy of this victory was celebrated with Judith."

If we prefer all along to make our exegesis on the subjective level, we can see that we are now parallel with the summits of the soul's perfection, where, as the mystics teach, the senses and lower faculties, "the people," become joyous and integrated in their turn through the infusion of grace. No longer hungry or thirsty, they enjoy God freely according to their nature, being delivered from the threat of Holofernes' soldiery—their former vices and temptations. (Who could ever exhaust the meanings of Scripture? There is so much wealth for mind and heart everywhere, the poor human who reads becomes as giddy as a six year-old let loose in a candy store.)

The inspired author troubles to tell us that Judith returned to her seclusion and lived "in her husband's house a hundred and five years." The number is no doubt symbolic, but I can't help dwelling on it for the benefit of anyone who might think contemplation, sackcloth and ashes don't provide a full life. Also, lest we think Judith's return to solitude was a retirement into inactivity, we note the author also says, "And all the time of her life there was none that troubled Israel, nor many years after her death." Her prayer, disclosed briefly to our sight in a national crisis, therefore continued, hidden and fruitful. Apparently doing nothing, she sustained and protected the very existence of the people of God, for "wisdom is more active than all active things: and reacheth everywhere by reason of her purity."

She does indeed dwell in "her husband's house," for this house is Holy Sion, the people of God themselves. In words the Church applies to the Blessed Virgin, God is shown as commanding wisdom,

"Let thy dwelling be in Jacob, and thy inheritance in Israel, and take root in my elect."

And she says, "I took root in an honorable people, and in the portion of my God his inheritance, and my abode is in the full assembly of saints."

In the atmosphere of peace in which the Book of Judith closes, the author slips in a little detail. He says that Judith "made her handmaid free, and she died, and was buried in Bethulia." This little handmaid is intriguing. She is given no name and not one line to speak, yet she alone was privileged to accompany her mistress to the tent of Holofernes "by night." She carried the provisions, she went with Judith to prayer in the valley, and it was she to whom Judith gave the head of Holofernes to carry, bidding her to "put it in her wallet." The little maid is obedient and silent always. Who is she? Is she the human will? Mystical theology has not yet defined whether the activity of the will "accompanies" the soul in the highest contemplation possible in this life, or whether eventually it is "left at the gate" with the other higher powers when the soul merges with God. Persons of experience tell me they incline to the view that the will does remain active all along, and if so, this doctrine would appear to be corroborated in Judith, where the handmaid is "set free" only when the will attains perfect freedom at death in the beatific vision.

Or is the handmaid the human body, the perfect instrument of Judith's perfect soul? Is her liberation at death perhaps a veiled reference to Our Lady's Assumption? Or if we chose all along to regard Judith as a figure of Divine Wisdom—Our Lord Himself—is the little maid not perhaps simply human nature? The Book of Judith is full of such wonderful ponderments. It would take seven volumes to go into them all, and the number here, too, is symbolic!

"Surely I shall not be condemned by any person of prudence for these different interpretations, so long as truth sustains them," said St. Bernard, apparently defending this sort of liberty.

> Charity, the rule for interpreting Scripture, will edify more readers, according as, in its work of edification, it discovers more meanings that are in conformity with truth. For why should anyone find this practice distasteful in adopting it in the use of things? For instance, to how many uses is water alone put for the good of our bodies? In the same was any divinely inspired statement will not fail of its purpose if it bears different meanings adapted to the various needs and habits of souls (Sermon LI on *Canticles*).

So there!

St. John of the Cross must have known the Book of Judith well, for see how he ends the Spiritual Canticle:

Que nadie lo miraba,
Aminadab tampoco parecía,
Y el cerco sosegaba,

Y la caballería
A vista de las aguas descendía.

"And there was a rest from the siege, and the cavalry came down at the sight of the waters." May God be praised in all things, as his friend St. Teresa used to say. Now the Bethulian aqueduct flows again!

"Vidi aquam!" exclaims the Church in wonderment every Easter. "I saw the water flowing from the right side of the temple, *Alleluia!* And all unto whom that water came were saved and they shall say, *Alleluia, Alleluia! ! ! !*

Holy Mary, *gratia plena,* Blessed Aqueduct, please keep the water flowing to us Bethulians, who are mice, and thirsty.

CARRY NATION, DON'T YOU DARE!

ALCOHOL was not one of my childhood problems. On visits to my French grandmother, I was duly served wine—one part to five parts water—because it was an integral part of the fare. Like St. Paul, Grandmother believed in "a little wine for thy stomach's sake," though I never knew her to quote the apostle on the subject. Such truths, she would have argued, are self-evident to sensible people by the light of natural reason, without appeals to the authority of Scripture.

This attitude of hers also used to get me a little port with ladyfingers on Sunday afternoons in the parlor. Not once was I cautioned about getting stinko and falling off my chair. I won't tell you how old I was before I heard that wine could make people drunk, because you might think I was retarded. The truth is, I was something like the little southern girl who was not told until puberty that the Confederacy had lost the Civil War. Nobody, I'm afraid, had even showed me what happens to a worm dropped in alcohol or explained to me the delicacy of stomach linings.

As I say, alcohol was simply not my problem, and presumptuous fool that I was, I concluded that alcohol was not a child's problem at all. This, I eventually learned, can be the poorest kind of preparation for motherhood. As it turned out, alcohol was a terrible problem to our first-born, but I never caught on until he was ten years old and already deeply affected.

The bomb burst at Christmas dinner, when the inevitable plum pudding and hard sauce made their appearance. After his first taste of this delicacy, the poor child leapt from his chair, gazed in horror at his lump of sauce and exclaimed, "Mother! This has *whiskey* in it!"

"Not whiskey," I said, "brandy." Whatever was the matter with children nowadays? Everybody knows good hard sauce isn't made with whiskey.

"But it's *alcohol!*"

"Of course it's alcohol. How else would you make hard sauce hard?"

"But I ate some," he wailed.

"Well, I should hope so. That's what I made it for." The boy, I suspected, had gone daft. "What's the matter with you? Since when can't you eat a dab of hard sauce without getting hysterical?"

"But I took the pledge!"

"You took the *what?*"

All other conversation around the table had ceased. Forks rested in mid-air. Daddy's jaw had dropped, and sister giggled.

"The pledge!" he repeated. I promised I'd never touch alcohol, *never—as long as I lived!*"

Good night, nurse. No matter how many child psych courses you take in school, you're never prepared for crises like this. We soon got the whole story. It was evident that Bishop Jansen and Carry Nation had been carrying on their nefarious work right under our very noses. The boy had been inveigled into joining the Temperance Society—grade school level—at the country schoolhouse down the road, and he could tell us all about worms and stomach linings.

"Now look, just forget that foolishness and finish your dessert."

"But I *promised*. I can't break a promise!"

"Just tell them you've resigned," suggested his father.

"If you resign, you won't get to go to the picnic!" reminded his sister, with lightning thrust. She had nothing to lose. She had joined up too, it developed, but her hard sauce had been consumed at a gulp, she being happily incapable of recognizing alcohol when she came across it.

This split the family neatly down the middle. Carry Nation's hatchet had struck again. We were "wets." Our children were "drys." A grisly deadlock ensued. If my grandmother had been there, I am sure she would have said something like, "You see what happens when you don't bring children up properly and let them have a little wine in their water. They get all sorts of ridiculous ideas."

"Look," I suggested sweetly, "just ask your teacher what it was Jesus turned the water into when He went to that wedding reception at Cana."

They said they would. At the end of the Christmas holidays, they came back with the answer. "It was grapejuice!" they announced triumphantly. "God wouldn't turn water into wine for people, because wine is *bad*. It makes people drunk!" (They also informed me that I was a drunkard, because I drank it.)

"Listen," their father offered, "it couldn't have been grapejuice. It had to be either wine or vinegar unless they drank it right off the wine-press. Learning how to keep grapejuice from fermenting is a miracle of modern science!"

"It was fresh, then," they said.

"The Bible says *wine;* it doesn't say grape-juice," I argued weakly, but helplessly, because that was just about all the Bible-quoting I had in those days. I couldn't hope to compete with well-read Temperance people, who obviously had inside information on Cana which I hadn't come across.

Today things are different. As you can see, I've been reading the Bible like crazy. Now that the crisis is past, I'm spilling over with quotations. For instance, I could nonchalantly quote Numbers 6:2–4. I could say,

> when a man [or a woman] solemnly takes the Nazirite vow to dedicate himself to the Lord, he shall abstain from wine and strong drink; he may neither drink wine vinegar, other vinegar, or any kind of grapejuice [heh! heh!], nor eat either fresh or dried grapes. As long as he is a Nazirite he shall not eat anything of the produce of the vine; not even unripe grapes or grape-skins.

There were other things Nazirites were not supposed to do, either. They were not supposed to cut their hair, or touch dead bodies, or mourn the departed. It seems to me the society was pulling its punches somewhat, being pretty free with that grapejuice, not to mention haircuts, vinegar and funerals. Why draw the line at wine? Let's face it, what our children had been asked to take was actually in the order of a Nazirite vow.

In Biblical times, this vow represented a special dedication to God. It was rarely taken for life, but usually only for a limited time, as by the great St. Paul himself, for instance. Even so, it was undertaken in a spirit of penance, much as we now go through Lent—not out of regard for the lining of the stomach. Only figures of extraordinary stature ever became Nazirites for life—such giants as Samuel, Samson, or St. John the Baptist, for instance, all of whom were consecrated to God or sanctified in the womb.

St. John especially, the very spirit of mortification and penance crying in the wilderness, is the pattern of perfect Nazirites. When announcing his birth to his father Zachary, the angel had indeed said "he shall drink no wine or strong drink." The solace of potable spirits, we soon learn, would have been quite superfluous in his case, for the angel adds, "He shall be filled with the Holy Spirit even from his mother's womb."

When Nazirites gave up drinking wine, vinegar and grapejuice forever and forwent mourning their dear ones, they didn't do so because those practices are bad, but precisely because they are so good, and so consoling. Giving them up is highly penitential and not to be expected of just everybody. As Cardinal Newman put it while still an Anglican, "Holy people fast lest they infringe on God's bounty, or by constant use forget how to do without." Fond and foolish as mothers can be, I couldn't honestly think that our children, aged ten and six respectively, should try to measure up to Nazirite standards all at once, and for life. Bubble gum, I thought, was better for a start, and nearer their quick.

"Well, perhaps you want your children to grow up and be alcoholics!" rejoins the Temperance Society.

Dear me, no. That's what I'm deathly afraid of, and nothing breeds alcoholism like a guilt complex. How many thousands of alcoholics feel compelled to keep on drinking just to drown their shame about drinking at all?

Most of all, however, I want our children to be Catholics.

And if they believe wine is bad, obviously they can't be, because this is heresy. It's that simple. Wine is a gift from God. He gave it to man just as He gave him laughter, and for the same reason: God is merciful. His justice decreed that we must suffer punishment, but His mercy makes the punishment bearable through many wonderful consolations. Wine is one of them. If Adam hadn't sinned, wine would never have made an alcoholic, or have been the occasion of gluttony.

"Bless the Lord, O my soul," sings the Psalmist in thanksgiving.

> You raise grass for cattle
>   and vegetation for man's use,
> Producing bread from the earth,
>   and wine to gladden men's hearts! (Ps. 104:14).

Bread and wine! Oh, Carry Amelia Nation, how could you? Would you lay your ax to the root of sacramental life? Would you destroy the priesthood? Must there be no Mass, no Redemption? No one will dispute that alcoholics should never touch alcohol, must indeed become quasi-Nazirites, because it does terrible things to them. They must forego the pleasure in the same way a diabetic forgoes sugar or someone allergic to tomatoes must eat something else, but does this mean sugar and tomatoes must be destroyed over the face of the earth? Oh, sugar and tomato-less our children may go, but wine-less, we pray God, never! Without wine, who can redeem the alcoholics?

"They have no wine!" the Blessed Virgin deplores at Cana, eternally importuning her Son. What a calamity! They have no wine, only sugar and tomatoes—and grapejuice. The

Blessed Virgin, who sees the lack, is Queen of Apostles. St. John Damascene called her the "unwatered vineyard of immortality's wine," so, "Rejoice O Virgin Mary, thou alone hast destroyed all heresies!"

The first time we hear of wine in Scripture is—of course—in Genesis. Like its companion, laughter, and everything most fundamental to mankind, it is introduced to us in those first mystical eleven chapters. Written so much later than the rest of the Pentateuch, they are the work of a spiritual writer who we have seen is a consummate artist. Inspired by the Holy Spirit, he compiled in nursery-tale language an overture in which may be sampled all the great themes to be found in the main Opus. Following on the serpent, the Tree of Life, the animal skins, the tower of Babel and the Ark, wine makes its entrance. And what an entrance!

One of the first things Noe did after the Flood, says Scripture, was to till the soil and plant a vineyard. Then reads the text, "When he drank of the wine, he became drunk and lay naked in his tent." Bless the Lord, O my soul! There's no euphemism here. This must have been really wine and not grapejuice. Grapejuice doesn't make you drunk.

We can't deny that the first fact about wine which is presented to us in Scripture is not that it "gladdens," or settles your queasy stomach, or kills pain, or makes parties convivial—all points brought out later—but that it makes you drunk. It inebriates. And who is inebriated? Certainly not Cain, or Lamech, or some alcoholic, but our second father, Noe, patriarch of the predestined, from whom, after the Flood, "the whole earth was peopled." Carry Nation must have had trouble with this passage if she read it aright.

To savor this marvel as we should, it might be well to vault the centuries into the first Pentecost of the Church, when she emerges at last from figure into fact, and where we find the apostles and disciples filled with the fire and fury of the Holy Spirit, speaking in foreign tongues to the Jews assembled from all nations for the feast in Jerusalem. As might be expected, many beholders accused them of being drunk.

"They are full of new wine," the mockers sneered, and St. Peter, as chief apostle, rose to defend them.

"These men are not drunk, as you suppose," he cried, "for it is only the third hour of the day!" (What a homely, human touch in the fisherman's discourse. It's obvious that, then as now, it wasn't considered good form to drink in the morning.) What the city was witnessing was certainly inebriation, but not caused by wine. St. Peter didn't say they weren't drunk; he said they weren't drunk *as you suppose.*

He went on to explain that their strange behavior was a spiritual drunkenness which was a fulfillment of a famous prophecy of the prophet Joel:

> And it shall come to pass in the last days, says the Lord,
>   that I will pour forth of my Spirit upon all flesh;
> And your sons and your daughters shall prophesy,
>   and your young men shall see visions,
>   and your old men shall dream dreams.
> And moreover upon my servants and upon my handmaids
>   in those days will I pour forth of my Spirit, and they shall
>   prophesy (Acts 2:17–18).

Three thousand souls were baptized in that first day's inebriation, "putting new wine into fresh skins," as our Lord had counseled. The mockers were more right than they knew. The Christians were full of new wine indeed, now no longer figuratively as in Noe's tent, but in reality.

"So now drunkenness is just dandy," fumes Mrs. Nation, "because it's a *figure!* Let me show *you* a few quotations from the Good Book!"

Oh no, Ma'am, please uncurl your lip. I'm not saying that. Nobody admires Noe for getting drunk. We just recognize that wine is hard to handle. Given our fallen nature, God's greatest gifts *are* hard to handle, you know—like that sunstroke in the barley harvest, for instance. That's just what the Bible is trying to teach us, that the Holy Spirit can do to us spiritually what wine does to us physically.

"Do not be drunk with wine," St. Paul admonishes the Ephesians, "but be filled with the Spirit!" Certainly the consolations of the Spirit can never find place in a soul perfectly satisfied with the earthly colsolations of alcoholic spirits.

Mrs. Nation thumbs her Bible expertly, and I know what she's looking for. It's probably Proverbs 23:

> Who hath woe? Whose father hath woe? Who hath contentions? Who falls into pits? Who hath wounds without cause? Who hath redness of eyes? Surely they that pass their time in wine, and study to drink off their cups. Look not upon the wine when it is yellow, when the color thereof shineth in the glass. It goeth in pleasantly: But in the end, it will bite like a snake, and will spread abroad poison like a basilisk. Thy eyes shall behold strange women: and thy heart shall utter perverse things. And thou shalt be as one sleeping in the midst of the sea, and as a pilot fast asleep, when the stern is lost. And thou shalt say: They have beaten me, but I was not sensible of pain: they drew me, and I felt not. When shall I awake, and find wine again? (29-35).

This is quite a case history, a whole lost weekend, in seven verses. In it we recognize all the trademarks of alcoholism—

the hangovers, chronic quarrels, bad family relations, delirium tremens, physical deterioration, unfortunate accidents and moral collapse, all ending with the well-known search for the hair of the dog the next morning. "When shall I awake," asks our drunkard, "and find wine again?" The Holy Spirit knows all about these things.

"Woe to you that are mighty to drink wine," charges Isaias, "and stout men at drunkenness!"

St. Paul, the same who recommends "a little wine for thy stomach's sake" to St. Timothy, tells the Corinthians categorically that "no drunkard . . . will possess the kingdom of God." Jeremias used drunkenness as a figure of worldliness. "Babylon hath been a golden cup in the hand of the Lord, that made all the earth drunk: the nations have drunk of her wine, and therefore they have staggered." Prophesying the destruction of Jerusalem, he says, "Thus saith the Lord: Behold I will fill all the inhabitants of this land . . . with drunkenness!"

There's no point in multiplying quotations to prove that drunkenness is evil. The Bible is full of invective against this sin. There is a fine distinction to be made, however, and not feeling qualified to argue the matter out with Mrs. Nation, I shall ask St. John Chrysostom to do it. In a homily on St. Paul's epistle to Timothy, he notes,

> He did not merely say, *"Use wine,"* but *"a little wine,"* and this not because Timothy required the advice, but because we do. Therefore, in writing to him, he limits and restricts wine drinking, telling him to drink as much as would overcome weakness and restore health to the body; not what would encourage another complaint. . . . For wine was given by God, not that we should be drunk with it, but that we should be temperate, that we should be made glad and

not sorry. Wine rejoices the heart of man, the Scripture says.
. . . This will be a useful argument against heretics who
attack what God has made. . . . And not against heretics
only is it good, but against our own simpler brethren, who,
when they see certain men degrading themselves by drink,
instead of blaming them, attack God's gift, saying, "Let
there be no wine." Then we may answer them: "Let there
be no drunkenness." For wine is God's, while drunkenness
is the devil's. It is not wine which makes inebriety, but
intemperance.

Ecclesiasticus, unfortunately one of the books missing from
Mrs. Nation's Bible, says gracefully, "How sufficient is a
little wine for a man well taught, and in sleeping thou shalt
not be uneasy with it, and thou shalt feel no pain," whereas,
"Watching, and choler and gripes are with an intemperate
man!" He tells us, "Wine taken with sobriety is equal life
to men: if thou drink it moderately, thou shalt be sober. . . .
Sober drinking is health to soul and body. . . . Wine was
created from the beginning to make men joyful, and not to
make them drunk!"—along with many other words in the
same vein.

He puts wine finally into its proper context in this
passage:

> The principal things necessary for the life of men are water,
> fire and iron, salt, milk and bread of flour, and honey, and
> *the cluster of the grape,* and oil, and clothing. All these
> things shall be for good to the holy, so to the sinners and the
> ungodly they shall be turned into evil (39:31–32).

Ecclesiasticus also chides us tight-lipped teetotalers with a
gentle, "Rebuke not thy neighbor in a banquet of wine and
despise him not in his mirth. Speak not to him words of
reproach," for therein lies spiritual pride. Even if the neigh-

bor goes beyond mirth and whoops it up loud, the beautiful example of Noe's good sons Sem and Japheth is always before us. Unlike the reprobate Ham, who tattled on his father lying "naked in his tent," they quietly "took a robe, and laying it upon their shoulders, went backward and covered their father's nakedness; as their faces were turned away, they did not see their father's nakedness," for charity loves especially to cover the sin of another.

Wisdom made Flesh saw fit to uphold both teetotalers and winebibbers, provided they were properly motivated. Himself accused of being a tippler by the Pharisees, our Lord retorted that there is no pleasing the holier-than-thou. "For John the Baptist came neither eating bread nor drinking wine, and you say, 'He has a devil.' The Son of Man came eating and drinking, and you say, 'Behold a man who is a glutton, and a wine-drinker, a friend of publicans and sinners' " (Lk. 7:33–4).

To us He confides in conclusion, "Wisdom is justified by all her children" (Lk. 7:35).

So, Mrs. Nation, shall we bury your hatchet?

The most important thing about wine we haven't even touched on yet, though our old friend Sirach hinted at it when he said wisely, "Sober drinking is health to *soul* and body." This phrase transports us suddenly into the very heart of the New Covenant of love, where our High Priest daily takes a goodly Chalice filled with wine into His holy and venerable Hands, saying, "Take ye all and drink of this!"

FOR THIS IS THE CHALICE OF MY BLOOD OF THE NEW AND ETERNAL COVENANT: THE MYSTERY OF FAITH, WHICH SHALL BE SHED FOR

YOU AND FOR MANY UNTO THE FORGIVENESS
OF SINS.

"Take ye all and drink of this!"

In vino VERITAS! Holy Wisdom has indeed "mingled
her wine and set forth her table."

"Come . . . drink the wine which I have mingled for
you," she pleads with the "unwise" (Prov. 9:2, 5).

How can anyone be so foolish as to refuse this invitation?
St. Chrysostom begs us to come forward quickly, explaining
that St. Paul didn't just counsel drinking a little wine, but
carefully prefaced his advice with, "Stop drinking water
only!" For God's sake, do. Instead of water, St. Paul could
just as easily have said to stop drinking grapejuice, for either
could be a figure of what he meant: plain, unfermented
natural life. The Christian must stop drinking water, not
entirely, but only, because his is a supernatural life, engrafted
on the natural, and it can be sustained only by supernatural
drink. Like Judith, we must carry a bottle of wine with us
into the enemy camp. Like Ruth and Esther, we drink wine
now with God.

At every Offertory our priests pour a few drops of water
into the chalice of wine to symbolize this union of Christians
with Christ, of the unfermented with the Fermented, which
is the life of the Mystical Body. "O God," they pray, "who
in a wonderful manner didst create and ennoble human
nature, and still more wonderfully hast renewed it; grant
that by the mystery of this water and wine, we may be made
partakers of His divinity who vouchsafed to become partakers of our humanity, Jesus Christ Thy Son, our Lord."

This ritual is no popish invention. Throughout Jewish

history, wine had been used in sacrifice always as a substitute for blood. Leviticus is filled with prescriptions of some
part of a *hin* of wine to be used in various rites, and we see
that, without wine, Jewish worship, like Catholic worship,
would have been literally impossible. It was an indispensable ingredient of the Passover. Beginning with the mysterious Melchisedech, King of Salem, who brought out bread
and wine as offerings after Abraham's victory over the four
kings, the priesthood of the true God has never thought of
using grapejuice.

Wine was created by God "from the beginning," as Ecclesiasticus says, for the express purpose of eventually being
transubstantiated into the Blood of His Son at a perfect
sacrifice—the Mass. "Isn't God wonderful?" we hear pious
people say, "He takes the simplest things—bread, oil, wine,
water and so on, and turns them into the stuff of sacraments!
And look how our Lord compared God to a mother hen
with chicks! God can use just anything that happens to be
lying around for His purposes."

This is silly. This is like the city kid who sees a lilac for
the first time and exclaims at how wonderful God is, who
can make flowers "just like the one on Mother's hat!" God
doesn't use just what happens to be lying around. Oppor-
tunists do that, not the Creator of the universe. It is much
truer to say that God created hens and chicks to be a figure
of His loving care of us (in a sense they *are* his loving care
for us in a special form) than to say He created them to lay
eggs, or run squawking across roads or be broiled on picnic
grills. Though it is true He created them for these purposes
too, they must always be secondary to the one great function

of all created things: to reflect God's perfections and draw us to Him.

A created substance with the high destiny of wine bears thinking about, for its natural properties must reveal somehow the supernatural properties of the Blood of God. God made wine red, mostly. (Leave it alone when it's yellow, Proverbs advised.) It looks like blood, the life principle of the body, according to the Jews. No one could overlook this analogy. St. Chrysostom mentioned that it overcomes weakness. It's medicinal. It aids digestion, say St. Paul and Grandmother. It makes palatable food which we might otherwise not be able to keep on our weak stomachs. It's an analgesic, allaying both physical and mental pain. In His death agony, our Lord was offered wine mixed with an opiate to alleviate his suffering, though this comfort He refused.

Most of all, however, wine makes us drunk. And lips that never touch liquor just might not touch God's lesson in it. The inebriation it produces is a pale figure of the action of God's Blood, which produces saints. Saints, drunk on the Blood of God, are notoriously irrational, because they have become super-rational. They act like crazy men, whose behavior goes by the name of "folly of the cross." They are full of a courage that never comes from grapejuice only. They become insensible to the world and its painful mockeries. They shout and cry and produce marvelous psalms of praise. As at Pentecost they literally stagger with the grace of God. They are so out of their wits they climb scaffolds cheerfully, smile when insulted, and give away all their property. That's being really "high." And being really high, they love *everybody*.

"*Sanguis Christi, inebria me,* Blood of Christ, inebriate me!" they pray, as did that inebriate Ignatius Loyola. They go around trying to persuade everybody else to have a Drink with them, because, of course, that's another of the properties of wine. It makes us convivial. Wine, as the fathers of the Church love to remind us, is pressed from many grapes, but all are One in the Chalice; and so do all who partake of the Cup tend to become One. This is true even at the lowest levels of unregenerate experience. As one of Arthur Godfrey's favorite jingles has it,

> The love of a beautiful maid,
> The love of a staunch, true man,
> The love of a baby unafraid
> Have existed since time began
> But the greatest love . . . The love of loves . . .
> Even greater than that of a mother . . .
> Is the tender, infinite, passionate love
> Of one drunken bum for another!

Ah, the wisdom of the gutter again!

But, "They have no wine!" The Blessed Virgin's concern at the wedding feast was well taken. She understood such a lack was a calamity of no mean proportions. For a wedding feast there must be mirth and fellowship and love and wine, because all weddings are a figure of one Wedding, where joy must be full.

"Write:" said the angel to St. John, "Blessed are they who are called to the Marriage Supper of the Lamb."

Like the chief steward at Cana, we may well exclaim, "Every man at first sets forth the good wine, and when they have drunk freely, then that which is poorer. But Thou hast kept the Good Wine until now!"

"But I say to you," He replies, "I will not drink hence-forth of this fruit of the vine until that day when I shall drink it new with you in the kingdom of my Father" (Mt. 26:29).

Against that joyous occasion, dear reader, I should like to propose a little toast. It's one I've developed over the years at parties, and it's part of our Family Joke. (Will you join us, Carry Nation?) It's simple, inoffensive and apostolic, and I pass it on gladly to anyone who might have occasion to use it.

"To us!" I say.

Anybody who will drink will drink to that. Christians, Communists, the lady next door, the bill collector, the snake charmer, your mother-in-law or His Excellency the bishop will find no fault with it. Anyone present who doesn't under-stand what drinking is really all about can't suspect, of course, but what I really mean is,

"To US!"

For we are gods, our Lord reminded us, and from now on we do our drinking with the Most Holy Trinity.

"Eat, O friends," invites the Bridegroom, "and drink, and be inebriated, my dearly beloved!"

And the Bride explains, "He brought me into the cellar of wine, He set in order charity in me."

"To US! . . . To US! . . . To US!"

Should the need be felt, there's a "drinking song" that goes very well with this toast. It's the *Splendor Paternae Gloriae,* which the Church's early morning inebriates inevitably sing at Lauds every Monday.

Laeti bibamus sobriam
Profusionem Spiritus!

goes the sixth verse. "Let's joyfully drink the sober drunkenness of the Holy Spirit!"

Be sober, be watchful, Carry Amelia Nation. It takes a little time to develop a head for this sort of thing if you're not used to it, and your adversary the devil goes about like a roaring lion trying his damnedest to break up the party.

AN ORDINARY DREAM

THERE'S one story in the Bible that always gives me a pain in the neck. It's the one about Jacob's Ladder, and the pain is real, not figurative. When I was about seven years old, I accompanied a Protestant friend to Sunday school once. They had been learning about Jacob, and when I entered the picture, they had just decided to act it out.

Various class members were designated to play the part of angels, but I, being the honored guest, was accorded the star role. I was Jacob, the teacher told me. (Actually I wasn't just Jacob. I was Catholic. And don't ask me what I was doing at Protestant Sunday school. What with all the washing, ironing and cooking around here I can't write more than one book at a time.)

"You're Jacob!"

"Yes, ma'am." Having never heard of Jacob until that moment, this was a pretty brave answer, I think.

A chair was overturned to represent a stone, and I was told to lie on the floor and put my head on the chair. If you think this is easy, try it. You'll see where the pain in the neck comes in.

"Jacob's asleep. Don't move, and don't open your eyes. You're dreaming."

I did as I was told, dreaming the best I could, what with

the pain in the neck and the awful racket that was going on. I figured this must be the angels doing their stuff. They seemed to know what to do, and I was dying to see what it was. I opened one eye, but all I could see was the chair bottom.

"Keep your eyes closed, Jacob! You're asleep!"

I shifted my neck a little, in sleep as it were.

"Don't move! You're dreaming about the angels climbing up and down the LADDER."

What ladder? When they let me up, it was all over. I never did find out how those angels did it. There certainly wasn't any ladder. Everybody seemed to know all about it but me. Anyway, they could answer the teacher's questions. What was Jacob lying on? The earth! What was under his head? A chair—no, a stone! Where were the angels going? Up and down!

I didn't want to show my ignorance by asking what ladder or who's Jacob, so I just waited for the refreshments to be passed around. As far as I was concerned, the whole thing was just a pain in the neck. It remained just a pain in the neck for some ten years, when I finally caught up with the story again, this time in college, in another Protestant religion class.

It was assigned, and I read it, but I can't say it made an impression nearly as penetrating into division of joints and marrow as the first one. To tell the truth, I was rather disappointed. The whole thing seemed pretty obvious. Certainly only people who believe in God would attach any importance to an ordinary dream like that, when you could be reading Freud. Jacob, I reasoned, was a primitive nomad on the run at the time. If he didn't make it up, it was probably something he ate, and anyway I was only taking the Bible course because it was required. I was certainly "gnawing the outer bark," for I was not, alas, a believer.

The next time I read Jacob's story, I was. Apparently, it was I who had been the primitive nomad on the run and it must have been something I ate, for suddenly by God's grace here is what the story said:

> Jacob left Bersabee and journeyed toward Haran. He came to a place where he spent the night because the sun had set. He took one of the stones of the place, put it under his head, and went to sleep there. He dreamed that a ladder was set up on the ground with its top reaching to heaven; angels of God were ascending and descending on it. The Lord stood beside him and said, "I am the Lord, the God of Abraham, your father, and the God of Isaac. I will give you and your descendants the land on which you lie. They shall be as the dust of the earth. You shall spread abroad to the west, to the east, to the north, and to the south; in you and in your descendants, all the nations of the earth shall be blessed. I will be with you and protect you wherever you go. I will bring you back to this land; indeed I will not forsake you till I fulfil my promise."
>
> When Jacob woke from his sleep he said, "Truly the Lord is in this place and I did not know it." Reverently he continued, "How awesome is this place! This is none other than the house of God; this is the gate of heaven."
>
> Jacob arose in the morning, took the stone which he had placed under his head, set it up as a memorial pillar and poured oil over it. He called the place Bethel; formerly the name of the city was Luza (Gen. 28:10–19).

This dream of Jacob's I can see now was ordinary beyond Freud, ordinary as God is ordinary who told us, "Should there be a prophet among you, in visions will I reveal myself to him, in dreams will I speak to him" (Num. 12:6), for this is God's ordinary way of doing. Jacob, too, was ordinary. So were the angels, and so was the stone. *Ordinary* is the word for Jacob's Ladder, because, if we are to believe Mr. Webster, *ordinary* is the word for "according to established order." This meaning is listed first. Believe it or not, "commonplace or inferior" comes last in the line of definitions.

If ordinary means the latter to you, have a care for your intonation around the bishop. He is the Ordinary in your diocese. He confers Holy Orders at Ordinations on ordinary men who will celebrate the Liturgy according to an *Ordo*. As shepherd of souls, he publishes ordinances so that nothing in his jurisdiction may become inordinate, and he wants everybody to be as ordinary as possible. Had I been ordinary in college, I would have caught on to Jacob's dream right away. Had I been *very* ordinary, I might have joined an Order.

(Believe me, if I couldn't have the Bible on that desert isle, I might settle for the dictionary. There is more forgotten wisdom locked up in any little word than you could ever find time to think about.)

Let's leap to conclusions. What makes people ordinary is never getting out of order. This tends, of course, to make them look dull when viewed from down here. They have an unhappy way of fading into the background if the background is as ordinary as it ordinarily is. It's only when everybody gets out of step but Willie that the ordinary Willie gets a chance to shine so you can see him. As a matter of fact, being ordinary takes so much stamina, it ordinarily leads to sanctity. We know Lucifer couldn't stand it. He had to be different. There is nothing ordinary about him. He is the Spirit of Disorder, and proud of it!

Knowing how hard it is to sell people on being ordinary, God gave us the vision of Jacob's Ladder to entice us. Through Jacob's closed eyelids we can glimpse for a moment the traffic of heaven, where higher being ceaselessly imparts to lower the gifts of God, lower being rendering thanks and praise in return.

Endlessly repeating, ascending and descending, the invisible almsgiving of the blessed proceeds "according to established order" from angel to archangel through principality and on up to seraph and cherub to God and back again. The exchange of gift and homage, freely accorded, provides perpetual replenishment through perpetual self-emptying. I am sorry always to harp on the same theme, but a book about the Bible has to, and of course here is the battle of the sexes again, as it takes place in angelic creation. In a form far simpler than ours, being so much closer to the Blessed Trinity, it can still be distinguished in the ascents and descents, the emptyings and fillings of angelic action and contemplation—their "acts and potencies."

Jacob couldn't have known it, of course, but this eternal two-way flow of love and knowledge is necessarily rooted in the Triune God, whose ceaseless production and procession of Persons are the exemplars of all activity visible or invisible. If we want to be ordinary, we must somehow take part in this divine harmony. Outside it there is no life, no God. The only question is, how ordinary can we get?

We're not very much at home up there with angels, things being the way they are, so let's run back down here to Jacob and the pain in the neck. The answer for us is bound to lie there, for Jacob was no angel. He was a human being like us. He never got completely off the ground, and

that is very important, if we are to take his view of the
matter. Lying on the earth at the foot of the Ladder with his
head on a stone, Jacob occupies the most equivocal, most
precarious spot in all creation. He is the nexus of matter and
spirit. Nobody would stay on that spot long unless he had
to, but that's where we are.

Like Jacob, we partake of a vast invisible world through
our spiritual faculties. His head, the story carefully explains,
was propped up on a stone. There's something special about
a man's head. It rarely lies with the rest of him "on the
ground,"—unless he wants it to. Isn't Scripture careful to
say that Jacob *put* the stone under his head? Presumably a
man who won't even prop up his own head won't be given
any higher view.

A man's head, nevertheless, is intimately connected with
his physical faculties, through which he is still very much
aware of the visible, material world lying under him and by
which he is bound. Jacob's senses in fact conditioned his
vision. He was sleeping because he had to. He was forced to
sleep at this particular spot not because he took a fancy to it,
but because the sun had set; he used a stone because he had
no pillow. Caught between these two worlds in the dark of
night (ah, night!), belonging to both yet not entirely to
either, Jacob is bound to be uncomfortable. Something has
to give, and until something does, human existence is
nothing but a pain in the neck. The devil saw to that, who
recognized the strategic importance of Jacob's location "in
the beginning," and infected it.

Now Scripture says Jacob came to a "place." If Jacob had
been an Englishman, this would probably mean "not much

of a place." Had he been American, this might mean "any old place." Jacob was Hebrew, however, and when a Hebrew comes to a place, he comes to a *place*. There was something there. When he took one of the stones of the place, he abstracted a stone from something. What?

Modern Biblical scholarship inclines to the view that here was a site of Chanaanite worship where a pagan shrine of some kind had existed from ancient times. One scholar at least suggests there may have been a Babylonian style ziggurat or stepped tower at nearby Luza which provided Jacob with the proper psychological preparation for his ordinary dream. Whatever it was, he took a stone from somewhere in or around it, put his head on it and dreamed of a ladder set up on the ground reaching to heaven.

When he woke up in the morning, he was astounded. "Truly the Lord is in this place and I did not know it!" he exclaimed.

Some cataclysmic dimension had been added to his understanding of his limited sense world. Looking upon his stone pillow with new eyes, he "set it up as a memorial pillar and poured oil over it." He was impelled to consecrate the stone which until now had seemed pretty much like any other, for suddenly Jacob saw what saints see. He saw that *matter is sacred*. How awesome is this place at the foot of the Ladder! This stone, this site of hitherto merely natural activity, is the gate of heaven! It is a means to God. Who would ever have suspected it? Without revelation, nobody.

Jacob saw something else too. He saw that it was imperative that he somehow take part in the traffic on the Ladder, for he made a vow without more ado:

"If the Lord is with me and protects me on my present journey, and gives me food to eat and clothing to wear, and a safe return to my father's house, the Lord shall be my God; and this stone which I have set up as a memorial pillar shall be the house of God. I will offer faithfully a tenth part of everything you give me" (Gen. 28:20–22).

For what God gave him from above, Jacob intended to make constant dutiful return from below. For a primitive nomad on the run, Jacob had rare insight. He made a free decision, prefiguring the free decision of all the elect, whose peculiar destiny it is to catch up everything below them into the sacred progressions above.

Vere dignum et justum est, aequum et salutare nos Tibi semper et ubique gratias agere, confirms the Church today at Mass, calling the angels to witness. And "What return shall I make to the Lord for all He hath given me?" asks the priest at Communion.

Jacob was on the right track, but his commitment could be only a figure of the great Commitment to come, made by a man who was God, in the name of all mankind. "A body Thou hast fitted to me. . . . To do Thy will, O my God, is my delight!" At the Incarnation the Son of God entered the uncomfortable trouble spot occupied by Jacob between matter and spirit. For pure love He took for Himself Jacob's and my pain in the neck, and divinized it. Jacob's vow became valid and sacramental. A proper return to God from our end of the Ladder became possible at last, for the divine Ladder had been extended through to the very depths of the earth, and man and matter had permanent fellowship with the angels.

"Truly the Lord is in this place."

Well might Jacob call it Bethel or "house of God." Its old name, Luza (akin to the Hebrew word for "waken") meant a kind of fruit tree. A fruit tree. Hm-m-m-m. Are we surprised to find Bethel had its roots in Paradise after all, or that the pain in the neck was Calvary? How ordinary.

"On this rock I build my church," says Christ, the Sacred Head resting where Jacob slept and dreamed, the Mystical Body stretched over the earth. "Did you never read in the Scriptures that the stone which the builders rejected [at Luza, perhaps?] has become the head of the corner?" (Mt. 21:42).

"Terrible is this place: it is the house of God and the gate of heaven!" marvels the Liturgy, echoing Jacob's words whenever a church is dedicated or an altar-stone anointed. And again, "This is the house of the Lord, built and well-constructed on solid rock!"

Through this awesome portal of matter we set foot forever on Jacob's Ladder and, fulfilling Jacob's vow, we take part in the traffic. We can see now that in a rudimentary and prefigurative way, Jacob had offered Mass at Luza. For a short while the invisible had opened to him as now it opens to us daily through "the mystery of faith" at the Consecration. God and man meet at last and make an exchange. Natural and supernatural come together and have knowledge of each other, for let's not forget the battle of the sexes—every Mass is a wedding feast.

But what is this invisible ladder like? The Hebrew word used here occurs nowhere else in the Bible in this sense. It could, I believe, mean "stairway" as well, or "steps," or even "stages." As long as we retain a connotation of degrees of ascent, I understand we are within our rights. Whatever the ladder was Jacob saw, it was the original stairway to the stars. The important new truth it taught was that the spiritual world has many gradations of being, and that constant mutual activity goes on between them, in the course of which heaven is linked to earth.

"In my Father's house there are many mansions," confirmed the new Jacob. Heaven is ordinary, but God had to tell us so, because we could never have found out for ourselves, never having been there. "Were it not so," He said, "I should have told you, because I go to prepare a place for you. . . . And where I go you know, and the way you know" (Jn. 14:2, 4).

The way, I'm afraid, is Jacob's Ladder. And do you know what kind of a "ladder" I think Jacob saw? I think he saw a *spiral staircase*. If Jacob's Ladder does what I think it does, and is what I think it is, it would have to *wind* upwards, as did in fact the ramps around the Babylonian ziggurat. The reason I think so is childishly simple. If material nature inevitably reflects spiritual nature, as faith tells us it must, then we can expect to find the progressions of Jacob's Ladder abundantly reproduced in the visible world. And so they are. And they all spiral upwards and downwards.

Anybody can see it for himself, anywhere. Time advances through a cycle of seasons, each bringing forth the next. Big fish eat little, for lower organisms feed higher, who in turn must die and supply food to the lower. The world of nature is so rife with illustrations of spiraling, I had better stop now before I get dizzy. The weary old philosopher Ecclesiastes sums it all up best anyway:

One generation passeth away, and *another* generation
cometh: but the earth standeth forever. The sun riseth, and
goeth down, and returneth to his place: and there rising
again, maketh his round by the south, and turneth again to
the north: the spirit [wind] goeth forward, surveying all
places round about, and returneth to his circuits. All the
rivers run into the sea, yet the sea doth not overflow: unto
the place from whence the rivers come, they return to flow
again (Eccl. 1:4–7).

The same is true in human activity. Political authority
descends in monarchies, ascends in democracies. Farmers
feed manufacturers who supply farmers—with thousands of
middlemen in between. History, language, arts, and science,
the battle of the sexes—everything spirals and pulses, ascends
and descends, withal always rising and growing by stages as
it cycles, mirroring endlessly Jacob's Staircase and the interior activity of the Trinity.

The most informal dinner invitation can't be accepted or
returned, the simplest question asked or answered, without
reference to this august Exemplar in the spiritual world. In
the Church the Liturgy will flow, swell and spiral from
Advent to Easter and around again until it has risen to the
Parousia. Even within our own souls we progress step by step
from Zara to Phares to Zara again, over and over in painful
ascents. Oh, it *must* have been a spiral stair Jacob saw!

In Ezechiel's apocalyptic description of the Holy of Holies
in the New Jerusalem, I think we find Jacob's staircase again.
The prophet says, in fact,

And there was a broad passage round about, going up by
winding stairs, and it led into the upper loft of the temple
all round: therefore was the temple broader in the higher

parts: and so from the lower parts they went to the higher by the midst (41:7).

Was there ever a more beautiful glimpse into the prayer of the blessed, "broader in the higher parts," that awaits us?

Explaining God's established order can get rather complicated, inasmuch as that entails explaining everything that goes on in the universe. It can't be done by word, says Ecclesiastes. The simplest and most basic parallel to the action of Jacob's Ladder is, however, very close to home. It is the ingestion and elimination of food, the truest reflection in nature of what theologians call the "illuminations and purgations" of angels. Like the sexual act, these bodily activities are so important that God attached specific pleasure to them lest we neglect them. I mention this parallel because our Lord did, and no servant is above his Master.

This happened one day when He rebuked the Pharisees for their legalistic cleanliness. Turning His back on these experts, He addressed the crowd in the plainest terms, saying, "'Hear me, all of you, and understand! There is nothing outside a man that, entering into him can defile him; but the things that come out of a man, these are what defile a man! If anyone has ears to hear, let him hear!'" (Mk. 7:15–16). Anybody, our Lord, thought, could understand this figure.

Indeed it seems impossible that the point of such plain speaking could be missed, couched in terms of a natural function common to all and so necessary to life, but the disciples did. Somehow, in the welter of Mosaic prescriptions in which they lived, they were unable to draw the simple spiritual lesson taught them every day by their own bodies.

"Are you also, then, without understanding?" asks the

Divine Simplicity in exasperation. Truth is indeed so simple most people can't grasp it unless it's camouflaged in philosophical verbiage or rabbinical shop talk. Our Lord has to go into detail for us, patiently drawing out the analogy. "The things that come out of a man are what defile a man," He repeats. Spiritually too, is this true.

> "For from within, out of the heart of men, come evil thoughts, adulteries, immorality, murders, thefts, covetousness, wickedness, deceit, shamelessness, jealousy, blasphemy, pride, foolishness. All these evil things come from within, and defile a man" (Mk. 7:21-23).

Our Lord taught here that man has within himself a most terrifying power: he can desecrate. Since the Fall, when the devil entered the trouble spot at the Ladder's foot, man can make clean things filthy simply by using them, by letting them, as it were, pass through him. His effluvia can be nauseous, because he can be nauseous.

Matter itself is utterly innocent in this process, for, as our Lord explains, "It does not enter his heart, but his belly, and passes on into the drain." (Carry Nation, are you listening?) Man, however, is not innocent. Standing at his crucial post, he can receive from above (and below) the best gifts of God and pass them on fetid to others on the Ladder, if he is not holy and does not put what he receives from God to holy uses. Could it be that a culture like ours today, so preoccupied with deodorants, mouthwashes, disinfectants and all manner of perfumed toiletries for both sexes might be trying to evade a little honest thinking along these lines? Have we perhaps become obsessed with washing the outside of the cup instead of honestly frequenting the Confessional?

There is properly no shame attached to the ingestion of

food, but we feel shame in eliminating it, as we feel shame in connection with our reproductive activity. Both processes mirror powerfully in flesh the action of the Ladder, and in both processes we reveal our sinful defectiveness in relation to the rest of God's creation. We pass on children stained by original sin, and so also, everything we receive on the Ladder is passed on corrupted by us to some degree. Now that we are able to put the Phutiphars in proper perspective in the cosmic action, we see why man fructifies defectively and woman nourishes defectively.

"Lie with me!" cries Mrs. Phutiphar.

"What's for dinner?" asks the Captain.

"My food is to do the will of Him who sent Me," said our Lord, giving us a clue to the two-sided mystery by asking us to His Wedding Dinner. There both our desires for Food and Union are destined to be satisfied eternally by God Himself, whom St. John of the Cross calls "la Cena que recrea y enamora"—the Supper which recreates and enamors. Theodoret came right out and said that when we eat the Body of the Bridegroom and drink His Blood, we consummate a nuptial union with Him.

Apparently, if we could receive God's will perfectly and perform it perfectly, we would no longer disrupt the ineffable flow of God's established order, and Adam's shames would no longer have place in us. If our reasoning is correct, therefore, it must follow that man also has power through his free will to make matter holy by his use of it, to sanctify it. Our Lord says as much when He uses the same figure again. Paraphrasing Isaias, He says, "He who believes in me, as the Scripture says, 'Out of his belly shall flow rivers of living water.' " Through incorporation with the Son of God, man's spiritual effluvia can be life-giving. God says so.

Apparently Jacob didn't see the whole Ladder. He saw only the upper part. The lower, stretching out beneath him in matter and time, is yet to be revealed to us, for its lower end rests not just on the ground, but in the transfiguration of creation at the end of the world, when Jacob will through God's power have caught up the entire visible universe and made it one with the invisible. Nature is destined, through man's cooperation with God, to become supernature. Jacob's stone will be consecrated—much as Roman temples became the first Christian churches, much as Judith sanctified the arms of Holofernes—to God's glory. Didn't Zacharias predict that in the New Jerusalem even the pots and pans and the bridles on the horses will be holy to the Lord?

Listen to Father Scheeben on this subject:

> God willed to sanctify and transfigure not only pure spirits, but also material nature which is visible to the senses, especially in man and with reference to man, by its union with the supernatural mystery placed in man. He wished to make not only spiritual, but material nature His temple, and through the Holy Spirit to admit this temple to participation in a supernatural sanctity and glory. By substantially uniting the spiritual with the corporeal in man, He brought spiritual and sensible nature together in the closest possible bond, in virtue of which corporal nature must have part in the supernatural elevation of the spiritual nature. But the glory with which material, corporal nature is to be invested was not meant to become immediately apparent. For the time being the supernatural is present only as a higher, heavenly, consecration, and is not to reveal its resplendent beauty until later; the divine seed lies dormant within material nature, and its abounding energy will burst forth only at the end of

time. In man particularly his visible body is sanctified along with his soul by the grace of the Holy Spirit abiding in him; that body possesses in this grace the seed of its future glorification, and so bears within itself a great mystery which at present we perceive only by faith. (Matthias J. Scheeben, S.J., *The Mysteries of Christianity,* translated by Cyril Vollert, S.J., B. Herder Book Co.).

To give us some inkling of this, the Son of Man took three apostles up a mountain with Him once so that privately they might see Him for what He was. They reported later that "His face shone as the sun, and His garments became white as snow." Please, I think the garments are important, in view of what Father Scheeben just said. Not only Jesus, but His garments were transfigured, and everybody knows garments are material. Isn't this a stupendous revelation? It makes one all shivery just to think of it, this power Incarnate Divinity gives mankind over whatever it comes in contact with.

What to do with this terrible power? Luckily for us, at the same time a voice spoke above the Transfigured Man and said, "This is my beloved Son in whom I am well pleased. *Hear him!"* He will tell us. And standing where Jacob stood, He tells us He is the Way. He is Jacob's Ladder. "No one comes to the Father but through Me." He is Pontifex between heaven and earth, and all traffic takes place in Him, angelic, human or material.

He explained how the Ladder works.

"Our Father," He said, "Thy will be done on earth as it is in heaven." Let everything down here be the way it is up there. Let the lower part of the Ladder reflect perfectly the upper. And "Forgive us our trespasses as we forgive those who trespass against us," for as He explained another time,

"With what measure ye measure it shall be measured to you. . . . Blessed are the merciful, for they shall obtain mercy."

"Do not judge, and you shall not be judged; do not condemn, and you shall not be condemned. Forgive and you shall be forgiven; give, and it shall be given to you; good measure, pressed down, shaken together, running over, shall they pour into your lap" (Lk. 6:37–38). And to illustrate this vital principle, our Lord told us a story about an unmerciful servant, and one about talents and another about gold pieces. Jacob's Ladder is a way of poverty and almsgiving, whose flow of goods must never be interrupted by us if we are to remain a working part of it.

The Old Testament was full of the same sublime lesson, which Proverbs chose to state this way:

> Some distribute their own goods, and grow richer: others take away what is not their own and are always in want. The soul which blesseth shall be made fat: and he that inebriateth, shall be inebriated also himself. He that hideth up corn, shall be cursed among the people: but a blessing upon the head of them that sell (Prov. 11:24–26).

"If thou wilt be perfect, sell what thou hast." Didn't Ruth give everything Booz gave her to her mother-in-law?

I feel unaccountably apologetic about it, but I am afraid I am going to have to mention just one more Old Testament widow. She is nameless. Formerly the wife of a God-fearing prophet, she had fallen prey to creditors who were threatening to sell her sons into slavery. She asked help of Eliseus, who, like our Lord before He multiplied loaves and fishes, inquired first what she had on hand.

She answered, "I thy handmaid have nothing in my house but a little oil, to anoint me."

For a great prophet, this was plenty. He told her, "Go, borrow of all thy neighbors empty vessels not a few. And go in, and shut thy door, when thou art within, and thy sons: and pour out thereof into all those vessels: and when they are full take them away."

She did, "And when the vessels were full, she said to her son: Bring me yet a vessel. And he answered: I have no more. And the oil stood." The story concludes with Eliseus' command to "Go, sell the oil, and pay thy creditor: and thou and thy sons live of the rest" (4 Kgs. 2–7).

This story is a Jacob's Ladder in miniature, for the widow receives as long as she pours out what oil she has. If we look beneath the surface meaning, we see that Jacob's Ladder is also a Ladder of Contemplation, as St. Bernard, St. John of the Cross, and many other souls of prayer knew it to be. It deals in the oil of grace, and shows that the real and essential traffic on the Ladder is an interior activity.

"When thou prayest," advised Christ, "go into thy room, and closing thy door, pray to thy Father in secret; and thy Father, who sees in secret, will reward thee" (Mt. 6:6).

Just so Eliseus tells the widow (Mother Church or any soul of prayer) to "go in and shut thy door," for this kind of multiplication is not done publicly and noisily, but in secret, as those other widows Ruth, Judith and Thamar did it. She is instructed to send her sons for all the empty vessels they could lay hands on, for this is what missionaries are sent for. Mother Church pours into any soul empty enough to receive grace, and stops pouring only when these "vessels" give out.

So here we are at the final transfiguration again, when the

creditor will be paid, and the oil of grace will stand in the saints through an endless Sabbath. You see, even Scripture spirals on Jacob's stairs, ascending and descending, its meanings now down here, now up there, depending on your point of view.

In our latter days, the figure of the widow has been swallowed up in the reality of Christ, who pours out, not oil, but Himself, and who commands, "Follow Me." The only human creature who approaches Christ in emptiness is the one we call Queen of Angels. She emptied herself of God, keeping nothing for herself, and she continues to do so as Mediatrix of Grace. This is being truly like God, who "emptied Himself, taking the nature of a servant," in order to serve all His creation. Lest there be any doubt in our minds as to which of the two functions possible to us on the Ladder is more important, He tells us straight out, "It is more blessed to give than to receive." Obviously giving is more God-like and proper to a super-naturalized being, and whoever would conform to God must give as He gives. Receiving, for a creature, is just doing what comes naturally.

As Father Scheeben also points out, Christ had to pour Himself out to the last drop of His Blood, if He were to represent perfectly in time the perfect outpouring of the Second Person of the Trinity in eternity. How well He understood the two-way duties of His Sacred Humanity on the Ladder! He tells His disciples, "As the Father has loved Me, I also have loved you." And He adds, "Abide in my love. If you keep my commandments you will abide in my love, as I also have kept my Father's commandments, and abide in his love."

Later He addresses the Father, saying, "Even as Thou

hast sent Me into the world, so I also have sent them into the world" (Jn. 17). Everything He has received He passes on to us, even His own vocation.

But we haven't rounded out the picture yet. Christ is Alpha and Omega, the beginning and the end of the Ladder. Through Christ man receives the supernatural, not only from above; now, he receives it even from below, for Christ willed to enter into matter itself. He made sacraments of it. Not only that, He became our Food.

To say now that what enters a man defiles him can be blasphemy. Who feeds on God can say truly his belly flows rivers of living water. This is what is so hard to explain, of course, to Captain Phutiphar. If you, too, find the figure too strong, I'm sorry. I didn't make it up, or create men the way they are. God did. I'm a housewife and rather close to essentials, I guess.

Father Scheeben puts it more decorously:

> Material nature, which ordinarily [sic!] tends to draw the spirit itself down from its native eminence, was raised so high by the Incarnation that henceforward, endowed with divine energy, it was to cooperate in effecting the supernatural elevation of the spirit. So great was the blessing which the incarnation of the God-Man shed over matter, that the flesh could become, and was made to become, the vehicle of the Holy Spirit. And the earth, to which man owes his bodily origin and his bodily nourishment, could become, and was made to become, his spiritual mother, while earthly elements were changed into spiritual, supernatural foods for him (*The Mysteries of Christianity*).

Not only does Jacob sanctify what is below him, but what is below can sanctify him. More incredible, I think it follows that he can pass on the life of God even to those above him. Suddenly he has a terrible new responsibility to the angels. I'll try to explain this as far as I see it.

We are seriously indebted to angels for what we receive from above, as Scripture often reminds us. In Ruth and Esther we saw how essential is their help as we advance in prayer. Tobias teaches the same doctrine more plainly, showing how they forward our prayer to heaven, protect us from their fallen colleagues, and heal our miseries. Our Lord gratefully accepted the help of angels after His temptation in the desert and again in His darkest hour in Gethsemani.

Scripture also records many instances of their appearance to men under unusual circumstances, but mostly they don't appear to men. They are invisible, and they enlighten our intellects and kindle our wills in the most ordinary way possible. Didn't Walter Hilton remark that God "by the ministry of angels" makes clear to us the hidden meanings of Scripture itself? I don't know very much about angels. All I do know is that without them I couldn't for one day run the house, let alone the children. If we are to believe St. Thomas Aquinas, we depend on angels not only for relations with God, but also for the well-ordered workings of the physical universe.

All this is, I believe, fairly obvious, or at least we have grown accustomed to hearing it. What is not so obvious is how angels depend on us. But what, you may well ask, can I do for an angel? Plenty. This approaches the realm of the fantastic, I'm aware. It is like the idea of giving God pleasure. But angels do need us, for through Christ we are their ordinary link with matter, now vivified by the Incarnation. Without us, their knowledge of God and His wonders cannot be complete. There is a certain kind of knowledge they can get only from us.

As pure intelligences endowed with free will, angels have no sense organs, no bodies. Their apprehension of a chair, or Jacob's stone, can only be intuitive. They grasp only what we might call "essence of chair," even though they could easily throw it around the room. They don't see or touch, or think by consecutive images or concepts—all attributes of creatures of sense who progress piecemeal in time. Everything an angel does, he does all of a piece. His prayer, for instance, can be only contemplative.

The sole common denominator between him and us is our spiritual part, our higher faculties. Through these an angel may presumably receive inside information on what a chair can be experientially, an object of certain color, shape or hardness. Only through us can an angel learn what a pain in the neck is like.

We may believe that the Incarnation at the foot of the Ladder opened a whole new world to angels—our world of matter and sensation—as much as it opened up their whole new world to us. Most important, it opened up to them sacramentality: the apprehension of God through the mysterious substance known as matter. No wonder they sang at the Savior's birth! After the Resurrection, Scripture tells us, the angel at the Holy Sepulchre "came down from heaven, and drawing near rolled back the stone, and *sat upon it.*" As far as I know, this is the first time an angel was seen to sit on anything earthly, and I like to think that he did this to symbolize for us and for the startled women the entirely new relationship which now existed permanently between himself and material things. How angels today must hover over Jacob's now truly consecrated stone!

This is quite beyond me, so I won't try to go into much detail. I just want you to know that when I dedicated this book to the angels, I wasn't being coy. They have every right to expect a little something even from me, inasmuch as angels depend on us specifically for the deployment of the riches and marvels of the Church, intrinsically embedded in matter as She is. I took my cue from St. Paul, who explained that he must preach the Gospel not only to enlighten men, but precisely "in order that through the Church there be made known to the Principalities and the Powers in the heavens the manifold wisdom of God, according to the eternal purpose which he accomplished in Christ Jesus our Lord" (Eph. 3:9).

If I'm wrong about this, please forgive me. There's certainly no doubt of St. Paul's important position on Jacob's Staircase. When he preached Christ in Jerusalem, from where does Scripture say he delivered his speech? It says, *"on the steps* . . . he addressed them in Hebrew." So also centuries before him the scribe Esdras, at the restoration of Israel following the Babylonian exile, read the Law "plainly in the street" to all the people, standing "on a step of wood, which he had made to speak upon" (Neh. 8:3,4), foreshadowing the Christ who now speaks plainly to us from His cross. So much for the steps. The Holy Spirit, I can't help repeating, is the Exemplar of literary craftsmen. He who deals in sparrows and the hairs of one's head will hardly overlook delicate details in composition!

"Truly the Lord was in this place and I did not know it!"

"In the morning," when the Ladder will be complete in

all its rungs, we will awaken like Jacob and be astounded. Even the angels will be amazed. How holy everything is! The Battle of the Sexes, the pain in the neck, stones, chairs, cherubim, genealogies, cocktails, comedians, St. Paul,—even the pork chops on Captain Phutiphar's table we shall see had their unique place on the Ladder. Who would have thought that Superman in the comic books was, after all, a homely figure of the Messias!

God, apparently, had been looking through the lattices at us all the time! He was the divine Joker in every deck of cards, in every game we called "of chance."

How holy everything is!

That four-year-old was right. God *was* in the sugar bowl.

Didn't He promise Jacob, "I will bring you back to this land; indeed I will not forsake you till I fulfill my promise"?

WAY DOWN UPON THE
RIVER CHOBAR

Now I am going to deliver some thoughts on the prophet Ezechiel. This should prove to you, (1) I have little scriptural background, (2) I have no humility, and (3) fools will rush in. I can't help having noticed that the more souls advance in learning and virtue, the less they feel qualified to decipher Ezechiel. The sublimity of his visions overpowers the virtuous, whereas the pyrotechnics of his style exhaust mere savants. Being unencumbered with much biblical learning and even less virtue, I therefore feel particularly qualified to worm my way forward. I shall proceed, though what I say about Ezechiel must, you understand, remain very much on the level of personal reaction.

My first reaction was simple enough: Block that metaphor! Reading his work for the first time is an excursion which can only be described as eating one's way through a large, moist, literary fruitcake. Almost anything is likely to turn up —flying books, cherubim, burning lamps, noisy bones, whirl-winds, eagles, vines, cedars, blood, or thunder. It has every-thing. There's even a Holofernes in it, though he goes by the name of Gog. Ezechiel had a skyrocket imagination whose equal the world has rarely seen, and when the Spirit of God roared through it, astounding effects indeed were produced:

And I saw, and behold a whirlwind came out of the north, and a great cloud, and a fire infolding *it!* And brightness was about it, and out of the midst thereof, that is, out of the midst of the fire, as it were the resemblance of amber. And in the midst thereof the likeness of four living creatures: and this was their appearance. *There was the likeness of a man* in them.

Every one had four faces, and every one four wings. Their feet were straight feet, and the sole of their foot was like the sole of a calf's foot: and they sparkled like the appearance of glowing brass. And they had the hands of a man under their wings on their four sides: and they had faces and wings on the four sides, and the wings of one were joined to the wings of another. They turned not when they went: but every one went straight forward.

And as for the likeness of their faces: there was the face of a man, and the face of a lion on the right side of all the four, and the face of an ox on the left side of all the four, and the face of an eagle over [or, "at the rear of"] all the four. And their faces and their wings were stretched upward: two wings of every one were joined, and two covered their bodies. And every one of them went straight forward. Whither the impulse of the spirit was to go, thither they went: and they turned not when they went.

And as for the likeness of the living creatures: their appearance was like that of burning coals of fire, and like the appearance of lamps. This was the vision running to and fro in the midst of the living creatures, a bright fire and lightning going forth from the fire. And the living creatures ran and returned like flashes of lightning.

Now as I beheld the living creatures, there appeared upon the earth by the living creatures one wheel with four faces. And the appearance of the wheels and the work of them was like the appearance of the sea: and the four had all one likeness: and their appearance and their work was as it were a wheel in the midst of a wheel. When they went, they went by their four parts: and they turned not when they went.

The wheels had also a size and a height and a dreadful appearance: and the whole body was full of eyes round about all the four. And when the living creatures went, the wheels also went together by them: and when the living creatures were lifted up from the earth, the wheels also were lifted up with them. Whithersoever the spirit went, thither as the spirit went the wheels also were lifted up withal, and followed it: for the spirit of life was in the wheels. When those went these went, and when those stood these stood, and when those were lifted up from the earth, the wheels also were lifted up together and followed them: *for the spirit of life* was in the wheels.

And over the heads of the living creatures was the likeness of the firmament, as the appearance of crystal, terrible to behold, and stretched out over their heads above. And under the firmament were their wings straight, the one toward the other. Every one with two wings covered his body, and the other was covered in like manner. And I heard the noise of their wings, like the noise of many waters, as it were the voice of the most high God. When they walked it was like the voice of a multitude, like the noise of an army: and when they stood, their wings were let down.

For when a voice came from above the firmament that was over their heads, they stood and let down their wings. And above the firmament that was over their heads was the likeness of a throne, as the appearance of the sapphire stone: and upon the likeness of the throne, was a likeness as of the appearance of a man above upon it. And I saw as it were the resemblance of amber as the appearance of fire within it round about: from his loins and upward, and from his loins downward, I saw as it were the resemblance of fire shining round about. As the appearance of the rainbow when it is in a cloud on a rainy day: this was the appearance of the brightness round about (Ez. 1).

This is a long quotation, but who can paraphrase or condense Ezechiel? You might as well try to stuff the proverbial dormouse in the teapot. What flamboyance! But also, what meticulous attention to detail. This is the literary genius of this prophet, who sounds like a poet, but who wrote almost exclusively in prose, and whose purple patches are simple evidence of a truthful man in an agonizing struggle with language.

He tells us that all the foregoing "was *the vision of the likeness of the glory of God,*" for he was above all a conscientious reporter. Those who might accuse Ezechiel of being unintelligible are simply not bearing this fact in mind. If he hadn't been such a good reporter, his visions would probably give us no trouble at all. We might be tempted to think that God is really quite comprehensible after all. As it is, his vision is a torment to exegetes, and utterly fascinating to everybody, just as God is. Ezechiel, we thank you.

Please don't think I'm so foolhardy as to take upon myself a detailed interpretation of what Ezechiel saw. As that great interpreter Daniel affirmed, "There is need of understanding in a vision" (Dan. 10:1). Until God sees fit to enlighten me properly, the best I can do is follow the example of the London schoolboy asked by his science teacher where elephants may be found. "Owing to their enormous size," he answered sagely, "they are seldom lost for any length of time." I shall confine myself therefore to certain enormous points in Ezechiel's vision which could hardly escape notice long.

The first of these is the fact that the prophet makes no claim, as Isaias did, of having seen "the Lord sitting upon a throne." Nor did he, like Moses, "speak with God face to face as one man to another," or even see His glory, as did Moses. Ezechiel is careful to say that what he saw was three steps removed from God as He is, namely, "a vision of the likeness of the glory of God." Throughout his faithful narration, we are struck by the insistent recurrence of the words "appearance of," "resemblance," "as it were," and "likeness." He seems to be mortally afraid of giving the impression that this was God Himself, or even God's glory, that he saw.

Then what did he see? I think if we really trust this conscientious amanuensis, the answer is right in the text. Ezechiel saw not God's glory, nor His likeness, as he says, but a vision of the likeness of His glory. Ezechiel, I do believe, saw a vision of Holy Scripture. As we said, Scripture is a vision of God, and Ezechiel is ours to prove it. I don't mean to say this is the only interpretation of Ezechiel's vision. God forbid! I merely suggest that this is a true interpretation.

Scripture is shown therein as manifold, coordinated, and one, wheels within wheels following the squared cherubim just as Old Testament and New Testament interlock, parallel and mutually explain each other, all parts moving separately in perfect freedom, yet all proceeding together hierarchically. The four living creatures who moved forward individually and yet simultaneously, being joined together, have long been recognized as probable figures of the four Gospels. The church so appropriates them in the liturgy. It's hardly surprising that "There was the likeness of a man in them," for Scripture is above all a revelation of Christ.

St. Paul gives us the best clue to Ezechiel's enigmatic words, for he tells us Christ is "the brightness of God's glory and the image of His substance." If Christ is God's glory, in fact its very "brightness," then Scripture can be said to be the likeness of this Glory who is Man, and what Ezechiel saw was a vision of this likeness. The prophet says that above the firmament over the creatures on a likeness of a throne was "a likeness as of the appearance of a man above it," and that the creatures themselves "had the hands of a man under their wings on their four sides." To ignore Christ, it would seem—to invert St. Jerome's dictum—is to ignore Scripture. He is the Key to the Scriptures, without which we unlock nothing of that sweetness the saint talks about. Doesn't our heart burn within us while He speaks to us on the road, explaining the Scriptures (Lk. 24:32)?

"The Bible," says Dom Celestin Charlier,

> contains both revealed truths and truths attainable by the unaided use of reason. But there is only one Truth, living and revealed, and that is the incarnate Word. Reflection on the concept of supernatural revelation will show that God can reveal nothing which is not His Son. God, alone and in Himself, is beyond the attainments of created reason. Outside God there are many truths which man has not attained, but none that he could not attain. In this sense truth is natural to man, it is within his scope. God alone lies outside that scope, and everything else insofar as it is rooted in God. He alone bestows Himself freely. The natural knowledge that we have of God brings God into our minds, but it does not place us in God as He is, in all His ineffable reality. If we are to know God in that way (and our whole being cries out for it, since He made us for Himself) then God must give us the knowledge He has of Himself. This Knowledge of God, subsistent and personal, is His Son. The eternal design of God from Paradise lost to the Parousia, the entire plan of salvation to which He invites us, consists precisely in this revelation of Himself in His Son. Thus when God reveals "something" in the Bible, that something can only be His Son, reduced to human and halting symbols. That something can only be a logical and historical preparation for the revelation of His Son in person, in the flesh.

Haven't we seen He is Jacob's Ladder?

. . . Christ is the focal point of the Scriptures as the *incarnation of the Word*. If God is to give Himself to man, He must come to man's level, the level of fallen nature. When man wrenched himself from God's grasp, he had nothing but himself to fall back on. From that time onward he knew only himself, and whatever else he knew beneath him only led him back to himself. If God would now take a hold on him again, He must stoop down to man's fallen level, and there offer His hand. The divine Word must be spoken in sounds that the human ear can hear; the divine Light must shine in a way that the human eye can see. The Bible is the Word of God become visible. Whether its function is to be heard or to enlighten, God has only one Word, and He speaks it only to give it. The pre-Incarnation of His Word in the Bible is the prelude to the Incarnation of the Word in the womb of the Virgin Mary (*The Christian Approach to the Bible,* Ch. VI, translated from the French by Hubert J. Richards and Brendan Peters, Newman).

Speaking of Scripture, Walter Hilton says,

This manner of seeing Him . . . does not reveal Him as He is, but clothed in the images of works and words, *per speculum etiam in aenigmitate;* through a glass and in an image, as the apostle says (1 Cor. 13:12). God is infinite power, wisdom and goodness, justice, truth, holiness and mercy, but what He is in Himself none can apprehend. He can only be seen in His works by the light of grace. His power is seen in the creation of all things out of nothing, His wisdom in the order in which He disposes them, His goodness in saving them, His mercy in forgiving sins. His holiness can be recognized in His gifts of grace, His justice in the punishment of sin, His truth in the rewarding of good works. All this appears in Scripture, and the soul sees it together with all His other attributes (*Scale of Perfection,* Bk. II Ch. 43, Benziger).

There are other enormous elephants in Ezechiel's vision. The wheels *upon the earth* by the living creatures, for instance. We are told these wheels had the spirit of life in them, and that they moved with the creatures. The wheels can surely be taken as symbols of the material universe, now vivified by the Incarnate God, who took material substance into Himself. Scripture (or Christ) and material creation mutually explain each other and move together, showing forth God's glory.

Christ the Man took matter into Scripture in a simple way we can all recognize when, for instance, He told a parable. Parables explain spiritual truths by means of material concepts, while at the same time the spiritual truths progressively unlock the hidden meanings of matter. They are truly "wheels within wheels full of eyes," as Ezechiel put it.

So too the beautiful passage about the creatures who both flew and covered their bodies with their wings. "The noise of their wings was as it were the voice of the most high God," relates the prophet, and "when a voice came from above the firmament . . . they stood, and let down their wings," just as happens on Jacob's Ladder, it would seem. I daresay that when St. Augustine or St. Francis of Assisi or you or I read a passage in Scripture that suddenly changes our whole lives, we can safely assume the creatures have "let down their wings" for us. Our destiny lies among the wheels in this life, I think, and it's comforting to read that "Whithersoever the spirit went, thither as the spirit went the wheels also were lifted up withal, and followed it." "Thy will be done on earth as it is in heaven," sums this up best, as we have seen. This is the mystery of the Transfiguration, promised to us and all creation at the end of time, but which actually takes place right now in Scripture for those who have eyes to discern it. I should like to continue with this absorbing subject, but it is, after all, a personal interpretation, and I seem suddenly to have run out of elephants.

Besides, there is so *much* in Ezechiel. In passing, I can't resist pointing out something else, which occurs in the last eight-chapter section dealing with the mystical measurements, descriptions, and prescriptions of the New Temple. Shortly after describing the winding staircase already mentioned, Ezechiel goes on to speak of the wall decorations of the august edifice. He notes,

> There were cherubims and palm trees wrought, so that a palm tree was between a cherub and a cherub, and *every* cherub had two faces. And the face of a man was toward the palm trees on one side, and the face of a lion was toward the palm tree on the other side: set forth through all the house round about. From the ground even to the upper parts of the gate, were cherubims and palm trees, wrought in the wall of the temple.

And again,

> There were cherubims also wrought in the doors of the temple and the figures of palm trees, like as were made on the walls: for which cause also the planks were thicker in the front of the porch without. Upon which were the oblique windows, and the representation of palm trees, on this side and on that side, in the sides of the porch, according to the sides of the house, and the breadth of the walls (41:18–20, 25–26).

Marvelous touches like these are the despair of the literalminded and must await full exegesis by mystics. "Ordinarily," I should not intrude an opinion here, but those palm trees (a favorite Old Testament symbol of the justified soul)

—set everywhere among cherubim and between a "man" and a lion who may be the Lion of Judah—are irresistibly suggestive. You see, the word for palm tree in Hebrew just *happens* to be—*thamar*. These *thamars* are evidently the special ornaments of God's Inner Temple. By God's grace, make of it what you will, for God wrote both Ezechiel and Genesis, and doesn't mix His metaphors.* Now I'm going back down here.

As Dom Charlier points out, the Bible reveals many things together with Christ. One of the things the Book of Ezechiel reveals is Ezechiel, a very human human being who enlists our sympathy immediately once we catch sight of him. He's something of a revelation all by himself. First of all, he's a writer. Though not the greatest of the sacred authors from a literary standpoint, he might easily have been patron of writers under the Old Dispensation, just as is St. Francis de Sales under the New. Like all real writers, he wrote because he couldn't help himself, not because he particularly wanted to.

Writing, with writers, is answering a call of nature. There's no reason to wax eloquent about it as a profession. The press of ingestion, plus that cathartic imagination of his, we feel would have been beyond Ezechiel's power to withstand, even without the Holy Spirit's prodding.

"Open thy mouth, and eat what I give thee!" God commands Ezechiel, much as a recalcitrant child is made to finish his dinner.

And poor Ezechiel tells us, "I looked, and behold, a hand was sent to me, wherein was a book rolled up: and he spread

---

* If this line of meditation intrigues you, you might glance at 3 Kgs. 6:29, 7:36 and 2 Para. 3:5.

it before me, and it was written within and without: and there were written in it lamentations, and canticles, and woe."

Then he is told, "Eat this book and go speak to the children of Israel!" "Purgation" follows on "illumination" with men as with angels. This is the Law of the Ladder.

Ezechiel was as much concerned about the food he ate as Captain Phutiphar, only more so, being a spiritual man. "And I opened my mouth, and he caused me to eat that book," he reports.

"Not by bread alone does man live, but by every word that comes forth from the mouth of God," retorted our Lord to the devil. We will have guessed by now that the book God gave Ezechiel to eat was no other than the Word of God, His only-begotten Son, destined to become our Food. (Every book written is food, and reflects Him, however defectively. Authors, take heed.)

"And he said to me: 'Son of man, thy belly shall eat, and thy bowels shall be filled with this book, which I give thee.'" Surprisingly enough, Ezechiel then discovers that this forced feeding "was as sweet as honey in my mouth," for doing God's will always turns out that way, unpleasant as it may seem at first.

We have seen that Scripture, which is Truth, isn't prudish about earthly figures, provided they're true. This one is very true, for writers, of all men, are the most "ordinary." Like earthworms and green leaves, they simply excrete what goes into them, acting on it and changing its form in passing. They maintain their footing on Jacob's Ladder precisely by changing the things around them, not into carbon dioxide or some other elements, but into words. As the English novelist St. John G. Ervine put it, "No one on earth and probably no one in heaven can prevent an author from making books while he has breath in his body and energy in his brain and fingers, therefore neglect will not greatly harm him."

"Who can withhold the words he hath conceived?" Eliphaz the Themanite asked of Job.

The flying book eaten by Ezechiel, however, wasn't just plain literary inspiration. It was divine literary inspiration, the most pressing kind a writer can suffer. If God's message goes into a writer, God help him! He becomes a Sacred Author, and it is a Sacred Message which he must somehow manage to cram into human speech.

"Thou art not sent to a people of a profound speech and of an unknown tongue," God tells Ezechiel, yet he must still find words that will transmit the ineffable to them, his own friends and neighbors. What a spot!

"Thou shalt hear the word out of my mouth and shalt tell it them from me," insists Almighty God, who also tells Ezechiel that if he doesn't, he will have to suffer the consequences, for the blood of his reading public will fall on his own head.

So Ezechiel himself, like all prophets, is the matter of a revelation. In him comes to the surface where we can see it the mystery of how God writes with writers without interfering in any way with their free will or their natural genius, inspiring them from the upper rungs of Jacob's Ladder.

St. John the Evangelist was also made to eat a book, as he tells us in the Apocalypse, and was commanded to "prophesy again to many nations and tongues and kings" (Apoc. 10:11). Scholars are fond of pointing to the many similarities between Ezechiel and the Apocalypse, especially in the matter of imagery. Anyone who can read can see that St. John must have liked Ezechiel and borrowed with great freedom from the prophet, never bothering to cite his source, either. The modern world calls this sort of thing plagiarism. That's because the modern world is materialistic and has forgotten some important things about writing.

Even pagans used to know better, for in classical times the greatest compliment one poet could pay another was to include some of his colleague's verses among his own. Great writers know there is no such thing as originality in writing, or for that matter, in anything human. (Even our so-called original sin, as I recall, is something we copied from the devil.) Ezechiel, who from down here looks overpoweringly original, took great pains to tell us he got it all from outside himself.

"My doctrine is not mine!" states even our Lord, who laid no claim to originality either.

Like Ezechiel, every author is a mouthpiece. What goes in comes out, good or bad, depending on the writer, who teeters like the rest of us on Jacob's Ladder. Only materialists dealing in a random world of isolated atoms could seriously believe that what springs from a man without visible antecedent must originate in him.

Wisdom is manifold, but one. The closer authors hew to her, the more they "communicate without envy," and the more they end up saying the same thing. Sacred authors do all say the same thing: CHRIST. By the same token, anyone who receives genuine lights in prayer that might seem un-believably original at the time, soon discovers them in Scrip-ture, in theology—or in some second-rate essayist whose heart is in the right place. (If he does not, he had better watch out!) Mystics not gifted with literary charisms are wont to utter platitude after platitude hopelessly trying to express what has gone into them, and eventually even the gifted ones lapse into silence.

Because they are humble, and avarice is far from them, holy people don't mind cribbing or being cribbed from. Just the other day I ran across a sermon by Cardinal Newman on God's goodness in giving us priests who are men, and not angels. It was a dead ringer for one on the same subject by St. Chrysostom. I only wondered idly at the time from whom St. Chrysostom might have cribbed his. My guess is St. Paul, barring the Holy Spirit. Oh, the freedom of the saints!

But what about all that imagery of Ezechiel's? Those burning coals and wheels full of eyes that are his individual form of expression? Isn't all that just a speck original? 'Deed not.

"What have you that you have not received?" snorts St. Paul.

Granted that God gave Ezechiel a spectacular imagination, still that faculty doesn't operate in a vacuum. It deals in sensory images that also have to come from outside. Where did Ezechiel get it all? That's easy. As you know, Jacob's Ladder works both ways. We receive from below as well as from above. That's why, in addition to the inspiration and the imaginative faculty, God gave Ezechiel the River Chobar. Before that, He had given him Jerusalem and everything in it.

Now, the River Chobar was way down here. It was so down here, it probably wasn't even a river. It may have been an irrigation canal that drew from the Euphrates—the last

place in the world where you would expect a great writer to
develop, so that's where God put him. As far as we know,
Ezechiel never wrote a line as long as he was in Jerusalem.
In fact, it wasn't until he got down on the Chobar, says
Ezechiel, "when I was in the midst of the captives," that "the
heavens were opened and I saw the visions of God."

He had been there some four years at this time. The notes
in the Confraternity edition of the Bible tell us, "He had
apparently functioned for some time as a priest when he was
deported to Babylonia with King Joachin and the first group
of Jewish exiles in 598 B.C. Here he lived with his wife in his
own house at the town of Tell Abib." His was a comfortable
though uprooted existence, lived among indifferent compatriots who had adapted themselves only too easily to the
worldly, idolatrous ways of their conquerors.

> By the streams of Babylon we sat and wept when we re-
> membered Sion.
> . . . How could we sing a song of the Lord in a foreign
> land?
> If I forget you, Jerusalem, may my right hand be forgotten!
> May my tongue cleave to my palate if I remember you not.
> If I place not Jerusalem ahead of my joy! (Ps. 136:1, 4-6).

Ezechiel the exile could have written this psalm himself,
so aptly does it fit his circumstances and state of mind on the
little Babylonian stream called the Chobar. He had reason to
mourn, for he had as little honor among his own people as
any other prophet.

God warns him,

> The children of thy people, that talk of thee by the walls,
> and in the doors of the houses, and speak one to another each

man to his neighbor, saying, 'Come, let us hear what is the word that cometh forth from the Lord.' . . . And thou art to them as a musical song which is sung with a sweet and agreeable voice: and they hear thy words and do them not.

So we see that Ezechiel had been granted a "white" martyrdom—an apostolate to the tepid. They said "Lord, Lord," and looked on Ezechiel as a welcome relief from boredom. For him the River Chobar was what we call nowadays "experience of life,"—the famous school of hard knocks. Even sacred authors can't do without this kind of instruction, for what they receive from below makes it possible for them to transmit what they receive from above. All the images come from below, sifted in the imagination and organized into symbols by the reason, the whole process mysteriously activated by suffering. In visions, I understand, God does the organizing in some measure for us, quickening the material at hand in the psyche. But to go on—

Dom Charlier says,

> We can no more separate the divine content and the human shape of the Bible or absorb one into the other than we can isolate the Word of God from the man Jesus, or confuse his divine nature and his human nature into one. In the Bible it is not possible to confuse or separate the levels at which they operate. We cannot say this is divine and that is human. Both activities work together in an order of harmony and balance to form a single work with a single meaning. The divine value of the Bible cannot be reached in isolation from its human meaning nor can the human meaning be stripped of its divinity.
>
> The ultimate reason why the Bible is consubstantial with eternal truth lies in the very nature of inspiration. Inspiration is essentially "theandric." The divine and human activities are not set in juxtaposition, nor does one substitute for the

other. The natural mechanism of the sacred writer's literary
activity remains undisturbed, even though its motive force
is the impulse given to his spiritual faculties. This basic
impulse dominates him, and permeates down through all his
work into the very last written word (*Op. cit.,* Ch. VII).

Doesn't this aspect of Scripture lead us to look at Ezechiel's vision in a new and still deeper perspective? Don't
the words "There was the likeness of a man in them" take
on added significance? If Ezechiel's vision is truly a vision of
Scripture, how it stresses this human, theandric element! The
four living creatures, says the prophet, "had the hands of a
man under their wings." Could anyone have capsulized
Dom Charlier's words better? Ezechiel was not just holy,
my friends; he was a real writer.

There was only one way for him to accomplish God's
purpose as God's writer, and he makes note of that, too. He
says, "And I came to them of the captivity, . . . to them that
dwelt by the River Chobar, and I sat where they sat: and I
remained there seven days mourning in the midst of them."
In other words, he came "down here."

"Being made in all things like unto us," the Word made
Flesh used the very same tactics, sitting where we sit, and
mourning in the midst of us. Even for God, there is no better
way to reach creatures composed of body and soul. This is
earthly existence, and in holy writers, work and life become
mysteriously integrated, personal salvation being inextricably
bound as it is with the accomplishment of a mission.

After his first great visions, Ezechiel made ready to speak
out to Israel. Even plain authors, we have already noted, are
almost impossible to stop when inspired, and Ezechiel was
no exception. God had to take very strong measures to rein

him in. No sooner had He granted the inspiration, than, believe it or not, He tells His spokesman he won't be able to utter a single word!

"Go in, and shut thyself up," He says, "in the midst of thy house," using almost the same words Eliseus used to the widow; but He adds, ". . . thou shalt be dumb."

Isn't this extraordinary? No. This is precisely the way God has always dealt with souls who surrender themselves completely to His purposes. God had to force Ezechiel to be quiet before his natural talent ran away with him under the force of the divine impulse. Even ordinary writers can't allow themselves to fritter away their gifts in idle talk, if they expect to write well. Writers are articulate. Nine times out of ten, they are loquacious, and Ezechiel probably was. He had to interiorize himself so as to gather his powers, to digest the flying book thoroughly, let's say, before passing it on. With an author as lush and prolific as he, this concentration was imperative. (Even allowing for faulty texts, he's still pretty repetitious.)

This painful inactivity cloaks a very mysterious process, closely allied to Ruth's dumb waiting in the dark at Booz's feet. It's as true in nature as in spirit. The grain must lie inert and die in the earth to yield fruit. Winter produces spring. Cold desolation precedes the delights of contemplation. St. Zachary utters the Benedictus only after a long period of dumbness. The Resurrection follows on the Entombment. Christ enters the Cenacle precisely when the doors are shut. God's humor rises to heights here that no human being can follow entirely. We must be content to laugh when God laughs, not really catching on, but not wishing to offend Him. So, "Shut thyself up in the midst of thy house!" Do you remember Judith? She did just that before tackling Holofernes. So did our Lord at Nazareth and in the wilderness. Great action, great messages, come forth only from solitude and silence. How aptly does Dom Hubert Van Zeller call Ezechiel's dumbness a contemplative's "ligature!"

What happens to poor Ezechiel in his predicament? The torrent of suppressed inspiration breaks through him anyway, but compressed and powerful. Rendered speechless, he proceeds to *act out* his message in a series of pantomimes that amuse the bored Chobarites no end and have perplexed for centuries readers who don't pray. This mummery was not more original with him than was his message. It was in the best tradition of Jewish prophets, who had often given their words extra punch by practical illustration. But it's safe to say Ezechiel outdoes them all. What a liturgy he plays! Using all sorts of props—iron pans, tiles, pieces of hair, and on one occasion even moving out all his furniture and tunneling his way through the wall to make his point, he prophesies willy-nilly to Israel in spectacular charades.

He himself is a charade, a charade on how action is a necessity of contemplation, the result of pent-up prayer, and not a superfluous adornment, as quietists would have us think. Every genuflection, every little sign of the Cross, all bodily postures during Mass should reflect this elementary truth as much as the most world-shaking works. Every human movement derives real potency only from spiritual pressure.

"When I shall speak to thee," God tells Ezechiel, "I will open thy mouth!" God's prophet speaks when God speaks.

All in good time. Who would speak truth must first of all

be silent. Speechless saints preach eloquent sermons; the fecundity of silence most reflects God's, who speaks only one Word, and that silently, says St. John of the Cross, also a writer.

Because he spoke Truth, Ezechiel of course delivered the same message God does: Christ. In practical terms, this means he told the Chobarites what all prophets have said—cleave to God and be made joyful, or leave Him and be destroyed. Very unoriginal. We must remember that Ezechiel was not only a writer. He was a prophet, one of the writing prophets like Isaias and Jeremias. His unoriginal message is prophecy.

Perhaps you think I'm talking down to you when I say something as obvious as that, but the fact is, I'm at a loss for words. (Holy angels on the Ladder, please help me.) The revelation that tugs at us here is stupendous. It's so stupendous God had to send one prophet in particular to tell us about it. Do you remember what St. Peter said when the Christians were accused of being drunk on Pentecost? He repeated those lines of the prophet Joel:

> "And it shall come to pass in the last days, says the Lord,
>   that I will pour forth of my Spirit upon all flesh;
> And your sons and your daughters shall prophesy,
>   and your young men shall see visions,
>   and your old men shall dream dreams.
> And moreover upon my servants and upon my handmaids
>   in those days will I pour forth of my Spirit,
>   and they shall prophesy!" (Acts 2:17–18).

"Your sons and your daughters shall prophesy. . . . My servants and my handmaids . . . shall prophesy!" This phenomenon, St. Peter assured his hearers, had already taken place. He was pope, too, and infallible. Since Pentecost, every Christian, man or woman, is a prophet—not a writer like Ezechiel, mind you, but a prophet like Ezechiel, or Joel. We have received "power from on high." The Spirit of God, which in the Old Dispensation had been vouchsafed only occasionally to a chosen few great souls like Ezechiel, Deborah, Jeremias, Elizabeth and Zachary or the Blessed Virgin, has now descended on *all flesh*. Can this really be?

This would mean that suddenly, with the wind and flames of Pentecost, everything we have said about Ezechiel applies to *us* personally, in the deepest sense—the River Chobar, the inspiration of God, the dumbness, the charades, everything! Are you with me? I am a prophet. So are you.

Once it had been reported to Moses that a couple of men* had apparently taken it upon themselves to prophesy "outside the camp," seemingly without proper authority. Josue turned to Moses and begged, "Stop them!" much as the apostles on a similar occasion forbade the man outside their group, whom they found casting out devils in Jesus' name. Like our Lord, Moses refused to constrain them. He replied surprisingly enough, "Would that all the people of the Lord were prophets! Would that the Lord might bestow his spirit on them all!"

Today this has come to pass; and of these prophets is expected prophecy. This doesn't mean simply foretelling the future, which is an incidental aspect of prophecy anyway. Being a *pro*-phet means speaking for someone else, being un-original. According to Webster, to prophesy means "to utter with divine inspiration." It also means "to give instruc-

---

* I'm sorry, but I must mention the names of these men. They were Eldad and Medad, meaning "God has loved" and "friend."

tion in religious matters; *expound the Scriptures.*" We have all become God's spokesmen to the world. Under the influence of the Holy Spirit, in fact, drunk as never before from the effects of baptism and confirmation, we must speak for God to the captives on the River Chobar. Driven by Pentecostal grace, we must "shut ourselves up in the midst of our house," leaving it only to act out the charade of a holy life in their sight, and speak when God opens our mouths. The gift of prophecy puts a terrible responsibility on us. St. Paul says:

> Aim at charity, yet strive after the spiritual gifts, but especially that you may prophesy. For he who speaks in a tongue does not speak to men but to God; for no one understands, as he is speaking mysteries in his spirit. But he who prophesies speaks to men for edification, and encouragement, and consolation. He who speaks in a tongue edifies himself, but he who prophesies edifies the Church (1 Cor. 14:1-4).

We, too, are not sent to a people "of profound speech and of an unknown tongue," but simply to our neighbors, just as Ezechiel was. That's hard. God, however, tells us what He told Ezechiel: "Behold I have made thy face stronger than their faces: and thy forehead harder than their foreheads. I have made thy face like an adamant and like flint: fear them not, neither be thou dismayed at their presence!"

"For behold, I am with you till the consummation of the world!" Christ promised, when He walked with us on the banks of the Chobar.

All we need fear is ourselves, not forgetting God also told Ezechiel,

> If the just man shall turn away from his justice, and shall

commit iniquity: I will lay a stumbling-block before him, he shall die, *because thou hast not given him warning:* he shall die in his sins, and his justices which he hath done, shall not be remembered: but I will require his blood at thy hand. But if thou warn the just man, that the just may not sin: living he shall live, *because thou hast warned* him, and thou hast delivered thy soul.

This is the hard part of being a prophet. It's easy to get killed doing this, and easy to get damned not doing it. Jewish tradition says Isaias was eventually put in a tree trunk and sawed in half. Jeremias may have been stoned to death.

Nevertheless, what St. Peter said had happened must have happened, because here I am, a plain handmaid, prophesying. I can foretell the future, just like Joel.

"It shall come to pass," I can say, not having to be original, "that whoever calls upon the name of the Lord shall be saved."

And I can predict, too, that God will come again to dwell with men. "And they will be his people, and God himself will be with them as their God. And God will wipe away every tear from their eyes. And death shall be no more; . . . nor pain any more!" (Apoc. 21:3–4).

What wonderful news for the River Chobar! The Spirit of the Lord has filled the whole earth! With just a few props, don't you think we could act this out for the captives?

I think God expects us to. He tells us in Ezechiel's book: "Ezechiel shall be unto you for a sign of things to come: according to all that he hath done, so shall you do, when this shall come to pass: and you shall know that I am the Lord God!"

XIII

GOD, THE GOOD HUSBAND

I MIGHT as well face it, the time is long past when I could read the Bible as a young girl reads it. I've never been able to read it as a man reads it, and never will—still less as a priest reads it. This means that some parts of Ezechiel must, without direct divine intervention, remain fairly abstract for me. Ezechiel was a priest, and for this reason he is able to present to priests the sins of priesthood with moving reality. Conversely, his description of the perfect pastor, rising to the messianic "I will set up one shepherd over them," which our Lord elaborated for us in a parable, is one of the most convincing and beautiful passages in Scripture. So also Ezechiel's last chapters on the New Temple could only be the work of one very familiar with the atmosphere of the sanctuary.

Of the priestly side of Ezechiel, I'm not qualified to judge. I can only believe and admire. But Ezechiel and I do have common ground, for he was not only a priest; he was also happily married. I'm happily married too, and that means I can read the Bible as the happily married do. Not everybody can do that. Not to everybody will certain parts of Ezechiel speak so plainly.

How do we know he was happily married? Well, he tells us so. He reports that God fortells him the sudden death of his wife, saying, "Son of man, behold I take from thee the desire of thy eyes with a stroke." Apparently, he loved her very much.

Then God, ordering him to prophesy the fall of Jerusalem in pantomime to the Chobarites, makes this extraordinary request: "Thou shalt not lament, nor weep: neither shall thy tears run down. Sigh in silence, make no mourning for the dead: let the tire of thy head be upon thee and thy shoes on thy feet, and cover not thy face, nor eat the meat of mourners" (Ez. 24:16–17).

What a terrible ascesis! Can the Nazirite vow be far behind? Blessed are they that mourn on the River Chobar! Let no one think that being a prophet is easy, before or after Pentecost. Being a perfect spokesman of the Most High requires great purity and great self-denial. God pruned Ezechiel to the heart. There was nothing spectacular about his martyrdom; it was quite banal, and excruciating.

Forgoing the emotional release of mourning the beloved "desire of his eyes" in his already lonely exile must have been crushing. It can only be compared with our Lord's grief over the impending destruction of the desire of His eyes, Holy Jerusalem. In his suffering, Ezechiel relates, "So I spoke to the people in the morning, and my wife died in the evening: and I did in the morning as He had commanded me."

For Ezechiel, this is pretty sparse comment. In my opinion, it is the most eloquent sentence he ever uttered. Between every evening and morning occurs a "night." These two, I suspect, were Ezechiel's "night of sense" and "night of the spirit," for he emerges purified. There are no fiery metaphors at this point, not even one little adjective, just dumb misery and perfect conformity to God's mysterious ways. Here we know Ezechiel has really become part of Scripture, his life and his mission perfectly integrated; the traffic on Jacob's Ladder can go upward and downward through his soul unimpeded.

The Chobarites were profoundly impressed. Their curiosity was aroused to the point of asking him, "Why dost thou not tell us what these things mean that thou doest?"

He prepares them for the fall of Jerusalem, the desire of *their* eyes, to which there is now no hope of return, and tells them they must react as he does to his wife's death. "And you shall do as I have done: you shall not cover your faces, nor shall you eat the meat of mourners. . . . You shall not lament nor weep, but you shall pine away for your iniquities, and every one shall sigh with his brother."

There have been various interpretations of this strange command, the most plausible being that the Chobarites were forbidden any public display of national feeling on foreign territory for political reasons. Whatever the historical motive, I think Ezechiel paints a perfect picture of the reaction of the tepid in the face of spiritual disaster. They don't react energetically, as do people who really care, they just "pine away for their iniquities," as inability to mourn is in itself a judgment of God. The lesson: the tepid are as bad as a man who doesn't even mourn the death of his wife.

"Because thou art lukewarm, and neither cold nor hot, I am about to vomit thee out of my mouth!" are the words St. John uses when speaking of God's own energetic reaction to tepidity in the Apocalypse. If the blood of martyrs is the seed of Christians, it may well be that tepidity is the soil of prophets.

Though his articulate style might fool us, I think the episode concerning his wife's death proves that Ezechiel the man was not "emotional" in the modern sense of the word (which seems now to be synonymous with lack of self control). He reserves his flaming figures of speech for exalted spiritual concepts that remain forever beyond his power to express adequately. His own feelings he keeps to himself. He might be saying, "This is a book by God, not by me. I am only a pro-phet."

"I live now, not I, but Christ liveth in me," was the way Paul, a later prophet, put it.

Still Ezechiel remains human, and he can't help betraying glimpses of himself. For instance in chapter sixteen, where God speaks of His love for His desired Jerusalem, he says:

> And when thou wast born, in the day of thy nativity thy navel was not cut, neither wast thou washed with water for thy health, nor salted with salt, nor swaddled with clouts. No eye had pity on thee to do any of these things for thee, out of compassion to thee: but thou wast cast out upon the face of the earth in the abjection of thy soul, in the day that thou wast born.
>
> And passing by thee, I saw that thou wast trodden under foot in thy own blood: and I said to thee when thou wast in thy blood: Live. I have said to thee: Live in thy blood.
>
> I caused thee to multiply as the bud of the field: and thou didst increase and grow great and advancedest, and camest to woman's ornament. Thy breasts were fashioned and thy hair grew: and thou wast naked and full of confusion.
>
> And I passed by thee and saw thee: and behold thy time was the time of lovers: and I spread my garment over thee, and covered thy ignominy. And I swore to thee and I entered into a covenant with thee, saith the Lord God and thou becamest mine.
>
> And I washed thee with water, and cleansed away thy blood from thee: and I anointed thee with oil. And I clothed thee with embroidery and shod thee with violet coloured

shoes: and I girded thee about with fine linen and clothed thee with fine garments. I decked thee also with ornaments and put bracelets on thy hands, and a chain about thy neck. And I put a jewel upon thy forehead and earrings in thy ears and a beautiful crown upon thy head.

And thou wast adorned with gold and silver, and wast clothed with fine linen and embroidered work and many colours: thou didst eat fine flour and honey and oil: and wast made exceeding beautiful and wast advanced to be a queen.

And thy renown went forth among the nations for thy beauty: for thou wast perfect through my beauty, which I had put upon thee, saith the Lord God (Ez. 16:4–14).

This is not God the Good Pastor speaking now, through Ezechiel the priest, but God the Good Husband, as must have been Ezechiel the man. Through these verses we can see Ezechiel buying earrings and bracelets and chains for the wife he loved, taking pleasure in seeing her well provided for and fashionably got up. He sounds indulgent, maybe a trifle foolish. When he looked at her, maybe he smiled rather fatuously as lovers do.

Is it possible that he was actually much older than his wife? That he really had first known her as a neglected child whom, who knows, he may have adopted in infancy? When she came of age, had his marriage to her perhaps been levirate, prescribed according to Mosaic Law to provide for an indigent female relation? In these modern days when only libido rules most courtships, we have little appreciation of "arranged" marriages, forgetting that God's will can be discerned most surely where inclination bows to reason, and self-will to proper authority.

Certain it is that marriages arranged by God and not by human passion do seem to produce Christ. Haven't we seen that Ruth's marriage to Booz was levirate? There is a strong suspicion that the Blessed Virgin's and St. Joseph's was too. We can't know for sure about Ezechiel's. For us the matter must remain speculative, but the figure of the foundling wife which he uses is unusual, and leads us to ponder how he came to think of it.

As we have seen, the portrayal of God as Husband is anything but unusual and well within the most ancient rabbinical tradition. It's a basic theme of Scripture. Beginning with Adam and Eve, rising to a climax in Canticles and ending with the Marriage of the Lamb in the Apocalypse, it can be detected in literally hundreds of guises. It comes plainly to the surface in the prophets Ezechiel, Osee and Jeremias—also Isaias.

The picture Ezechiel paints of a cherished wife is that of humanity raised by grace, whom God adorns fondly with gifts and virtues, just as a doting husband bestows trinkets upon and supplies sustenance for a beloved spouse. For her he does everything Captain Phutiphar didn't do but should have, and much more besides. Though the imagery is human, it's hardly haphazard, for the Holy Spirit doesn't write that way.

In Ezechiel's little vignette is hidden the story of the fall and Redemption of Israel and every individual soul. The wife-to-be is shown as an infant cast off and abandoned in pitiable condition by her natural parents, just as humanity was cast off by its parents Adam and Eve. She is portrayed as an infant left exposed, unwashed, unsalted, and naked, lacking in other words the water, the salt and the baptismal robe of the saving sacrament. The helpless baby is picked up out of pure pity by the husband-to-be, who helps her grow to

fine natural maturity, figuring God's care of Israel throughout the Old Dispensation.

At the fullness of puberty, called here "the time of lovers,"
the man suddenly becomes aware of his foundling as a
woman. As Ruth had asked Booz to do, he "spread his
garment over her," and entered into a binding marriage
contract with her, a formal Hebrew betrothal. "And thou
becamest mine," he said. They became one flesh, as in the
fullness of time we too became one Flesh with Almighty
God through Christ—in whom the Word married human
nature.

What follows is highly prophetic of the New Covenant.
Ezechiel could never have explained it as well as we can,
who have the key to it all. In Ezechiel's imagery converge
most powerfully two main concepts of Scripture: Israel as
the adopted child of God and Israel as the bride of God. Her
betrothed husband "washes her with water," and "anoints
her with oil," prefiguring baptism and confirmation. He puts
earrings into her ears, through which faith must enter. In
fact, present scholarship shows us he arrays her with all the
trappings of the Hebrew bride, who traditionally wore a
necklace and crown during the wedding ceremony and as
much finery as her family could afford.

"And I saw the holy city, New Jerusalem, coming down
out of heaven from God," echoes St. John, "made ready as a
bride adorned for her husband!"

Like the valiant woman in Proverbs, Ezechiel's wife is
clothed in fine linen, the garb of the sanctified, whose Lord
was laid in a fine linen cloth awaiting His Resurrection. As
did other prophets, Ezechiel liked the figure of linen, the

traditional garb of the priesthood. In describing the dress of priests in the New Temple he says particularly, "They shall be clothed in linen garments . . . linen mitres on their heads, and linen breeches on their loins, and they shall not be girded with anything that causes sweat." Sweat, dear me, was one of the heavy punishments laid on Adam and Eve. Thank goodness, one day it shall be no more.

At the risk of laboring the point, it's clear that Ezechiel's wife has as many jewels and ornaments as Judith. Like Ruth she eats the "fine flour" of the Eucharist provided by her Husband. Like Esther, she had a beautiful crown on her head and was "advanced to be a queen." The point of the whole story is that God is a Husband like no other. His care for His intended dates from the first moment of natural life. He provides for her upbringing, He makes her one flesh with Himself, and adorns her with all manner of expensive adornments beyond any interest or help from her natural parents. All she has is from her Husband. He pays the entire cost of the wedding, reception and all. Even her beauty, God says, is His. "Thou wast perfect through my beauty," for His wife, like all wives, shares absolutely in all her Husband's goods.

"Be perfect, as your heavenly Husband is perfect," our Bridegroom might have said.

Using much the same imagery in reverse, Isaias explains what happens when a soul falls into sin:

> In that day the Lord will take away the ornaments of shoes, and little moons, and chains, and necklaces, and bracelets and bonnets, and bodkins, and ornaments of the legs, and tablets, and sweet balls, and earrings, and rings, and jewels hanging on the forehead, and changes of apparel, and

short cloaks, and fine linen, and crisping pins, and looking glasses, and lawns, and headbands, and fine veils. And instead of a sweet smell there shall be stench, and instead of a girdle, a cord, and instead of curled hair, baldness, and instead of a stomacher, haircloth! (Isa. 3:18-24).

What a catalogue! Nobody can say Isaias didn't live in the world and notice things. He was married too.

When the cherished wife proves unfaithful, Ezechiel accuses her, on the other hand, of taking all these beautiful things her husband gave her and giving them to her lovers, much as the sinner misuses God's gifts. Any wife knows this is hitting bottom. She falls lower than a harlot, because "gifts are given to all harlots, but thou hast given hire to all thy lovers and thou hast given them gifts to come to thee!" he says. And again, "trusting in thy beauty, thou playedest the harlot because of thy renown, and thou prostituted thyself to every passer-by, to be his . . ." committing "fornication with the Egyptians thy neighbors, men of large bodies." A Captain Phutiphar? Well, maybe. We know he was carnal.

Ezechiel, no doubt imagining his reaction if his own wife acted this way, easily parodies the sentiments God might entertain toward His wayward Jerusalem. He waxes indignant and doesn't mince words, visualizing apostasy as simple infidelity to the marriage vow: "Thou art thy mother's daughter, that cast off her husband and her children," he thunders, "and thou art the sister of thy sisters, who cast off their husbands and their children! . . . Thy sister Sodom herself and her daughters have not done as thou hast done, and thy daughters."

Among her misdemeanors, he specifically accuses her of infant sacrifice: "Thou hast taken thy sons and thy daughters, whom thou hast borne to me: and hast sacrificed the same to [false gods] to be devoured!"

This isn't just one of Ezechiel's alarming metaphors. In the company of two Moslem emirs saying their beads, I was once privileged to visit an ancient graveyard in present-day Lebanon. It adjoins the site of a Phoenician temple where infant sacrifice had been practiced for centuries. Protruding from the earth here and there were literally hundreds of burial urns containing tiny bones. Like so many broken clay wombs, they expose their contents today to the horrified gaze of any sightseer who can bear the sight. I was expecting a child at the time, and I assure you, this was one experience I am not likely ever to forget.

The historian Diodorus tells us the mother of the young victim took a prominent part in the ritual of immolation, standing by the priest as he slit the child's throat and then proceeded to consign the body to the furnace within the idol itself. Today this sort of infanticide before false gods goes under the name of Contraception or Medical Abortion—not Moloch—and the rite is no longer performed in public. God's injunction to His chosen wife has not changed, however, for all her children still belong to Him, their rightful Father.

"Thus saith the Lord," says Jeremias, "a voice was heard on high of lamentation, of mourning, and weeping, of Rachel weeping for her children, and refusing to be comforted for them, because they are not," for Mother Church continues to bewail her Holy Innocents.

Ezechiel promises the bad wife in God's name, "I will judge thee as adulteresses, and they that shed blood are judged: and I will give thee blood in fury and jealousy. . . .

They shall stone thee with stones, and shall slay thee with their swords!" Under Jewish law, adulteresses were literally stoned to death if convicted, for this was considered a sin unpardonable by a mere husband.

Playing the same theme, Jeremias reveals that only God the Good Husband is capable of such forgiveness. "Return!" He says to sinful Israel, "for I am your Husband!" Such clemency is patently beyond nature, for he notes,

> It is commonly said: if a man put away his wife, and she go from him, and marry another man, shall he return to her any more? Shall not that woman be polluted and defiled? But thou hast prostituted thyself to many lovers: nevertheless return to me, saith the Lord, and I will receive thee.

Only an omnipotent God could dare be so abject!

It's clear that Jeremias thinks this is astounding. He was celibate, however, and lacking in practical experience. Perhaps he didn't realize as profoundly as he might have, in his bones—as a married man would—the height of mercy required for this sort of thing. He makes use of the figure, but he doesn't elaborate.

The prophet Osee does. Osee tells us he was actually married to an adulteress, a statement we are at liberty to take literally. He it was who put into God's mouth the words: "Behold, I will allure her, and will lead her into the wilderness: and I will speak to her heart." He doesn't merely say he will receive the adulteress if she returns; he seeks her out, follows her, makes love to her, pleads with her, *begs* her to return to Him.

What suffering must lie behind these words! Only a great prophet would dare speak of God's love in such words, and only a very unhappily married man could ever have found them. Somehow, I feel the unhappily married must understand Osee very well, and I do wish Mrs. Phutiphar could have read him. What makes Osee's message universal, however, is that he wrote for adulteresses too, and that takes in every sinner who ever strayed. Like Mary Magdalene, we can love much to whom much has been forgiven, once we have been taken back.

Now, like Osee and Jeremias, Ezechiel also talks about forgiving adulteresses. He too announces God's forgiveness. As a priest, perhaps he had had occasion to judge such women according to the Law, and he may have known others, but somehow his terms lack the agony of Osee's and bespeak no emotional entanglements with any. After enumerating a series of dire and just punishments due to fall on the unfaithful wife, he just says quietly, "My indignation shall rest in thee: and my jealousy shall depart from thee and I will cease and be angry no more." Then he goes on to talk about a new covenant with Israel, and that's all. As I say, Ezechiel gives every evidence of having been a happily married man. We suspect husbandly love in the face of infidelity was a trial he never had to undergo. We feel convinced Ezechiel's wife was faithful and easily loved, a well hedged-about vineyard, the "desire of her husband's eyes," and most cruelly missed when she died.

It is also clear that Ezechiel entertained a spiritualized concept of marriage, like Tobias, who was told by the angel Raphael, "For they who in such manner receive matrimony as to shut out God from themselves, and from their mind, and to give themselves to their lust, as the horse and mule, which have not understanding, over them the devil hath power." In similar fashion, Ezechiel describes a harlot precisely as a soul "mad with lust after lying with them whose flesh is as the flesh of asses: and whose issue is as the issue of horses." Already in the Old Dispensation we see stirring the marvelous new creation which is sacramental Christian marriage, where the mainspring of the fleshly union is God Himself.

Mrs. Ezechiel, being married to such a man as the prophet, may have suspected many things that every Christian wife can now know for sure. She may have divined what it means to be the wife of a theandric husband, as is every Christian husband since Pentecost. We can't help wondering, too, how much of the prophet's book she may have written without knowing it. The interplay of personalities in marriage is so mysterious! Though never dignified by the title "prophetess" as was Mrs. Isaias, Mrs. Ezechiel was "the desire" of her husband's eyes, and that means she possessed the one thing necessary: love.

Spiritual literature is rich in "marriage" lore where it concerns the union of souls consecrated to God in religion. A cloistered nun makes her profession quite properly in a wedding dress, and wears a wedding ring. Tell any monk he's a bride of Christ, and he'll understand you perfectly, but tell that to an insurance salesman with ten children, and he might try to take a swing at you. Strangely enough, it's married Christians who seem least aware of God as Good Husband, though they are certainly those to whom this aspect of God should be most meaningful, most incarnate. True, in the sacrament of marriage they are married to Him through the medium of another human being, and not directly through a vow as are religious, but they are married to Him nonetheless. Their earthly married life should be a living meditation rooted in the mystery of marriage, unfolding constantly in and through them. This is *their* charade to act out.

The details of married life which were once only figures of spiritual reality have since the Great Betrothal become true sacramentals. With living faith, Christ's love flows freely through them *in a special way*. Through the hands of a human husband each wife now receives earrings and bangles—or a new dishwasher—from God Himself, acting not only as Divine Providence, but as Husband. As a husband He scolds her, praises her and takes her out to dinner. His homecoming every evening assumes the proportions of a little parousia, a sacramental pledge of the great Parousia at the end of time, when Mother Church's Husband comes home for good. Through a good husband, God reveals what He is; through a bad one, He reveals what He is not. We can't lose. When enough earthly husbands realize that the role they play in their families is God's—well, girls, stand by for a sudden rash of male saints. Nobody can imitate God without being perfect.

> Husbands, love your wives, just as Christ also loved the Church, and delivered himself up for her, that he might sanctify her, cleansing her in the bath of water by means of the word; in order that he might present to himself the Church in all her glory, not having spot or wrinkle or any such thing, but that she might be holy and without blemish. Even thus ought husbands to love their wives as their own bodies. He who loves his own wife, loves himself. For no one ever hated his own flesh; on the contrary, he nourishes and cherishes it, as Christ also does the Church (because we are members of His body, made from His flesh and from His bones) (Eph. 5:25-30).

Can you hear this, Captain Phutiphar?

This is just the beginning of the wonders to be found in the sacrament of matrimony, full exposition of which must await more complete definition by theologians. In the meantime, most fruitful meditation on the subject can be drawn from pondering the virginal marriage of the Blessed Virgin and St. Joseph, where the essentials of human sacramental union stand out most clearly because free of carnal incidentals. Theirs, perfect in all these essentials, most truly produced Christ by means of Christ. As a most perfect earthly instance of "one Christ loving Himself," the Holy Family must contain the whole mystery of spiritual generation within marriage.

In any human union, the husband (or wife) is simply the fleshly instrument used by God in the real marriage, which can only be with God as Partner and Procreator. In Our Lady's virginal marriage the fleshly secondary causality is over-passed, but this does not alter the reality of the marriage. Every child is after all sired by God, from whom is all fatherhood. In our Lord's case, the Child was wholly so, without benefit of human carnal help from any earthly father, but *not* without benefit of human *spiritual* cooperation, as provided by St. Joseph within the sacrament of marriage.

Our Lord was not born out of sacramental wedlock, nor was He conceived outside it. Isn't Scripture careful to note that our Lord's conception took place in "a virgin betrothed to a man called Joseph?" She was not unmarried in the modern sense at the time, for we know Jewish betrothals gave the future husband full marriage rights according to a valid contract, the very matter of the sacrament. As St.

Bernardine of Siena notes in his superb sermon on St. Joseph, the Blessed Virgin was well aware of the important part her husband played in Christ's generation. She doesn't hesitate to refer to him as the Child's father when they find Him in the Temple (much as He was found in her!). She says plainly, *"Thy father* and I have sought thee sorrowing." It is even true to say our Lord was also of Joseph's flesh, for we know he and his blessed Wife were both of the same physical stock, of the line of David, and most likely closely related.

Relegating St. Joseph to the role of a convenient "perfect gentleman" of dubious masculinity whose main function in the Holy Family appears to have been the preservation of appearances is monstrous. This negative concept of a heroic saint entrusted with the care of the Universal Church belongs to a deranged piety that does him little honor, and we would do well to beg his forgiveness.

Quite the contrary, would it be going too far to suggest that the marriage of St. Joseph and the blessed Mary produced Christ carnally as the *necessary fruit* of a human spiritual generation so perfect, so God-imbued, its like has never been seen before or since? It was after all the Spirit of God—not a combination of material elements—which produced matter from the void in the first place, as the first chapter of Genesis makes plain. Matter always necessarily derives from spirit; matter itself is not needed to produce matter where God is the worker.

To Mary's query, "How shall this happen, since I do not know man?" wasn't the angel Gabriel careful to answer, "The Holy Spirit shall come upon thee and the power of the Most High shall overshadow thee?" She was betrothed at the time. Isaias had not prophesied that a spinster would conceive, but "a *virgin* shall conceive and bear a son, and his name shall be called God-with-Us." This virgin was a married woman, one flesh with St. Joseph in the fullest, most real spiritual sense, of which carnal union is only a representation. How, therefore, could the virginal St. Joseph have been excluded from participation in so eminently spiritual a generation? Is this consonant with the concept of the Holy Family as the most perfect reproduction of the Blessed Trinity possible within a frame of human relationships?

In St. Matthew's genealogy of our Lord we read, "And Jacob begot Joseph, the husband of Mary, and of her was born Jesus, who is called Christ." It's interesting to learn that this is a disputed text. Believe it or not, one of the variants runs as follows: "Jacob begot Joseph. Joseph, to whom the virgin Mary was betrothed, begot Jesus, who is called Christ." Commenting on this, Father Karl Adam remarks,

> . . . Joseph is referred to as Jesus' true father. But it is remarkable that the text nevertheless speaks of the *Virgin* Mary, and that she was merely betrothed. We might well think that if the author of this variant seriously wanted us to regard Joseph as Jesus' real father, he would have to omit the expression "virgin" as well as the reference to her betrothal. For if Joseph is Jesus' real father, the reference to Mary's state of virginity is simply meaningless, and so is the reference to her being Joseph's betrothed, for it was Jewish law and custom that the affianced bride should live as a virgin, and might not yet live in wedlock. (*The Christ of Faith: the Christology of the Church*, Ch. XV, translated by Joyce Crick, Pantheon).

Father Karl Adam concludes that the word "begot" must

have been used figuratively. I'm a housewife, not a theologian; but, I wonder, could it be true *sacramentally*? Understood, of course, that God is the real Progenitor of our Lord, could this be the pre-eminent exemplar of Juda superseding Sela?

Arguing more superficially, we might also note that in marriage, all goods are held in common. In a perfect marriage, how far is this true of spiritual goods? Doesn't it follow that any child begotten of the Holy Spirit by Mary would also be her husband's? Is it too much to suppose that our Lord bore a decided physical resemblance to St. Joseph? Isn't He the carpenter's son we all know?

Carrying this reasoning into our own homes, can Christian spouses therefore produce purely spiritual progeny within their sacrament as religious do within their marriage with God? What other end, after all, does marriage have but to produce Christ to the limits of the partners' capacity for projecting life? Can they through its agency save the souls next door—or in China? Does a guest invited into a Christian home maintained purely for God's glory come momentarily into the aura of the marriage sacrament?

What part did Mrs. Ezechiel perhaps play in the spiritual productions of her husband? Was she just an innocent bystander? Heavens! Bearing in mind that literary production is analogous to eating rather than to procreation, still is it possible that even this meager literary effort you are now reading depended somehow on the sacramental cooperation of my husband? Isn't this his book as well as mine? (Just wait till he hears!)

According to God's plan, parents should generate spiritually the offspring they produce carnally. This is simply

Christian education, and requires little explanation. Is it logical to suppose, however, that childless parents really have no children at all of their sacramental union? Scripture expressly extols "the barren and the desolate." Isn't it more logical to suppose that Christian marriage is capable of spiritual procreation as such? Aren't all the souls of the saved the children of the Blessed Virgin and St. Joseph through their marriage as unprecedentedly vivified by Christ? If the sacrament can't generate purely spiritually, how can it be a sacrament of marriage?

Oh, dear. If any theologian should run across this, would he please set me straight? It's awkward, not knowing. How can we be satisfied with a mere dozen or so kids we can see, when we might aspire to thousands more we can't see, in the order of grace?

Not long ago, I ran across a paragraph written by an outstanding religious to the effect that marriage is fine because most incarnate, but its sphere of action limited and less spiritual than other vocations'. Marriage, I read, actively extends only to a circle of children, friends, and relatives. (The milkman wasn't mentioned.) I confess I find this puzzling. I will be the first to admit that this state of affairs is true in the great majority of cases, but to say that this is true of marriage as a sacrament sounds to me like dangerously setting limits to God's grace and quite overlooking the hidden universe of prayer. Whatever its source, I have always understood that grace keeps right on flowing until blocked by an obstacle, or the widow's vessels give out, and in marriage the source is constant and never failing. Who knows what the milkman might take it into his head to do, anyway?

I don't know why Christian parents aren't potential

"founders" of great spiritual organizations as truly as St. Francis or St. Ignatius, just because their "foundations" may not happen to be visible. Sometimes they are visible, though they are not organizations in the accepted sense. (Parents, through the grace of the Holy Spirit, will, I trust, remain unorganized in the eyes of the world!) Mr. and Mrs. Martin, parents of the Little Flower, certainly were sources of the Little Way, and, as far as I am concerned, the spiritual parents of all those who trudge along it. When I think of St. Anne and St. Joachim, whose union was dignified by an Immaculate Conception, indeed I see that our very Redemption was the fruit of marriage "from the beginning."

These holy parents can hardly be said to have had an incarnate, but limited influence! True, in their case, as in that of the Martins, the full force of grace flowed through a child of flesh, as it did with the Blessed Mother and St. Joseph. Perhaps this is what is meant by the "limit" of the sacrament. I don't know; I'm just asking. (My goodness, I wonder what it must be like in heaven to be the parents of the Queen!)

"Shall not I that make others to bring forth children, myself bring forth? saith the Lord. Shall I, that give generation to others, be barren?" (Isa. 66:9).

"Go, call thy Husband!" Our Lord commanded the Samaritan woman.

She answered, "I have no husband," and because she was a graceless adulteress at the time, our Lord agreed with her.

"Thou hast spoken truly," He said. "For thou hast had five husbands and he whom thou now hast is not thy Husband."

A soul in sin literally has no husband. She is Jezabel, the

"unhusbanded," doomed to spiritual sterility—doomed, that is, until the Christ declares His intentions to her.

Alluring her and speaking to her heart as Osee said He would, He confides gently to the Samaritan, "I who speak with thee am He."

As we prophets now know, this was her first real proposal.

"Can he be the Christ?" she marvelled.

She would have been a fool not to accept.

XIV

MY FAVORITE PUBLISHER

THIS, they tell me, is the Hour of the Laity. Whether I like it or not, I have to *do* something for Christ. From now on, I have to come out of my quiet cobwebby corner and be *active*. Suddenly the fate of the entire pagan world depends upon my powerful involvement in it at all levels.

I may even have to learn to play Bridge to reach some hard-to-penetrate sectors, or, worse still, organize weekly barbecue suppers with square dancing, mailing out invitations to people I don't know and can't reach by phone. I can distribute pamphlets, make speeches on Christian values, sing at funerals, be a den mother, teach catechism, sell raffle tickets, collect used clothing, elect more (and more) officers, raise children, learn to tango, and above all, *keep informed*. No sacrifice of selfish peace and privacy, I am reminded, is too great for Christ. If I acquire the proper virtuosity—proper, that is, to great saints—I may find a few minutes every single day to PRAY.

When the pitch gets particularly frenzied around here, it helps to remember that one of the laymen I admire most in the Bible began a very effective apostolate as a raving lunatic. In pious parlance he is the Gerasene demoniac. He came out all right, so maybe I can. His story, which I ponder with increasing earnestness, must be significant, for all three synoptic evangelists take cognizance of it.

Our Lord came across him "in the country of the Gerasenes"; that is, in the region called Decapolis lying east of Galilee across the Lake. A loose political confederation of some ten autonomous Greek towns of which Gerasa was presumably one, its population was predominantly pagan. Though trade there between Jew and Gentile was brisk, relations were strictly business.

Here is St. Mark's account of the meeting:

> And they came to the other side of the sea, to the country of the Gerasenes; and as soon as He stepped out of the boat, there met him from the tombs a man with an unclean spirit. This man lived in the tombs and no one could any longer bind him, even with chains; for often he had been bound with fetters and chains, and he had rent the chains asunder and broken the fetters into pieces. And no one was able to control him. And constantly, night and day, he was in the tombs and on the mountains, howling and gashing himself with stones (Mk. 5:1–5).

St. Luke, the physician with an eye for significant details, notes that our friend "wore no clothes and lived in the tombs, not in a house." Today, any amateur psychiatrist would unhesitatingly diagnose these symptoms as evidence of advanced psychosis. Here certainly is a personality split to sub-human levels. The fundamental sense of shame, and therefore of sin, which is Adam's legacy, is missing entirely. Though the evangelists don't come right out and say so, we can be sure the poor man had long ago lost his sense of humor.

He's violent, noisy and utterly disorganized in his responses. It's fitting that he live in tombs and not in a house. It's interior souls like Judith who live serenely "in the upper part of her house shut up with her maids," or like the Prophet Ezechiel "shut up in the midst of his house" to digest God's message in his very bowels. People who are at home in their houses, in the innermost citadel of their own souls, are content in one place because being with God is being every place.

Our demoniac lived in the tombs—not just one tomb, but "in tombs." In his condition, how could he stay put anywhere very long? Random restlessness, rage and hasty multiplicity are the "action" of the disintegrated. The tomb is the devil's substitute for a house, the natural theater of operations for a soul become so exterior to himself he has no home. His body and spirit yearn to part company like a married couple hell-bent for the divorce court. (Did you think I'd forget the battle of the sexes in dementia, where you can see it gone wrong more dramatically than anywhere else?)

St. Luke adds that our poor man would often be "driven by the devil into the deserts"—perhaps whenever he showed signs of settling down into one particular tomb. Aping the action of God who "leads us into the wilderness to speak to our heart," the devil perverts the divine stratagem and drives his victims to the desert to ravish and destroy them. Even our Lord, "led by the Spirit" into the desert, found Satan waiting for Him there.

Possession is a distilled picture of the ultimate state of sin in this life. Though not necessarily acquiesced to in this instance, it is still the heightened abnormal condition which shows us what sin does if allowed to pursue its course, unhindered, to its logical conclusion. The wages of sin are not only death, but life in tombs, the living death which is damnation.

Our demoniac can go through only motions of hatred, for his members are completely in the power of Satan. Set against God, he is also set against his fellow men, for St. Matthew describes him as "so exceedingly fierce that no one could pass by that way." It follows he is suicidal as well, detesting even himself, "howling and gashing himself with stones." He exhibits all the characteristics of the deeply disturbed. There is here a revolt against legitimate authority which has reached the nadir of breaking even the material fetters which might control him. All semblance of orderly life gone, he turns night into day, in the tombs and roaming the mountains "constantly" as the evil spirit moves him.

Even sleep is denied him.

As I say, he would today be quickly written down as criminally insane by anyone who didn't know any better. He would be given such drugs as might soothe, and confined to a padded cell. As for the devil, who is a liar and an impostor from the beginning, he would be the first to go along with this limited diagnosis. Baudelaire put it very deftly when he remarked that the devil's grandest gambit is persuading us he doesn't exist. This leaves him free to do pretty much as he pleases without interference from us.

Developing this idea brilliantly in *The Devil's Share,* the Swiss Protestant Denis de Rougemont says,

> The Devil's first trick is his *incognito.*
> God says, "I am He who is." But the Devil, ever jealous of God and bent on imitating Him, even though it be in reverse

(since he sees everything from below) says to us, like Ulysses to the Cyclops, "My name is *Nobody*. There is nobody. Of whom should you be afraid? Are you going to tremble before the nonexistent?"

In England in the sixteenth century there was circulated a woodcut inspired by the impish creations of Breughel and Bosch. It represented a character with a horned head and two cloven feet, whose body was invisible. And the title was, *No-body*.

Like the Cheshire cat in *Alice in Wonderland,* the Devil has in our day completely disappeared, leaving hovering in the air only a grin, which is imperceptible to people in a hurry.

Yet the Bible proclaims the Devil's existence on every page, from the first, where he appears in the form of the serpent, to the next-to-the-last, where we see Satan bound a thousand years. . . . The Bible—this is a fact too little known—speaks much less of *evil* in general than of the *Evil One* personified (at least in the original texts). If one believes in the truth of the Bible, it is impossible to doubt the reality of the Devil for a single moment.[1]

So the devil walks among us unsuspected, taking on the protective coloration of whatever suits his purpose, and nothing suits his purpose so well as modern "nerves" and nervous activity leading us to overlook him. Only souls whom God enlightens can catch him at his impostures.

Before continuing with this subject, however, let me state clearly that I am not proposing that all insane persons are possessed! Nor are all epileptics, or persons suffering from other nervous disorders. Nevertheless, it would be to fly in the face of the truth God teaches to deny that the devil is particularly adept at faking nervous symptoms or hiding

[1] Denis de Rougemont, *The Devil's Share,* translated by Haakon Chevalier, Pantheon Books, pp. 17–18.

behind real ones. One has only to read the accounts of our Lord's healing of demoniacs and take note of the details to see this for ourselves.

Not neglecting ultimately that Christ came to drive out Satan, and that He gave this power to His apostles to pass on, does it therefore seem likely that we should never have need of it? How many unfortunates in our mental hospitals are more in need of exorcism than psychiatry? How many are beyond the reach of real help because they are trapped by the fixed ideas of materialists who deny sin or the existence of any spiritual beings whatever, good or bad?

Why, exactly, can the effects of dementia and those of possession be so similar? The answer is so easy for a Christian! As we have already seen, when the devil chose irrevocably to try to win creation for himself, he took for his base of operations that key spot between the material universe and the spiritual one at the foot of Jacob's Ladder. He entered mankind—by way of woman. When he enters an individual, it follows that he pursues the same tactic. He enters at the point of connection between soul and body, through the body, into that mysterious zone where body is somehow able indirectly to influence spirit as Eve influenced Adam.

What follows is disintegration of what should be a perfect marriage. This can happen as the result of disease, trauma, alcoholism, plain lovelessness or some thousands of other secondary causes, complicated or not by diabolic factors. The fact remains that possession is bound to look the same because the effects are the same. And let's be realistic. The genuine cause is always the same: the devil. Though the sin may not be personal in individual cases, it is always at least original. Every ill in the world, from snakebite to total war, is an effect of sin and the devil.

In possession as in plain temptation the body under the tutelage of the devil seeks to boss the spirit, as under the tutelage of the devil Eve tried to boss Adam. The devil has no direct power over the human will, but as he reached Adam through Eve, he can exert plenty of psychological pressure on the soul through the body.

In the beginning Satan's victory occurred precisely "in the middle of the garden" where stood both the tree of life and the tree of knowledge of good and evil, where a dreadful choice was made. In us, the middle of the garden is simply "the heart of man" of which our Lord spoke, from which come "evil thoughts, adulteries, immorality, murders . . ." and all manner of uncleanness. Anyone inclined to look upon the Redeemer's Sacred Heart as a mere sentimental aid to prissy piety doesn't see the intimate and fundamental relationship here between physiology, psychology and theology as revealed in Scripture. God, promising through His prophet Ezechiel to replace our hearts of stone with ones of flesh (36:26), gave us His Son's Heart, that like Him we might "know to refuse the evil and to choose the good" (Isa. 7:15). With this new Heart in us, we can conquer Satan.

In the Book of Job, when God asks the devil where he comes from, the devil answers, "I have gone round about the earth, and walked through it." He is the prince of this world, and matter is his oyster. In human beings, he can stir up emotions, and cloud the senses and the imagination to such a degree that the information they supply the intellect, and therefore the will, can be completely or partially false. This is brainwashing. The devil invented it, and he teaches it to his followers. A subject our day is just beginning to explore, it reeks with "the mystery of iniquity."

Hasn't the Book of Judith already told us how the devil goes "round about" to capture a city?

"Now Holofernes, in going round about, found that the fountain which supplied them with water, ran through an aqueduct without the city on the south side: and he commanded their aqueduct to be cut off" (Jud. 7:6).

He looks for natural weaknesses. He can't enter the city unless allowed, but he can try to force its capitulation by playing hob with its supply system, attacking always "from the south side," as he attacked Adam. He is well aware that even the grace of God enters the soul by way of the body in the sacraments, and faith itself by way of the ear.

Being a housewife, and therefore a demonologist only at the grass roots level, I shall let someone better qualified fill out the picture in proper language:

> This very close union between the nervous system, which pertains to the body, and the sensibility, which is a faculty of the soul, permits the transmission of the commands of the will to the body and its movements. It is this union that is dissolved by death. It is this union that is weakened by mental disorders; for these are definable as disorders of the nervous system, carrying *ipso facto* a disorder of the same importance into the sensibility, and resulting at the limit in madness. Then the will finds all the machinery of command put out of action and no longer controls either the sensibility or the nervous system, which are both abandoned to their only two alternatives of dazed depression or of furious excitement.

Now it is precisely at this point of intersection and liaison between soul and body that the theologians locate the action of the devil. He cannot, any more than other creatures, act directly on the intelligence or the will: that domain is strictly reserved to the human person himself and to God his Creator. All that the devil can do is to influence the higher faculties indirectly, by provoking tendentious representations in the imagination, and disordered movements in the sensitive appetite, with corresponding perturbations in the nervous system, synchronized as it is with the sensibility. Thereby he hopes to deceive the intelligence, especially in its practical judgments, and still more especially to weigh in on the will and induce its consent to bad acts. As long as things stop there we have "temptation."

But—with God's permission, accorded for the greater supernatural good of souls, or to put no constraint on the freedom of their malice—things need not stop there. The devil can profit from a disorder introduced into the human composite by a mental malady. He can even provoke and amplify the functional disequilibrium, and take advantage of it to insinuate and install himself at the point of least resistance. There he gets control of the mechanism of command, manipulates it at his pleasure, and so indirectly reduces to impotence both the intelligence and, above all, the will; which for their proper exercise require that the sensible data shall be correctly presented and that the means of transmission shall be in good working order. Such are the main lines of the theory of diabolic possession worked out by Catholic theology. . . . By fastening, in possession, on the precise point at which body and soul are knit together but can be disassociated, he maintains the line of operations that he chose from the start in order to wage his war against humanity.

If all this is correct, we shall have to infer with the theologians that all true diabolic possession is accompanied, in fact, and by a quasi-necessity, by mental and nervous troubles produced or amplified by the demon, and yet having manifestations and symptoms which are practically and medically identical with those produced by neuroses . . . (Msgr. F. M. Catherinet, "Demoniacs in the Gospels," *Satan,* Sheed & Ward).

So also, speaking of the action of the devil on those advanced in prayer, the great St. John of the Cross warns, "The evil one takes his stand with great cunning on the road which leads from sense to spirit" (*The Living Flame of Love,* Stanza III, 55). Here the devil tries to divert souls from Ruth's arid waiting by feeding them "cataracts of knowledge" and sensible consolations in spiritual guise in order to lure them from higher good by inducing them to cling to good things of sense. This is why the saint always preached the way of *nada* which Judith walked. It's the only safe road.

Bearing all this in mind, was the Gerasene perhaps given to us not so much for the early days of the Church as for the latter ones ahead, when the full force of Satan's cunning will be unleashed on us? Let's continue the story according to St. Mark:

> And when he saw Jesus from afar he ran and worshipped him, and crying out with a loud voice he said, "What have I to do with thee, Jesus, Son of the most high God: I adjure thee by God, do not torment me!" For he was saying to him, "Go out of the man, thou unclean spirit."
> And he asked him, "What is thy name?" And he said to him, "My name is Legion, for we are many." And he entreated him earnestly not to drive them out of the country.

A few more remarks by M. de Rougemont might be pertinent here:

> If the Devil is Legion, this means first of all that while remaining *one,* he can assume as many diverse aspects as there are individuals in the world.

But this may also mean that the Devil is the anonymous mass. It may mean, finally, that being everyone, or anyone, he will appear to us as being No One in particular. And this brings us back to the first of his tricks, which was to make us doubt his very existence.

The name of Legion evokes, from another point of view, the Hellenic myth of Proteus. We have just enumerated the principal roles which the Devil assumes in the Bible: they are all in some manner *disguises* of his original misfortune. Satan fears to show himself as he is; that is obvious, since he fears even to exist in our eyes; therefore he will confront men only with masks which are by turns reassuring or flattering. "Disguise, I see thou art a wickedness, wherein the pregnant enemy does much" (Shakespeare, *Twelfth Night,* II:2).[2]

Legion, let's say, is multiple. Through him the devil apes and perverts the manifold effects of the Holy Spirit in the mystical body of Christ.

"For the Body is not one member, but many," explained St. Paul to the Corinthians, but prefacing this with, "We were all given to drink of one Spirit."

"My name is Legion," confesses the devil, "for we are many." In the satanic kingdom there is no unity, not even in the head.

But there is more than that in the gospel story. We read next:

> Now a great heard of swine was there on the mountainside, feeding. And the spirits kept entreating him, saying, "Send us into the swine, that we may enter into them." And Jesus immediately gave them leave. And the unclean spirits came out and entered into the swine; and the herd, in number about two thousand, rushed down with great violence into the sea, and were drowned in the sea (Mk. 5:11-13).

[2] *Ibid.,* pp. 43-44.

This is a frightful scene, evidently terrifying to the witnesses. Even if the evangelists hadn't told us, we would know we were in pagan territory by the mere presence of two thousand swine, animals legally unclean for Israelites under Mosaic Law. What our Lord encounters here is a situation faced by every missionary bringing Christ among idolaters and devil worshippers. It stands to reason the devils don't want to leave a district where they are propitiated and entertained. They will cause as much commotion as possible to prevent dislodgment.

Even as our Lord approached the Decapolis by boat there had been such a tempest on the Lake as occasioned one of His outstanding miracles—the calming of wind and waves at a word. Were the apprehensive evil spirits the cause of the storm, aggravating incognito the natural turbulence of this low pressure body of water, unpredictable at best? Perhaps. This is the method they use with unstable human beings, and we know devils have such power as God permits over natural forces. In this case He even permitted a whole herd of swine to drown as He permits untold natural disasters every day.

Here, however, we are shown what can sometimes be the cause. The whole aim of the devil is negation and destruction. Although these demons didn't drive our Gerasene over the brink as Satan drove Achitophel and Judas, the swine couldn't stand it caught between God's power and the devil's. They went "whole hog." They bolted.

There is so much mystery here, however, it's useless for me to probe deeper. I return to the more understandable human aspects in the story:

But the swineherds fled and reported it in the town and in the country; and people came out to see what had happened. And they came to Jesus, and saw the man who had been afflicted by the devil, sitting clothed and in his right mind; and they were afraid. And those who had seen it reported to them how it had happened to the possessed man, and about the swine. And they began to entreat Him to depart from their district (Mk. 5:14–17).

A great miracle has been performed, but those standing very much to benefit by deliverance from the menace of a maniac consider the price too high. For them two thousand swine are too much for peace, and "they were afraid." God's power may well terrify the superstitious. The Man who came as Sign of Contradiction, bringing no peace without the sword, will always, like Achior, cause disturbance in the Enemy's camp. Like the woman searching for her precious lost drachma, He had just lit a lamp and *swept the house,* in fact, turned it upside down, and these pagans didn't like it.

He is asked please to go away, and hurry. Let us be, they plead. We like things as they are. Let's have the devils and the pigs back. You frighten us. Go away! "All the people," says St. Luke, "of the Gerasene district besought Him to depart from them; for they were seized with a great fear."

Well, all the people, that is, except one—the dear demoniac, my favorite lay apostle. He's sitting clothed and in his right mind, at peace. He has just become an "ordinary" man. Like Adam, he has just discovered to his consternation that he is strip, stark naked. Humility and the vital sense of humor rush into the vacuum, and he is not only healed, but converted. Possibly it was our Lord Himself who had handed him the clothing he is now wearing, as the Lord God had given the "garments of skin" to the demoniac's progenitor in Eden. It's true, clothes do make the man. Neither angels nor animals wear them.

In his right mind, body and soul restored in their holy wedlock, the Gerasene follows his divine Benefactor to the boat as He prepares to heed the people's wishes and leave. A poignant little scene follows, wherein, "the man who had been afflicted by the devil began to entreat Him that he might remain with Him."

And the Christ refuses him point-blank. Isn't this *incredible?* So many much worse candidates than the poor demoniac had certainly been allowed to follow Him! Mark well. We have here nothing less than a disappointed religious vocation. We have even more than that. We have a disappointed vocation to the cloister. The erstwhile demoniac, now at peace with God and himself, wants *to remain with Him,* no more, no less!

He may be entirely unsuited to religious life for one reason or another, or maybe he has long-standing obligations dating from palmier days, but I don't think that's the whole truth. I think this is an instance of the divine Juda refusing Sela to Thamar, for I am sure our demoniac is a Thamar. Goodness, don't we know already how violent and aggressive he could be? Nothing so betrays character as its abnormalities! Converted, he is prepared to leave everything, joyously and absolutely, to "remain with Him."

For the Gerasene, this would be too easy. This wouldn't be giving everything, which is what Christ requires. Our Lord asks of him something very hard for a person of his temperament. He asks him, out of love, to stay put. He tells him, "Go home to thy relatives, and tell them all that the Lord has done for thee, and how He has had mercy on thee."

"Trust in God and stay in thy place," counsels the Wise Man, aware of where the heights of renunciation lie for some of us, and ultimately, for all of us. Nobody who hasn't groped for these heights can appreciate how hard it is to give up serving God the way one wants to serve Him and to be content with serving Him the way He wants to be served. For God, sometimes the lion must munch like a rabbit, the eagle flutter like a hen. This is the agony of the three hours on the cross—staying put in spite of all temptations to come down and show what we can do!

"Fiat," said a dedicated Virgin once, informed she was to become a mother.

To prove how much of a Thamar my friend really was, he too accepted the "lesser" call. Our would-be monk acceded to God's command. He would work in the world. In doing so he finally sold the very last thing he possessed—his own will—and truly followed His new-found Lord. He who had roamed the mountains constantly, living in tombs, had now a vocation to stay home. He was to remain in a secular, pagan world where devils reigned and "tell" God's mercy.

Can you imagine a man burning with the zeal of a Charles de Foucauld or a Francis Xavier being told to put on a gray fedora, marry his mistress, take a course in business management and settle down to spreading the Gospel in suburbia on Saturday nights? Well, I think my hero's vocation was something like that. It had been bestowed on him by our Lord Himself, as surely as today a layman can receive a mandate from his bishop. The Gerasene didn't waste any time on self-pity, for the Gospel tells us clearly, "He departed and began to publish in the Decapolis all that Jesus had done for him. And all marvelled."

He was ordered, says St. Luke, to "return to thy house." Oh, the mercy of God! *To thy house.* No more tombs, but in his own house, like Judith and Ezechiel. He had indeed already returned to his house. His apostolate, begun as a madman long before he knew it, first took shape at the feet of our Lord, where he had just preached an eloquent sermon by sitting peaceful and cured for all to see, a living witness to the power and goodness of God.

After our Lord left, how did he go about "publishing"? It's evident from the Gospels that he had been living a long time outside society, but still he had ties. Our Lord told him to return to his family. I wonder what happened. I seem to remember our Lord's own brethren and neighbors trying to push Him off a cliff when He returned to tell the Good News in Nazareth. Indeed, relatives can be exceedingly dangerous folk. Our Lord recognized what little honor a prophet has in his own country, and noted wryly that a man's worst enemies are those of his own household.

Standing Christlike and alone among one's own relatives and countrymen requires all the fortitude even a Thamar can muster. We may be sure our Lord chose this particular apostle with care. There was nothing second rate about his vocation, just because he was a layman living the active life. No vocation from God is ever second rate. Whatever the calling, "From me is thy fruit found," as Osee prophesied, speaking specifically of the conversion of the Gentiles (Os. 14:9).

There are so many things we don't know about the

Gerasene. Was he an old man? A young man? Married? Could he wiggle his ears and fascinate toddlers? Did he have a trade? Was he a hog farmer? Did he write books, or was he illiterate? Was he actually pagan, or maybe Jewish? Was he rich? Handsome? Could he sing? What was his position in society? Was he handy with tools? Did he have any children? Could he really have been a publisher? Maybe.

Whenever we meet anyone in Scripture who is mentioned prominently but about whose personal life we know so little, we may suspect his example is meant to have wide application. It doesn't matter what the details were, for what he teaches us can apply to any walk of secular life. Isn't it particularly fitting that he should be anonymous? He is a shining type of the hidden lay saint, who everywhere publishes without attracting much notice to himself, leavening where he happens to be, doing only what he does.

He, too, is legion. He is the "legion of little souls" St Thérèse calls to her standard, the only answer to the hordes of Satan. He is "the mice" the divine Judith called out to rout the footsoldiers of Holofernes. Though the deadly General was overcome on Good Friday, there is a gigantic "mopping up" operation still to be done. Our Gerasene, former maniac in a house divided against itself, is a dean of lay apostles.

So "ordinary" that he is more incognito than the devil, the layman has as many faces as there are laymen. God creates no duplicates. Like Thamar and Judith, his disguises deceive even the master impostor himself and all his tricksters, who, looking for many, always find only One.

"For as the body is one and has many members, and all the members of the body, many as they are, form one body, so also is it with Christ," explains St. Paul (1 Cor. 12:12).

Entreated to leave the Decapolis before causing further disturbance, our Lord did so. Unlike the Adversary, He never forces Himself on His creatures. Being the Christ, however, He cannot forsake them, so He left them only apparently. He stayed very much in the Decapolis, for He stayed in the Gerasene. (I wonder, if the Gerasenes had allowed our Lord to remain among them, would He have granted our demoniac his request? Who knows? God doesn't reveal this secret.)

As it was, the man possessed by devils was now possessed by Christ, who condescended to have need of him. Through him He had the entry He ardently desired into the hearts of these heathen who were so terrified of His power they refused Him the most rudimentary hospitality. Through the Gerasene He could now talk familiarly with them over pork chops (!) at the dinner table, put His arms around their children, and tell them His love in thousands of little ways. He could make them yearn for the mercy He had shown the Gerasene.

Whatever methods our friend employed to allow His God speech, he was successful. Avoiding His enemies in His own country, our Lord returned some time later to the Decapolis. We are astounded to learn that this time,

> great crowds came to Him, bringing with them the dumb, the blind, the lame, the maimed, and many others; and they set them down at His feet, and He cured them; so that the crowds marvelled to see the dumb speak, the lame walk, and the blind see.

Isaias' prophecy, in other words, had been now fulfilled among the Gentiles as it had been among the chosen people.

The Gerasenes said, "He has done all things well. He has made both the deaf to hear and the dumb to speak " (Mk. 7:37). St. Matthew says they went even further: "They glorified the God of Israel." This, from people who a short time before couldn't even abide Christ's presence!

Curing on the same occasion a deaf and dumb boy whose case seemed particularly hopeless, St. Mark reports our Lord "charged them to tell no one." We are informed, however, that "the more He charged them so much the more did they publish it!" By accepting his vocation to stay put and do what he could, it seems our Gerasene by God's grace had performed a propaganda miracle. Where there had been one solitary "publisher" there were now thousands. Could he ever have suspected so much depended on him?

Our Lord had only told him to go home and tell his relatives. He did that, but he didn't stop there, because I guess one thing rather led to another. St. Luke says he went "publishing throughout the whole town." St. Mark says he did it throughout the Decapolis, and that included ten towns. That's a Thamar for you. They always have to go the limit. Didn't our Lord know His man! He had given him one gold piece to invest, and now look!

"Well done, good servant, because thou hast been faithful in a very little, thou shalt have authority over ten towns." The Decapolis? "To every one who has shall be given," added our Lord, propounding the law of Jacob's Ladder from another angle.

How do we know that the "publishers" now numbered in the thousands? Well, the Gospel says there were "four thousand men, apart from women and children," who hung around Jesus here for three days. Having compassion on them in this desert spot, we are told furthermore that Christ was moved to another epiphany to the Gentiles. He performed among them a miracle similar to one He had performed some time before for the Jews of Galilee, multiplying "seven loaves and a few little fishes" to fill their empty stomachs. Christ was a Man, remember. To Him food was always important!

"By their fruits you shall know them," He said, and by these fruits I know both my God and my favorite lay apostle. He's the real article.

We admit we don't know what his procedures were, but that doesn't mean we don't know anything about his apostolate. Of one thing above all others we can be certain. He didn't need St. Paul to tell him "our wrestling is not against flesh and blood, but against the Principalities and the Powers, against the world-rulers of this darkness, against the spiritual forces of wickedness on high " (Eph. 6:12). He knew the lay apostolate was the Battle of Bethulia. He was a man once possessed by Satan, with personal experience of diabolic divide-and-rule, of the fatal severing of Phares from Zara, of destroying the one thing necessary by too many things unnecessary.

Our Gerasene couldn't afford to fall into this old trap. Judging by his results, we know his Catholic Action never degenerated into Catholic Activism. He was a man who wanted above all else to "remain with Him," and I think he did, willy-nilly, somehow or other.

To our shame, didn't a pope use the word *Americanism* once as the epitome of active zeal gone nuts? It's the standing temptation of outwardly directed westerners, and especially of a western laity insufficiently grounded in spirituality. With us, Phares easily runs off with the whole show. For us, the mystical Christ is not so much a living organism as an organization. Organization is our national δαίμων, our genius, as the whole world tells us. That means it can easily become our demon. Maroon three Americans on a desert isle, and what's the first thing they do? Search for food? Well, yes, but only after electing a President, a Vice-President in charge of public relations and a Corresponding Secretary.

Jacob lets go of Esau's heel, and Martha gets Mary to do a lot of cooking that nobody eats. Rachel wastes valuable time envying Leah her numerous visible progeny; the divine Judith is put in man's uniform and set to guarding a dozen mountain passes at once, waging hand-to-hand combat with soldiers bound to overpower her; Thamar is persuaded into a sterile, boondoggling widowhood crocheting afghans for the moths to eat, and Ruth spends her time chasing all the young men whose outward persons happen to be more attractive than Booz's.

Behind all this stands his satanic majesty, the King of Divorce. At all costs he must divorce man from God, the Church from Christ, husband from wife, soul from body, action from contemplation and Antiochene from Alexandrian. It's not surprising that there is close statistical correlation between atheism, heresy, divorce, mental disease, and the sterile apostolate. All are aspects of the same thing, and all the work of the devil. Once he succeeds in engineering a divorce on any level, he simply closes in for the kill.

To accomplish his purpose in the field of the apostolate, he has two choice feints. He can pretend to espouse the cause of Zara, persuading us to dispense with Phares. Phares, he tells us, is coarse and vile, for the lower classes. It's only the spirit that counts, mind over matter. He leads us into morbid asceticism, angelism, Jansenism, quietism and all the related heresies which despise matter as useless or evil. This leads eventually to the overthrow of any genuine scholarship or formal dogma as trammeling to free spirit; and if carried farther, it accomplishes the destruction of the sense of sin and can bring on outright dementia. We then have Catholic Inaction.

The devil's other feint accomplishes the same ends by the opposite method. Better suited to America and "man's world," it's the one we need most to guard against. In this one, he espouses the cause of Phares and drives him into a debilitating frenzy of personal and communal effort. Zara is elbowed aside as an awfully nice but ineffectual chap who is always mooning in corners, gazing vacantly into space, and thereby hopelessly obstructing all vital movement. The devil's favorite catch-phrase now becomes, "Work is prayer," and he will shout it at you until you're dizzy. This is meant to dispense you from untold wasted hours on your knees. It eliminates in one fell swoop all difficulties and distractions in prayer by eliminating prayer.

This means we can teach more and more hours of catechism by freeing the teacher from any self-centered "private piety" concerned with the selfish problems of her own spiritual formation—a really superfluous preparation for catechesis, says the devil. A teacher is formed by teaching, says he, the virtuoso at half-truths. So, too, the singing of Gregorian is taught as music and nothing else, and on down the line of every endeavor requiring interior discipline.

Though clearly recognized as an active work by the fathers of the Church, the common performance of the Liturgy is presented by the fallen angel as a *complete substitute* for individual prayer. If you've made the responses good and loud, and stayed awake, you've been to Mass, says he.

Phares, with Satan behind him, soon drives us out of our house. He runs us into tombs and has us howling like banshees on the mountains, because we can't go home any more. We have forgotten the lesson of Judith, who returned to her house as soon as her job outside was finished; and the lesson of Ezechiel, whose words and liturgical acts are always the vehicles of spirit, and spirit only; and the lesson of the Blessed Virgin, who, leaving "the hill country" as soon as her cousin Elizabeth no longer needed her, immediately "returned to *her own* house," and not someone else's!

We must beware of Phares. Though good in himself, he can be harder to handle than Zara, for Phares is on our "south side." He has our whole carnal nature rooting for him. Without meaning to, he appeals to our worst appetites, our ambitions, our need for distraction and our legitimate sensual preoccupations. He can't help hoping we'll "come down from the cross" and do something extraordinary that will gratify him.

Without Zara's guidance, Phares falls into materialism and stultifying reliance on natural means to attain supernatural ends. He leans to a spiritual torpor far more dangerous than the physical inertia Zara might be guilty of. He says, "Do! Don't just sit there and suffer! Work is prayer!" Phares is pretty naive. Like Leah, he has weak eyes. He doesn't see who puts these damnable words into his mouth. "You have it backwards," whispers Zara, "prayer is work. Work isn't prayer unless the worker is a soul of prayer." Poor Zara can't be heard, however, unless Phares can be made to stop talking a minute. Phares is a terrible listener.

Our Gerasene, who knew what activity gone mad could become, surely learned to listen. Like Job he well knew that "man's life on earth is a warfare," and he knew against whom it is waged. Security lies, strangely enough, only in this warfare. Through it all the inseparable twins must fight shoulder to shoulder, but never forgetting "the older serves the younger." Action must serve prayer, because prayer has the red cord binding us to God, who gives the orders.

The greatest battles against the powers of darkness are waged not on the speaker's platform, but in one's own house, where one meets one's worst enemies in mortal combat. By God's grace, my Gerasene has kept this housewife off many, many, useless committees! Though doing a little "publishing," now and then, I dasn't stray too far from the life-giving waters of my own kitchen sink. I therefore take this opportunity of publicly thanking my friend, whoever he was on earth, in the presence of the angels, good and bad.

Though Phares may be running off with me even as I congratulate myself (this chapter does seem rather long), I feel I must mention one disturbing element in the Gerasene's story, which I have put off until now. In St. Matthew's account, *two* possessed men were liberated by our Lord, whereas St. Mark and St. Luke speak only of the one we have been talking about. What can mean this alarming discrepancy among inspired authors?

The explanation occurring is that there were in fact two demoniacs. St. Matthew, an apostle, was probably an eye-witness of what transpired. He would hardly err in this respect. Also, he wrote his Gospel some years before his two colleagues, who must have heard the tale second hand. Their stories, however, are more fulsome than his, which mentions no conversation at the boat, nor our hero's later activities.

Where could they have gleaned their information? Whatever their other sources, it's my guess that the Gerasene himself may have been one. Though his identity is concealed from motives of delicacy, he may have been well known to them, even personally. He may be known even to us in early hagiography under some other aspect. Certainly he above all others could have revealed the private conversation with our Lord at the lakeside. Years later, he alone figures in the Gospels of Mark and Luke because he is the only one of the two men they had ever heard of, or considered important.

Now, the only question that remains could be a terrible one. What happened to the other man? That other potential lay apostle? Why was he never heard from? Did he die soon after his release from Satan? Did he too wish to remain with Christ, but was he unable to duplicate the act of humility his companion made? Was he simply not called to an active apostolate? Or was he the "Zara" of the two, rendering fruitful the apostolate of the other man, the "Phares," by living a life of hidden prayer?

Or did he lay his gold piece up in a napkin? Is it of him our Lord may have prophesied, saying, ". . . From him who does not have, even that which he has shall be taken away?" Did he start out bravely enough, but fall prey to one of the devil's feints? The following parable might apply to him:

> But when the unclean spirit has gone out of a man, he roams through dry places in search of rest, and finds none. Then he says, "I will return to my house which I left"; and

when he has come to it, he finds the place unoccupied, swept and decorated. Then he goes and takes with him seven other spirits more evil than himself, and they enter in and dwell there; and the last state of that man becomes worse than the first (Mt. 12:43–45).

May God have mercy on us! Is the missing apostle the real lesson to be found in the Gerasene's story?

Or could this invisible man be a figure of the human soul? If we were to reread the story now, searching for mystical meaning, what deep truths might we discover? Well, that would take another chapter. You can see how it is with Scripture. Like its Author, its "wisdom has no limit" (Ps. 146).

THE DONKEY'S TALE

ALTHOUGH she hasn't even been mentioned thus far, there's one biblical character above others who has been in my mind all the while I set down the foregoing pages, and I'm going to mention her now. She is Balaam's Ass. I think I've derived more lowdown comfort from contemplating this creature than from all the Judiths, Ruths, Thamars, Esthers or other females whatever, because she's right down here with me. She's just my speed and just my size.

A wise and holy monk—whose opinion I value among other reasons because he isn't given to handing out compliments—was the one who put me on to this beast. Apropos of an untutored sinner like myself writing spiritual books, he said by way of encouragement, "Well, you never can tell. You might do some good. After all, even Balaam's Ass spoke the truth, you know."

That she did. Determined to take the creature for my model, I first took the precaution of brushing up on her story as it occurs in Numbers. It's a wonderful tale. When her master Balaam the prophet fell so low as to accept pay from the King of Moab to curse Israel, the stubborn ass, seeing the angel of the Lord barring Balaam's way, just plain refused to go. In the best donkey tradition, "she turned off the road and went into the field." When Balaam beat her back on course,

> the angel of the Lord took his stand in a narrow lane between vineyards with a stone wall on each side. When the ass saw the angel of the Lord there, she shrank against the wall; and since she squeezed Balaam's leg against it, he beat her again. The angel of the Lord then went ahead, and stopped next in a passage so narrow that there was no room to move either to the right or to the left. When the ass saw the angel of the Lord there, she cowered under Balaam. So, in anger, he again beat the ass with his stick.
>
> But now the Lord opened the mouth of the ass, and she asked Balaam, "What have I done to you that you should beat me these three times?" "You have acted so wilfully against me," said Balaam to the ass, "that if I but had a sword at hand, I would kill you here and now." But the ass said to Balaam, "Am I not your own beast, and have you not always ridden upon me until now? Have I been in the habit of treating you this way before?" "No," replied Balaam.
>
> Then the Lord removed the veil from Balaam's eyes, so that he too saw the angel of the Lord standing on the road with sword drawn; and he fell on his knees and bowed to the ground. But the angel of the Lord said to him, "Why have you beaten your ass these three times? It is I who have come armed to hinder you because this rash journey of yours is directly opposed to me. When the ass saw me, she turned away from me these three times. If she had not turned away from me, I would have killed you; her I would have spared" (Num. 22:28–33).

That's consoling. I don't know about Balaam, but speaking for myself, I can only offer this volume as proof that I too have "turned off the road," and have been having a wonderful time nibbling happily in the succulent scriptural fields of Mother Church, now and then even venturing into the vineyards between the stone walls for a ripe cluster or two. I've been half expecting her to come chasing after me with a big broom, like David Copperfield's aunt, shouting, "Janet! Donkeys!"—but she hasn't. Quite the contrary, she has favored me with a *Nihil obstat*. "Nothing stands in the way," says she, neither Balaam nor angel of the Lord.

I think Mother Church likes donkeys. In a tight spot once, Samson killed a thousand Philistines with the fresh jawbone of one of these creatures, and she remembers it. Samson, being an exuberant man who loved puns and jokes—especially practical ones—made up a jingle to commemorate the occasion:

"With the jawbone of an ass
  I have piled them in a heap
With the jawbone of an ass
  I have slain a thousand men."

This is very funny, you know, killing a thousand enemies with an ass' jawbone. (What makes the jingle funny is that the words for "ass" and "heap" are the same in Hebrew.) Scripture says,

> As he finished speaking he threw the jawbone from him; and so that place was named Ramath-Lehi. Being very thirsty, he cried to the Lord and said, "You have granted this great victory by the hand of your servant. Must I now die of thirst or fall into the hands of the uncircumcised?" Then God split the cavity in Lehi, and water issued from it, which Samson drank till his spirit returned and he revived.

The Vulgate has it, *"Aperuit itaque Dominus molarem dentem in maxilla asini, et egressae sunt ex eo aquae"*—the Lord therefore opened a molar in the jaw of the ass and from it issued waters. It's a good thing I'm not on a Biblical Commission, because even in the interests of accuracy it would cost me a pang to bow to improved scholarship and forego this rendition of the text, so delightful do I find the idea of life-giving water springing from the jaws of an ass. This is sentimental and unworthy, I know, but somehow a donkey sniffs truth here, and her big ears catch the unmistakable though muffled sound of God's glorious laughter over Ramath-Lehi, "the heights of the Jawbone."

Bless the Lord, O my soul! Not only do you give man wine to gladden his heart, but

> You send forth springs into the watercourses
> that wind among the mountains,
> And give drink to every beast of the field,
> till the wild asses quench their thirst.

These wild ass forebears of Balaam's beast were native to North Africa, and no doubt it was one of them that provided Samson with his unusual weapon in a most unlikely spot. They stand about four feet high, are freedom-loving and solitary by nature, and can live on next to nothing on the most rugged terrain. They are infinitely tougher than their cousins the horses, and are intelligent, swift and sure-footed. From what I read about them in our children's encyclopedia, I can see that being asinine may not be a bad thing at all.

The ass has somehow earned himself a reputation for stupidity and obstinacy, which would lead us to believe the poor creature is as badly off as a creature can be, being defective in both intellect and will. The encyclopedia assures me, however, that donkeys become stubborn only if badly treated. Be that as it may, I might add, from what I learn in Balaam's story, they also become mighty stubborn when divinely enlightened!

Like a woman, the will is a blind, yearning faculty which is made to follow the lead of its head and husband, the intellect. (Don't think we can forget the battle of the sexes in our last chapter, just because we're talking about donkeys.) Mother Eve disobeyed God by disobeying Adam, for being created after her husband, it was through him and not directly from God that she received the command not to eat the fruit of the tree. Ever since this happened, the human will, a "female" faculty, has tended to wander from the authority of the intellect, a "male" faculty which in its turn is defective in knowledge through the sin of Adam.

This is a sad situation only God can remedy, and when He does, Balaam's Ass teaches us the marvelous results. An ass whose mind is flooded with light couldn't possibly be obstinate, because an ass doesn't have free will to go off the track as we do. As stupidity gives way to vision, obstinacy is transmuted into fortitude and sticks up for truth in spite of any kicks and beatings to the contrary. That is the way things should be. Whatever you say about Balaam's little donkey, she wasn't wishy-washy. By all means, be asinine!

When domesticated and illumined, the wild ass becomes an incomparable work animal, slow and patient, excellent for riding and pulling. He's not so dumb, either. He "knows his Master's crib," says Isaias, and that's more than a lot of human beings know, right there, for "Israel hath not known me, and my people hath not understood." Through this prophet the Holy Spirit promises, too, that a day will come when "the ass colts that till the ground shall eat mingled provender as it was winnowed in the floor" (Isa. 30:24).

Well, I'm just asinine enough to know this is mighty tasty! Didn't Father Jacob foretell of the Messias in his blessing of

Juda that "He tethers his ass to the vine, his ass's colt to the choicest vine?"

"Rejoice greatly," says Zacharias, "O daughter of Sion, shout for joy, O daughter of Jerusalem: BEHOLD THY KING will come to thee, the just and saviour: he is poor, and riding upon an ass, and upon a colt the foal of an ass."

And so it proved, for there happens to be a story in the Gospels about an ass colt. On Palm Sunday, our Lord said to His disciples, "Go into the village opposite; on entering it you will find a colt of an ass tied, upon which no man ever yet sat; loose it and bring it. And if anyone ask you, 'Why are you loosing it?' you shall answer him thus, 'Because the Lord has need of it.'"

Imagine God *needing* a little donkey! Was there ever a God like ours?

> And they brought it to Jesus, and throwing their cloaks over the colt they set Jesus on it. And as he went, they kept spreading their cloaks upon the road. And when He was drawing near, being by now at the descent of the Mount of Olives, the whole company of the disciples began to rejoice and to praise God with a loud voice for all the miracles that they had seen, saying,
>
> "Blessed is he who comes as king,
>   in the name of the Lord!
> Peace in heaven,
>   and glory in the highest!" (Lk. 19:35–38).

This time bearing not Balaam but Truth Himself upon her back, the little ass entered the Holy City in triumph. Docile as you please, she trod daintily on the carpet of cloaks laid before her Master, serenely accepting as her due the donkey's share of His glory.

If even the stones would cry out under the pressure of Truth at such a moment, can Balaam's ass be silent?

Joel didn't say God's spirit of prophecy would rest only on people. He said on "all flesh." Since Pentecost all creation is endowed with prophetic utterance. From Adam to ziggurats and zygotes, everything says, "There is a God! He speaks. He utters *us*. Listen!"

"Come," says Balaam's ass, "let's prophesy. The Lord has need of us."

"Brethren, at least, *let us bray!*"

A NOTE ON THE TYPE

IN WHICH THIS BOOK WAS SET

This book has been set in Granjon, a lovely Linotype face, designed by George W. Jones, one of England's great printers, to meet his own exacting requirements for fine book and publication work. Like most useful types, Granjon is neither wholly new nor wholly old. It is not a copy of a classic face nor an original creation, but rather something between the two—drawing its basic design from classic Garamond sources, but never hesitating to deviate from the model where four centuries of type-cutting experience indicate an improvement or where modern methods of punch-cutting make possible a refinement far beyond the skill of the originator. This book was composed by Progressive Typographers, Inc., York, Pa., printed by Wickersham Printing Company of Lancaster, Pa., and bound by Moore and Company of Baltimore. The design and typography of this book are by Howard N. King.